**PRENTICE HALL MA...**

## COURSE 2

# Study Guide & Practice Workbook

**PEARSON**

**Prentice Hall**

**Boston, Massachusetts**
**Upper Saddle River, New Jersey**

ISBN: 0-13-125456-1

22   17

# Study Guide & Practice Workbook

## Contents

**Answers appear in the back of each Grab & Go File.**

# Contents (cont.)

# Reteaching 1-1

One way to estimate a sum, difference, or product is to round numbers to the nearest whole number. Then add, subtract, multiply or divide.

| Round to the largest nearest whole number | | Round to the largest nearest whole number | |
|---|---|---|---|
| 1.6 | → 2 | 17.2 | → 20 |
| + 4.4 | → + 4 | × 7.3 | → × 7 |
| | 6 **Estimate** | | 140 **Estimate** |

You can get a quick estimate if you use *compatible numbers* to compute mentally.

$$\begin{array}{r} \$24.27 \\ - \ \ 8.79 \end{array} \longrightarrow \begin{array}{r} \$24.00 \\ - \ \ 9.00 \\ \hline \$15.00 \ \textbf{Estimate} \end{array}$$

---

**Estimate each sum, difference, product or quotient.**

|  | | **Estimate** | | | | **Estimate** |
|---|---|---|---|---|---|---|
| **1.** | 9.265 +6.840 | → → | 9 + 6.7   16 | **2.** | 12.91 − 7.80 | → → − |
| | 16.105 | | | | | |
| **3.** | $16.49 − 5.25 | → → | 16.00 − 15.00   $11.00 | **4.** | 2.362 + 0.815 | → → + |
| **5.** | 2.4 × 5.2 | → → | 2.0 × 5.0   10 | **6.** | 6.5 × 0.9 | → → × |
| **7.** | $12.09 − 10.55 | → → | $12.00 − 10.00   $2.00 | **8.** | 6.147 + 0.715 | → → + |
| **9.** | 65.4 − 22.2 | → → | 65.0 − 22.0   43 | **10.** | 27.14 × 3.1 | → → × |
| **11.** | 9.21 ÷ 3.95 | → → | 9.00 ÷ 4.00   2.25 | **12.** | 110.2 ÷ 10.8 | → → ÷ |

# Practice 1-1

**Use rounding to estimate the nearest half-dollar.**

**1.**   $4.85   $5.00
        + 1.47   + 1.50
                  $6.50

**2.**   $6.79
        − 3.95

**3.**   $14.19  14.20
        + 5.59   5.60
                $ 19.80

**4.**   $25.43
        − 21.20

**Use front-end estimation to find each sum.**

**5.** 4.76 + 6.15   4.76
                 6.00   6.15
                 5.00   10.91

**6.** 1.409 + 3.512

**7.** 2.479 + 6.518

**8.** 3.17 + 2.72

**9.** 9.87 + 2.16

**10.** 5.89 + 7.21

**Estimate each sum.**

**11.** 8.9 + 9.01 + 9.3 + 8.7 + 9.15

**12.** 5.7 + 6.3 + 5.9 + 6.12 + 5.87

**13.** $24.79 + $25.79 + $25.02 + $24.10 + $25.19 + $24.59

**14.** $66.93 + $72.18 + $69.18 + $71.94 + $65.75

**Use any estimation strategy to calculate. Tell which strategy you used.**

**15.** 93.26 − 69.78

**16.** 51.12 × 87.906

**17.** 43.19 + 26.87

**18.** 457.03 + 592.8

**19.** 702 ÷ 61

**20.** 81.19 × 38.69

**21.** 12.87 + 14.31 + 15.09

**22.** 536 ÷ 41

**23.** 526.89 − 417.26

**Find each estimate.**

**24.** A rare truffle once sold for $13.20 for a 0.44 oz can.
Approximately how much would 1 lb of this truffle cost?

**25.** The length of the longest loaf of bread measured 1,405 ft $1\frac{3}{4}$ in. It
was cut into slices $\frac{1}{2}$ in. thick. How many slices were there?

# Reteaching 1-2

**Adding and Subtracting Decimals**

Add 3.19 + 6.098 + 2.67.

① Round to estimate.

$$3.19 \rightarrow 3$$
$$6.098 \rightarrow 6$$
$$+\ 26.7 \rightarrow +\ 27$$
$$\phantom{+\ 26.7 \rightarrow}\ 36$$

② Line up the decimal points.

$$3.19$$
$$6.098$$
$$+\ 26.700$$

③ Add zeros. Then add.

$$3.190$$
$$6.098$$
$$+\ 26.700$$
$$35.988$$

Compare to make sure your answer is reasonable: 35.988 is close to 36.

Subtract 8.7 − 4.97.

① Round to estimate.

$$8.7 \rightarrow 9$$
$$-\ 4.97 \rightarrow -\ 5$$
$$\phantom{-\ 4.97 \rightarrow}\ 4$$

② Line up the decimal points.

$$8.7$$
$$-\ 4.97$$

③ Add zeros. Then subtract.

$$8.70$$
$$-\ 4.97$$
$$3.73$$

Compare to make sure your answer is reasonable: 3.73 is close to 4.

**Estimate first. Then find each sum or difference.**

| | | |
|---|---|---|
| **1.** $46.2 - 34.09$ | **2.** $3.31 + 9.075$ | **3.** $9.06 - 7.2$ |
| **4.** $84.32 + 6.94$ | **5.** $8.037 + 1.9$ | **6.** $10.6 - 4.59$ |

**Find each sum or difference.**

**7.** 4.102 + 7.7 _____

**8.** 5.4 − 1.6 _____

**9.** 7.09 + 4.3 + 20.1 _____

**10.** 0.392 − 0.26 _____

**11.** 15.64 − 8.5 _____

**12.** 8.709 + 3.2 _____

**13.** 6 + 0.497 _____

**14.** 95.1 + 6 _____

**15.** 0.004 − 0.0005 _____

**16.** 0.2408 − 0.051 _____

**17.** 0.36 + 4.7 + 6 _____

**18.** 5.306 − 0.78 _____

# Practice 1-2

**Adding and Subtracting Decimals**

**Identify each property shown.**

1. $(8.7 + 6.3) + 3.7 = 8.7 + (6.3 + 3.7)$

_____

2. $9.06 + 0 = 9.06$

_____

3. $4.06 + 8.92 = 8.92 + 4.06$

_____

4. $0 + 7.13 = 7.13 + 0$

_____

5. $(8.4 + 12.6) + 4.7 = 8.4 + (12.6 + 4.7)$

_____

6. $0 + 17.96 = 17.96$

_____

**Find each sum.**

7. $4.6 + 8.79$

_____

8. $14.8 + 29.07$

_____

9. $20.16 + 15.703$

_____

10. $36.12 + 5.793$

_____

11. $8.9 + 2.14 + 7.1$

_____

12. $3.6 + 5.27 + 8.93$

_____

13. $107.5 + 6$

_____

14. $15.26 + 13.29 + 38.96$

_____

15. $46.21 + 53.942$

_____

16. $83.14 + 96.72$

_____

17. $58.01 + 74.94$

_____

18. $9 + 0.638$

_____

**Find each difference.**

19. $8.7 - 2.03$

_____

20. $53.86 - 4.02$

_____

21. $14.59 - 8.3$

_____

22. $27.13 - 18.9$

_____

23. $42.75 - 26.36$

_____

24. $53.86 - 16.47$

_____

25. $56.89 - 48.91$

_____

26. $23.5 - 18.079$

_____

27. $5.06 - 3.297$

_____

28. $3.4 - 2.768$

_____

29. $5.002 - 4.3$

_____

30. $0.2406 - 0.058$

_____

**Use the advertisement at the right. Find each cost.**

| | |
|---|---|
| 2 eggs, toast, bacon, milk | $2.75 |
| 1 egg, toast, bacon, milk | $2.20 |
| toast, milk | $0.90 |
| toast, bacon, milk | $1.65 |
| 1 egg, toast | $0.95 |

31. 1 egg _____

32. toast _____

33. bacon _____

34. milk _____

35. 1 egg and milk _____

36. 1 egg and bacon _____

# Reteaching 1-3

**Multiplying and Dividing Decimals**

Multiply 5.43 × 1.8.

① Multiply as if the numbers were whole numbers.

② Count the total number of decimal places in the factors.

③ Place the decimal point in the product.

$$
\begin{array}{r}
5.43 \\
\times \ 1.8 \\
\hline
4344 \\
+\ 543 \\
\hline
9.774
\end{array}
$$

5.43 } **3 decimal places**

9.774 ← **3 decimal places**

Divide 38.25 ÷ 1.5.

① Rewrite the problem with a whole number divisor.

$1.5\overline{)38.25}$
↓

② Place the decimal point in the quotient.

$1.5\overline{)38.2.5}$
**Move 1 place each.**

③ Divide. Then check.

$$
\begin{array}{r}
25.5 \\
15\overline{)382.5} \\
-30 \ \ \ \\
\hline
82 \ \\
-75 \ \\
\hline
7\,5 \\
-7\,5 \\
\hline
0
\end{array}
$$

$25.5 \times 15 = 382.5$ ✔
**Multiply to check.**

---

## Find each product.

1.
$$
\begin{array}{r}
1.42 \\
\times \ 7.2 \\
\hline
\end{array}
$$

2.
$$
\begin{array}{r}
2.2 \\
\times 4.1 \\
\hline
\end{array}
$$

3.
$$
\begin{array}{r}
5.11 \\
\times \ 0.3 \\
\hline
\end{array}
$$

4.
$$
\begin{array}{r}
3.68 \\
\times \ 5.8 \\
\hline
\end{array}
$$

5. $2.8 \times 0.05$

_____

6. $1.45 \cdot 0.7$

_____

7. $(2.07)(4.9)$

_____

8. $9.3(0.56)$

_____

9. $0.006(3.75)$

_____

10. $3.8 \times 912$

_____

## Rewrite each problem so the divisor is a whole number.

11. $5.1\overline{)351.9}$ _____

12. $1.8\overline{)14.9}$ _____

13. $0.32\overline{)39.68}$ _____

14. $0.06\overline{)0.948}$ _____

15. $0.8\overline{)2.112}$ _____

16. $0.49\overline{)9.457}$ _____

## Find each quotient.

17. $2\overline{)15.8}$

18. $0.4\overline{)2.2}$

19. $0.09\overline{)0.99}$

20. $2.7\overline{)12.15}$

21. $0.14\overline{)28.14}$

22. $0.08\overline{)0.64}$

Name _____ Class _____ Date _____

# Practice 1-3

**Multiplying and Dividing Decimals**

**Find each product.**

**1.** $28 \times 6$

**2.** $7.3 \cdot 0.9$

**3.** $58 \cdot 2.1$

**4.** $15(187)$

**5.** $6.6 \times 25$

**6.** $(1.8)(0.7)$

**7.** $0.91 \cdot 2.7$

**8.** $4.6(3.9)$

**Rewrite each equation with the decimal point in the correct place in the product.**

**9.** $5.6 \times 1.2 = 672$

**10.** $3.7 \times 2.4 = 888$

**11.** $6.5 \times 2.5 = 1625$

**12.** $1.02 \times 6.9 = 7038$

**13.** $4.4 \times 6.51 = 28644$

**14.** $0.6 \times 9.312 = 55872$

**Name the property of multiplication shown.**

**15.** $3 \times 4 = 4 \times 3$

**16.** $9 \times (6 \times 3) = (9 \times 6) \times 3$

**17.** $2 \times 0 = 0$

**18.** $10 \times 1 = 10$

**Find each quotient.**

**19.** $0.7 \div 100$

**20.** $4.85 \div 0.1$

**21.** $7.08 \div 10$

**22.** $3.5 \div 0.1$

**23.** $847 \div 0.01$

**24.** $0.3 \div 0.1$

**25.** $32.6 \div 0.01$

**26.** $5.02 \div 0.1$

**27.** $2.1\overline{)12.6}$

**28.** $29.75 \div 0.7$

**29.** $37 \div 0.2$

**30.** $4.74 \div 0.06$

**31.** $1.414 \div 1.4$

**32.** $0.78\overline{)0.16614}$

**33.** $0.154 \div 5.5$

**34.** $0.85\overline{)0.0527}$

**Solve.**

**35.** Alicia paid $1.32 for a bag of pinto beans The beans cost $.55 per lb. How much did the bag of pinto beans weigh?

**36.** Nina and 3 friends ate lunch at a cafe. They decided to split the bill evenly. The total bill was $17.84. How much was each person's share?

 *Course 2* Chapter 1

All rights reserved.

© Pearson Education, Inc., publishing as Pearson Prentice Hall.

# Reteaching 1-4

The **metric system** of measurements uses *prefixes* to describe amounts that are much larger or smaller than the base unit. The base units for measuring length, mass, and volume are shown in the table below.

| ÷ 1,000 | ÷ 100 | ÷ 10 | base unit | × 10 | × 100 | × 1,000 |
|---|---|---|---|---|---|---|
| kilo- | hecto- | deca- | meter gram liter | deci- | centi- | milli- |
| × 1,000 | × 100 | × 10 | base unit | ÷ 10 | ÷ 100 | ÷ 1,000 |

To change a unit in the metric system, you multiply or divide by a power of 10.

① Change 34,000 mL to L.  $\qquad$ 34,000 mL = ? L

② Look at the table. To convert mL to L, divide by 1,000.  $\qquad$ 34,000 ÷ 1,000 = 34

③ Answer:  $\qquad$ 34,000 mL = 34 L

**Write the number that makes each statement true.**

1. 16 grams = __?__ milligrams

   Are you converting from a smaller unit to a larger unit or a larger unit to a smaller unit?

   _____

   Will you multiply or divide?

   _____

   What number will you multiply or divide by?

   _____

   16 grams = _____ milligrams

2. 1,600 meters = __?__ kilometers

   Are you converting from a smaller unit to a larger unit or a larger unit to a smaller unit?

   _____

   Will you multiply or divide?

   _____

   What number will you multiply or divide by?

   _____

   1,600 meters = _____ kilometers

3. 6 meters = _____ centimeters

4. 162 kilograms = _____ grams

5. 4,000 milliliters = _____ liters

6. 25,000 millimeters = _____ meters

**Choose a reasonable estimate.**

7. width of a dime:
   1 m, 1 cm, 1 mm

   _____

8. height of a building
   50 m, 50 cm, 50 mm

   _____

# Practice 1-4

**Choose a reasonable estimate.**

| | | | | |
|---|---|---|---|---|
| 1. | Length of a calculator | 18 m | 18 cm | 18 mm |
| 2. | Length of a football field | 100 km | 100 m | 100 cm |
| 3. | Thickness of a paperback book | 25 km | 25 m | 25 mm |
| 4. | Capacity of a bottle of shampoo | 250 mL | 250 L | 250 kL |

**Write the number that makes each statement true.**

5. 0.7 km = _____ m      6. _____ L = 40 mL      7. 83 m = _____ mm

8. 9,500 m = _____ km      9. 8 g = _____ kg      10. _____ m = 800 km

11. 1 km = _____ cm      12. 4,000 mm = _____ m   13. 9 kg = _____ g

**Change each measurement to the given unit.**

14. 43 km 14 m to kilometers _____

15. 84 m 15 cm to centimeters _____

16. 9 kg 421 g to kilograms _____

17. 14 L 7 mL to liters _____

**Write the metric unit that makes each statement true.**

18. 9,850 kg = 9.85 _____      19. 87.43 m = 8,743 _____

20. 10,542 mL = 10.542 _____   21. 8.42 mm = 0.842 _____

22. 2,347 m = 2.347 _____      23. 0.356 m = 356 _____

**Solve.**

24. The capacity of a beaker is 150 mL. How many beakers can be filled from a 4 L container?

_____

25. Vitamin C comes in pills with a strength of 500 mg. How many pills would you need to take if you want a dosage of one gram?

_____

26. Your science teacher mixes the contents of two beakers containing 2.5 L and 800 mL of a liquid. What is the combined amount?

_____

27. A teaspoon of common table salt contains about 2,000 mg of sodium. How many grams of sodium is this?

_____

# Reteaching 1-5

**Problem Solving: Using a Problem-Solving Plan**

The three-step problem-solving plan is a step-by-step approach you can use to solve problems.

**Step 1: Read and Understand** the problem
**Step 2: Plan** how to solve the problem. **Solve** it.
**Step 3: Look back** and **check** to see if your answer makes sense.

A volunteer organization finds that on the average, 2.87 of every 100 families need advice from the agency. About how many families can they expect to advise in a town of 966 families?

**Read and Understand**

What are you asked to find?

**About how many families need advice from the volunteer organization?**

Do you need to find an exact answer or an estimate?

**Estimate.**

**Plan and Solve**

Use compatible numbers to estimate about how many 100s there are in 966. Write an equation.

**1,000 ÷ 100 = 10**

What number sentence shows about how many families need advice?

**10 × 3**

About how many families need advice?

**30 families**

**Look Back and Check**

What strategy can you use to check your answer? Show an example.

**Make a table.**

| 3 | 6 | 9 | 12 | 15 | 18 | 21 | 24 | 27 | 30 |
|-----|-----|-----|-----|-----|-----|-----|-----|-----|-------|
| 100 | 200 | 300 | 400 | 500 | 600 | 700 | 800 | 900 | 1,000 |

**Use the problem-solving plan to solve each problem.**

1. In the seventh grade at Howard Middle School, 2.14 out of every 100 students play the trumpet. There are 400 seventh graders at Howard. About how many students play the trumpet?   _____

2. Tyrone, Brett, Gabe, and Mario compete in a softball throwing contest. Tyrone won the contest with a distance of 79.25 meters. Brett threw 10.65 meters less than Mario. Gabe threw 6.9 meters further than Brett but 2.75 meters less than Tyrone. How many meters did Mario throw the softball?   _____

# Practice 1-5

**Use the problem-solving plan to solve each problem.**

1. What are two whole numbers whose product is 1,224 and whose sum is 70?

   _____

2. If it costs $3.20 to make one cut on a log, how much would it cost to cut a log into 4 pieces?

   _____

3. At the fair, the chickens and the rabbits were placed under the same tent. The chickens and the rabbits have a total of 360 legs. If there were 105 animals, how many were rabbits?

   _____

4. There are 18 students standing in a circle, evenly spaced and consecutively numbered. Which student is directly opposite student 1?

   _____

5. In a soccer tournament, there are 22 entries. The tournament is single-match elimination; that is, two soccer teams compete at the same time, and the loser is eliminated. How many games will be played to determine the champion?

   _____

6. A license plate has a three-digit number printed on it. The product of the digits is 210, their sum is 18, and the numbers appear in descending order from left to right. What is the license plate number?

   _____

7. Two students started a phone club. It was decided that once a month each member would call every member of the club. They also decided to expand the club by adding one new member each month. How many phone calls would be made during the month in which the fifth member was added?

   _____

# Reteaching 1-6

**Comparing and Ordering Integers**

The numbers 2 and −2 are opposites. The numbers 7 and −7 are opposites.
**Integers** are the set of positive whole numbers, their opposites, and zero.

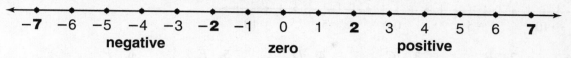

You can use the number line to compare integers.

−2 is less than 0.                    7 is greater than 2.
−2 < 0                                7 > 2

| Numbers to the left are less. <br> −2 is farther left than 0. | Numbers to the right are greater. <br> 7 is farther right than 2. |
| --- | --- |

The **absolute value** of an integer is its distance from zero on the
number line. Distance is always positive.

The absolute value of −5 is 5.              The absolute value of 3 is 3.
$|-5| = 5$                                  $|3| = 3$

**Compare using <, >, or =.**

1. 4 ☐ 2

2. −3 ☐ −2

3. 3 ☐ −4

4. −1 ☐ −2

5. 0 ☐ 5

6. 0 ☐ −4

7. −6 ☐ 4

8. −8 ☐ −2

9. 3 ☐ 0

10. −7 ☐ −10

11. −10 ☐ 10

12. 1 ☐ −1

**Find each absolute value.**

13. $|-6| = $ _____

14. $|3| = $ _____

15. $|-8| = $ _____

16. $|9| = $ _____

17. $|-5| = $ _____

18. $|0| = $ _____

19. $|6| = $ _____

20. $|-10| = $ _____

21. $|-20| = $ _____

**Order the numbers from least to greatest.**

22. −4, 5, −2, 0, 1

_____

23. 6, −3, −5, 4, −6

_____

24. 3, −5, 4, −4, −7, 0

_____

25. 1, 3, −7, −6, 5, −2

_____

Name _____  Class _____  Date _____

# Practice 1-6

**Name the integer represented by each point on the number line.**

**1.** A     **2.** B     **3.** C     **4.** D     **5.** E     **6.** F

**Compare. Use <, >, or =.**

**7.** $-8$ ☐ $8$     **8.** $4$ ☐ $-4$     **9.** $|5|$ ☐ $|-5|$     **10.** $-8$ ☐ $0$

**11.** $-6$ ☐ $-2$     **12.** $-1$ ☐ $-3$     **13.** $|-4|$ ☐ $0$     **14.** $|-3|$ ☐ $2$

**Graph each integer and its opposite on the number line.**

**15.** $-9$

**16.** $5$

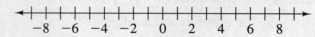

**17.** $6$

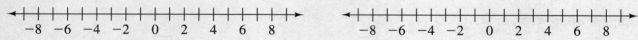

**18.** $7$

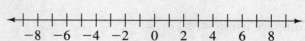

**19.** $8$

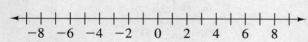

**20.** $-2$

**Find each absolute value.**

**21.** $|2|$     **22.** $|-3|$     **23.** $|-38|$     **24.** $|-2+5|$     **25.** $|-44|$

_____    _____    _____    _____    _____

**26.** $|5|+4$     **27.** $|-5|+4$     **28.** $|5+2|$     **29.** $|-16|$     **30.** $|3-7|$

_____    _____    _____    _____    _____

**Write an integer to represent each situation.**

**31.** a gain of 5 yards     **32.** a debt of $5     **33.** 4 degrees below zero

_____    _____    _____

**34.** a temperature of 100°F     **35.** 135 feet below sea level     **36.** a loss of $30

_____    _____    _____

# Reteaching 1-7

**Adding and Subtracting Integers**

Use these rules to add and subtract integers.

### Adding Integers

| Same Sign | Different Signs |
|---|---|
| • The sum of two positive integers is positive.<br>  Example: $6 + 16 = 22$<br>• The sum of two negative integers is negative.<br>  Example: $-9 + (-3) = -12$ | • First find the absolute values of each number.<br>• Then subtract the lesser absolute value from the greater.<br>• The sum has the sign of the integer with the greater absolute value.<br>  Example: $-10 + 9 = -1$ |

### Subtracting Integers

• To subtract integers, add the opposite.
• Then follow the rules for adding integers.
  Example: $6 - (-3) = 6 + 3 = 9$

---

**Find each sum.**

**1.** $8 + (-2)$ _____

**2.** $-9 + 4$ _____

**3.** $3 + (-2)$ _____

**4.** $-1 + 11$ _____

**5.** $12 + 13$ _____

**6.** $-9 + 5$ _____

**7.** $7 + 2$ _____

**8.** $-1 + (-7)$ _____

**9.** $-3 + 0$ _____

**10.** $-1 + (-1)$ _____

**11.** $6 + 5$ _____

**12.** $3 + (-2)$ _____

**Complete.**

**13.** $-3 - 4$  Change to addition:  $-3 +$ _____ $=$ _____

**14.** $5 - 2$  Change to addition:  $5 +$ _____ $=$ _____

**15.** $-6 - (-10)$  Change to addition:  $-6 +$ _____ $=$ _____

**16.** $8 - (-2)$  Change to addition:  $8 +$ _____ $=$ _____

**Find each difference.**

**17.** $4 - 5$ _____

**18.** $-5 - 4$ _____

**19.** $-8 - (-7)$ _____

**20.** $19 - (-6)$ _____

**21.** $-10 - 12$ _____

**22.** $-12 - 10$ _____

**23.** $-4 - (-5)$ _____

**24.** $-2 - (-3)$ _____

**25.** $9 - (-7)$ _____

**26.** $0 - 3$ _____

**27.** $6 - 8$ _____

**28.** $0 - (-10)$ _____

# Practice 1-7

**Adding and Subtracting Integers**

**Find each sum.**

**1.** $-2 + (-3)$

**2.** $8 - 7 + 4$

**3.** $8 + (-5)$

**4.** $15 + (-3)$

_____

**5.** $-16 + 8$

**6.** $7 + (-10)$

**7.** $-9 + (-5)$

**8.** $-12 + 14$

_____

**Find each difference.**

**9.** $9 - 26$

**10.** $-4 - 15$

**11.** $21 - (-7)$

**12.** $27 - (-16)$

_____

**13.** $-16 - (-43)$

**14.** $47 - 19$

**15.** $-156 - 98$

**16.** $-192 - 47$

_____

**17.** $0 - (-51)$

**18.** $-63 - 89$

**19.** $-12 - (-21)$

**20.** $92 - (-16)$

_____

**21.** $72 - 15$

**22.** $-86 - (-19)$

**23.** $17 - (-46)$

**24.** $-78 - (-53)$

_____

**Find the value of each expression.**

**25.** $3 + 8 + (-4)$

**26.** $2 + |-3| + (-3)$

**27.** $9 + 7 - 6$

_____

**28.** $56 + (-4) + (-58)$

**29.** $-4 - 3 + (-2)$

**30.** $|-8| - 15 + (-8)$

_____

**Use >, <, or = to complete each statement.**

**31.** $-9 - (-11)$ ☐ $0$  **32.** $-17 + 20$ ☐ $0$  **33.** $11 - (-4)$ ☐ $0$  **34.** $-19 + 16$ ☐ $0$

**35.** $28 - 19$ ☐ $0$  **36.** $52 + (-65)$ ☐ $0$  **37.** $-28 - (-28)$ ☐ $0$  **38.** $-28 - (-53)$ ☐ $0$

**Solve.**

**39.** The highest and lowest temperatures ever recorded in Africa are 136°F and −11°F. The highest temperature was recorded in Libya, and the lowest temperature was recorded in Morocco. What is the difference in these temperature extremes?

_____

**40.** The highest and lowest temperatures ever recorded in South America are 120°F and −27°F. Both the highest and lowest temperatures were recorded in Argentina. What is the difference in these temperature extremes?

_____

# Reteaching 1-8

**To multiply integers:**

- If the signs are alike, the product is positive.

$$2 \cdot 3 = 6$$
$$-2 \cdot -3 = 6$$

- If the signs are different, the product is negative.

$$2 \cdot -3 = -6$$
$$-2 \cdot 3 = -6$$

**To divide integers:**

- If the signs are alike, the quotient is positive.

$$6 \div 3 = 2$$
$$-6 \div -3 = 2$$

- If the signs are different, the quotient is negative.

$$6 \div -3 = -2$$
$$-6 \div 3 = -2$$

**Study these four examples. Write positive or negative to complete each statement.**

$$7 \cdot 3 = 21 \qquad\qquad 7 \cdot -3 = -21$$
$$-7 \cdot -3 = 21 \qquad\qquad -7 \cdot 3 = -21$$

1. When both integers are positive, the product is _____.

2. When one integer is positive and one is negative, the product is _____.

3. When both integers are negative, the product is _____.

$$21 \div 3 = 7 \qquad\qquad -21 \div -3 = 7$$
$$21 \div -3 = -7 \qquad\qquad -21 \div 3 = -7$$

4. When both integers are positive, the quotient is _____.

5. When both integers are negative, the quotient is _____.

6. When one integer is positive and one is negative, the quotient is _____.

**Tell whether each product or quotient will be *positive* or *negative*.**

7. $4 \cdot 7$

8. $-4 \cdot 7$

9. $-4 \cdot -7$

10. $4 \cdot -7$

11. $-28 \div 4$

12. $28 \div 4$

13. $-28 \div -7$

14. $28 \div -7$

15. $10 \cdot -4$

16. $-25 \div 5$

17. $-2 \cdot -2$

18. $100 \div 10$

# Practice 1-8

**Multiplying and Dividing Integers**

**Complete each statement. Then write two examples to illustrate each relationship.**

**1.** positive ÷ positive = ?

_____

**2.** negative · positive = ?

_____

**3.** positive · positive = ?

_____

**4.** negative ÷ negative = ?

_____

**5.** negative ÷ positive = ?

_____

**6.** positive · positive = ?

_____

**7.** positive ÷ negative = ?

_____

**8.** negative · negative = ?

_____

**Estimate each product or quotient.**

**9.** $-72 \cdot 57$

**10.** $-92 \cdot (-41)$

**11.** $-476 \div 90$

**12.** $-83 \cdot 52$

**13.** $538 \div (-63)$

**14.** $-803 \cdot (-106)$

**15.** $49 \cdot 61$

**16.** $479 \div (-61)$

**Find each product or quotient.**

**17.** $\frac{-36}{9}$

**18.** $\frac{-52}{-4}$

**19.** $(-5) \cdot (-20)$

**20.** $\frac{-63}{-9}$

**21.** $(-15) \cdot (2)$

**22.** $\frac{22}{-2}$

**23.** $(13) \cdot (-6)$

**24.** $\frac{-100}{-5}$

**25.** $(-60) \cdot (-3)$

**26.** $\frac{-240}{30}$

**27.** $(43) \cdot (-8)$

**28.** $\frac{-169}{-13}$

# Reteaching 1-9
**Order of Operations and the Distributive Property**

You can remember the order of operations using this phrase:

**P**lease, **M**y **D**ear **A**unt **S**ally

**P**arentheses **M**ultiply **D**ivide **A**dd **S**ubtract

① First, do operations within parentheses.

$7 + 8 \cdot \boxed{(5 + 3)} - 1$          $3 \div \boxed{(5 - 2)} + 36$

$7 + 8 \cdot \quad 8 \quad - 1$          $3 \div \quad 3 \quad + 36$

② Next, multiply and divide from left to right.

$7 + \boxed{8 \cdot 8} - 1$          $\boxed{3 \div 3} + 36$

$7 + \quad 64 \quad - 1$          $\quad 1 \quad + 36$

③ Then, add and subtract from left to right.

$\boxed{7 + 64} - 1$          $\boxed{1 + 36}$

$71 \quad - 1$          $37$

$70$

---

**Complete.**

**1.** $3 + 2 \cdot 4$

$3 + $ _____

_____

**2.** $5 \cdot 4 + 3 \cdot 2$

_____ $+$ _____

_____

**3.** $(5 \cdot 4) + 3 - 2$

_____

_____

**4.** $5 + 7 \cdot 2$

$5 + $ _____

_____

**5.** $8 \cdot 6 + 4 \cdot 4$

_____ $+$ _____

_____

**6.** $(6 \cdot 2) + (12 \div 2)$

_____ $+$ _____

_____

**Find the value of each expression.**

**7.** $8 + 5 \cdot 6 + 2$

_____

**8.** $7 - 4 + 5 \cdot 3$

_____

**9.** $9 + 3 \cdot 7 - 5$

_____

**10.** $(15 + 9) \div (8 - 2)$

_____

**11.** $80 - 6 \cdot 7$

_____

**12.** $15 \div (5 - 2)$

_____

**Find the missing numbers. Then simplify.**

**13.** $8(5 + 2) = \boxed{\phantom{0}}(5) + \boxed{\phantom{0}}(2) = \boxed{\phantom{00}}$

**14.** $\boxed{\phantom{0}}(5.6) = 4(6.0) - 4(\boxed{\phantom{0}}) = \boxed{\phantom{00}}$

**15.** $\boxed{\phantom{0}}(3.4 + 7) = 5(3.4) + 5(7) = \boxed{\phantom{00}}$

**16.** $4(6 + 7) = \boxed{\phantom{0}}(6) + \boxed{\phantom{0}}(7) = \boxed{\phantom{00}}$

**17.** $9(3 + 6) = 9(\boxed{\phantom{0}}) + 9(\boxed{\phantom{0}}) = \boxed{\phantom{00}}$

**18.** $\boxed{\phantom{0}}(10 - 5) = 4(10) - 14(5) = \boxed{\phantom{00}}$

# Practice 1-9

Order of Operations and the Distributive Property

**Find the value of each expression.**

**1.** $(8 + 2) \times 9$

**2.** $5 - 1 \div 4$

**3.** $(6 + 3) \div 18$

**4.** $80 - 6 \times 7$

_____

_____

_____

_____

**5.** $4 \times 6 + 3$

**6.** $4 \times (6 + 3)$

**7.** $35 - 6 \times 5$

**8.** $8 \div 3 + 6$

_____

_____

_____

_____

**Find the missing numbers. Then simplify.**

**9.** $5(9 + 6) = 5\,(\underline{\;?\;}) + 5\,(\underline{\;?\;})$

**10.** $4(9.7 - 8.1) = \underline{\;?\;}(9.7) - \underline{\;?\;}(8.1)$

_____

_____

**11.** $\underline{\;?\;}(3.8) = 9(4) - 9(\underline{\;?\;})$

**12.** $\underline{\;?\;}(17.1 + 12.6) = 6(17.1) + 6(12.6)$

_____

_____

**Find each product mentally using the Distributive Property.**

**13.** $3(6.4)$

**14.** $5(7.1)$

**15.** $5(8.9)$

**16.** $6(9.8)$

_____

_____

_____

_____

**17.** $4(9.2)$

**18.** $9(11.1)$

**19.** $7(8.9)$

**20.** $8(20.1)$

_____

_____

_____

_____

**Copy and place parentheses to make each statement true.**

**21.** $6 + 6 \div 6 \times 6 + 6 = 24$

**22.** $6 \times 6 + 6 \times 6 - 6 = 426$

_____

_____

**23.** $6 + 6 \div 6 \times 6 - 6 = 0$

**24.** $6 - 6 \times 6 + 6 \div 6 = 1$

_____

_____

**25.** $6 + 6 \div 6 + 6 \times 6 = 6$

**26.** $6 - 6 \div 6 \times 6 + 6 = 0$

_____

_____

**27.** A backyard measures 80 ft $\times$ 125 ft. A garden is planted in one corner of it. The garden measures 15 ft $\times$ 22 ft. How much of the backyard is not part of the garden?

_____

# Reteaching 1-10

**Mean, Median, and Mode**

Alexis, Rita, Ming, Mario, and Jewel are in the Library Club.
During the summer they read the following numbers of books.

11, 6, 11, 8, 3

To find the **mean,** or average, number of books read
by the Library Club members:

① Find the sum of the numbers of books read.          $11 + 6 + 11 + 8 + 3 = 39$

② Divide the sum by the number of readers, 5.          $39 \div 5 = 7.8$

The mean is 7.8 books.

To find the **median,** or middle value, of the data set:

① Arrange the numbers in order.                         3, 6, **8**, 11, 11

② Find the middle number.                                      ↑

                                                         8 is the middle number.

The median is 8 books.

The **mode** is the number that occurs most often.       3, 6, 8, **11, 11**
In this data set, 11 occurs twice. The mode is 11.

---

**Use the table to complete Exercises 1–4.**

1. Jerry plays basketball. What number would
   you divide by to find the mean number of
   points Jerry scored per game?              _____

2. What is the mean number of points Jerry scored?

   _____

3. Write the data in order. Then find the median number of points
   Jerry scored.

   _____

4. What is the mode of the data?  _____

| Game Points Scored by Jerry | | |
|---|---|---|
| 10 | 11 | 15 |
| 18 | 9 | 16 |
| 10 | 12 | 10 |

**Find the mean, median, and mode for each situation.**

5. the miniature golf scores for 7 friends:

   23, 30, 39, 32, 35, 14, 23

   mean _____    median _____    mode _____

6. the scores for a geography quiz:

   7  8  6  9  9  8  10  6  9  8  9  7

   mean _____    median _____    mode _____

# Practice 1-10

**The sum of the heights of all the students in a class is 1,472 in.**

1. The mean height is 5 ft 4 in. How many students are in the class?
   (1 ft = 12 in.)

   _____

2. The median height is 5 ft 2 in. How many students are 5 ft 2 in. or taller?

   _____

   How many are shorter?

   _____

**The number of pages read (to the nearest multiple of 50) by the students in history class last week are shown in the tally table at the right.**

| Pages | Tally |
|-------|-------|
| 50 | I |
| 100 | |
| 150 | II |
| 200 | ℍℍ I |
| 250 | |
| 300 | ℍℍ |
| 350 | III |
| 400 | IIII |
| 450 | I |
| 500 | I |

3. Find the mean, the median, and the mode of the data.

   _____

4. What is the outlier in this set of data? _____

5. Does the outlier raise or lower the mean? _____

6. Would you use the mean, median, or mode to most accurately
   reflect the typical number of pages read by a student? Explain.

   _____

**A student hopes to have a 9-point average on his math quizzes.
His quiz scores are 7, 6, 10, 8, and 9. Each quiz is worth 12 points.**

7. What is the average quiz score?

   _____

8. There are two more quizzes. How many more points will be needed to give a 9-point quiz average?

   _____

**Find the mean, median, and mode for each situation.**

9. number of miles biked in one week
   21, 17, 15, 18, 22, 16, 20

   _____

10. number of strikeouts per inning
    3, 2, 0, 0, 1, 2, 3, 0, 2

    _____

**Find the outlier of each data set. Describe how the outlier affects the mean.**

11. 22, 21, 20, 11, 23, 27, 25, 22 _____

12. 27, 25, 22, −20, 20, 23, 21, 25 _____

# Reteaching 2-1

**Evaluating and Writing Algebraic Expressions**

To evaluate an *expression,* substitute a value for the *variable* and compute.

Evaluate $5y - 8$ for $y = 7$.
$$5y - 8$$
$$5 \times 7 - 8 \quad \leftarrow \textbf{Substitute } y \textbf{ with 7.}$$
$$35 - 8 = 27 \quad \leftarrow \textbf{Compute.}$$

You can use key words to write a word phrase for an algebraic expression.

| | | |
|---|---|---|
| $a + 5$ | $\rightarrow$ | $a$ plus 5 |
| | or | $a$ increased by 5 |
| $2n$ | $\rightarrow$ | the product of 2 and $n$ |
| | or | 2 times $n$ |

**Evaluate each expression using the values $m = 3$ and $x = 8$.**

1. $4m + 9$
   Substitute $m$: $4 \times$ _____ $+ 9$

   Compute: _____ $+ 9 =$ _____

2. $4x - 7$
   Substitute $x$: $4 \times$ _____ $- 7$

   Compute: _____ $- 7 =$ _____

3. $5x + x$
   Substitute $x$: $5 \times$ _____ $+$ _____

   Compute: _____ $+$ _____ $=$ _____

4. $x + 2m$
   Substitute $x$ and $m$: _____ $+ 2 \times$ _____

   Compute: _____ $+$ _____ $=$ _____

**Evaluate each expression using the values $y = 4$, $z = 8$, and $p = 10$.**

5. $3y + 6 =$ _____

6. $4z - 2 =$ _____

7. $p + 2p =$ _____

8. $3z \times z =$ _____

9. $5z - y =$ _____

10. $2p + y =$ _____

11. $8p - p =$ _____

12. $3y + 2z =$ _____

**Write a word phrase for each algebraic expression.**

13. $9 + x$

   _____

14. $6x$

   _____

15. $x - 8$

   _____

16. $\frac{x}{5}$

   _____

**Write an algebraic expression for each word phrase.**

17. $x$ newspapers plus 10

   _____

18. 4 less than $x$ teabags

   _____

19. 3 more than $x$ envelopes

   _____

20. 6 times $x$ school buses

   _____

# Practice 2-1

**Evaluating and Writing Algebraic Expressions**

**Evaluate each expression using the values $m = 7$, $r = 8$, and $t = 2$.**

**1.** $5m - 6$      **2.** $4t + 18$      **3.** $4m + t$      **4.** $r \div t$

_____      _____      _____      _____

**5.** $m \times t$      **6.** $35 \div m$      **7.** $5t + 2m$      **8.** $r \times m$

_____      _____      _____      _____

**9.** $3m - 5t$      **10.** $m + r - t$      **11.** $(m \times r) \div t$      **12.** $mrt$

_____      _____      _____      _____

**13.** Complete the table below. Substitute the value on the left for the variable in the expression at the top of each column. Then evaluate each expression.

| | $w + 5$ | $3(w + 4)$ | $5w$ | $8(3w)$ | $3(w - 2)$ |
|---|---|---|---|---|---|
| $w = 2.7$ | | | | | |
| $w = 9.05$ | | | | | |

**Write a word phrase for each algebraic expression.**

**14.** $n + 16$      **15.** $3.2n$      **16.** $25.6 - n$

_____      _____      _____

**17.** $n \div 24$      **18.** $\frac{45}{n}$      **19.** $15.4 - n$

_____      _____      _____

**Write an algebraic expression for each word phrase.**

**20.** 12 more than $m$ machines

_____

**21.** six times the daily amount of fiber $f$ in your diet

_____

**22.** your aunt's age $a$ minus 25

_____

**23.** the total number of seashells $s$ divided by 10

_____

**24.** You and four friends plan a surprise party. Each of you contributes the same amount of money $m$ for food.

    **a.** Write an algebraic expression for the total amount of money contributed for food. _____

    **b.** Evaluate your expression for $m = \$5.25$. _____

# Reteaching 2-2

**Using Number Sense to Solve Equations**

**One way to solve some equations is to use mental math.**

| | |
|---|---|
| Solve $t + 9 = 13$. | Solve $y - 7 = 15$. |
| Ask yourself, what number added to 9 is 13? | Ask yourself, what number minus 7 is 15? |
| $4 + 9 = 13$ <br> So, $t = 4$. | $22 - 7 = 15$ <br> So, $y = 22$. |
| Solve $\frac{a}{3} = 9$ | Solve $3y = 15$. |
| Ask yourself, what number divided by 3 equals 9? | Ask yourself, what number multiplied by 3 is 15? |
| $\frac{27}{9} = 3$ <br> So, $a = 27$. | $3 \cdot 5 = 15$ <br> So, $y = 5$. |

**Solve each equation using mental math.**

**1.** $4t = 24$

_____

**2.** $3w = 45$

_____

**3.** $p + 8 = 16$

_____

**4.** $a + 2 = 11$

_____

**5.** $\frac{h}{3} = 7$

_____

**6.** $\frac{g}{4} = 7$

_____

**7.** $y - 7 = 15$

_____

**8.** $d - 6 = 14$

_____

**Solve each equation using mental math or estimation.**

**9.** $d + 7 = 21$

_____

**10.** $c - 21 = 4$

_____

**11.** $a + 9 = 50$

_____

**12.** $q - 43.94 = 400.12$

_____

**13.** $3 + b = -6$

_____

**14.** $91 + r = 100$

_____

**15.** $28 - n = 20$

_____

**16.** $16.3 + s = 36.94$

_____

# Practice 2-2

**Identify a solution for each equation from the given set of numbers.**

**1.** $30p = 900$; 3, 20, 30, or 60

_____

**2.** $\frac{h}{9} = 11$; 3, 30, 72, or 99

_____

**3.** $t + 32.4 = 62$; 29.6, 31.4, or 18.6

_____

**4.** $r - 17 = 40$; 23, 57 or 63

_____

**Solve each equation using mental math.**

**5.** $5t = 25$

_____

**6.** $8w = 64$

_____

**7.** $9y = 81$

_____

**8.** $p + 5 = 12$

_____

**9.** $a + 2 = 15$

_____

**10.** $w + 8 = 20$

_____

**11.** $\frac{h}{6} = 4$

_____

**12.** $\frac{g}{8} = 16$

_____

**13.** $\frac{a}{7} = 3$

_____

**14.** $y - 11 = 28$

_____

**15.** $d - 4 = 12$

_____

**16.** $w - 10 = 15$

_____

**17.** $18 - t = 14$

_____

**18.** $21 + y = 31.64$

_____

**19.** $18.43 + x = 123.4$

_____

**20.** The seventh-grade class has been collecting aluminum cans for recycling. The class has collected 210 cans. Their goal is to collect 520 cans. Write an equation and estimate the number of aluminum cans needed to reach their goal.

_____

**21.** A seamstress bought some bolts of fabric at $25.30 each. She spent a total of $227.70. Write an equation and estimate the number of bolts of fabric that she purchased.

_____

**22.** For your party you purchased balloons for $.79 each. You spent a total of $11.85. Write an equation and estimate the number of balloons purchased.

_____

# Reteaching 2-3

**Solving Equations by Adding or Subtracting**

**Follow these steps to solve equations.**

|  | | Solve: $n + (-2) = 11$ | Solve: $n - 6 = -36$ |
|---|---|---|---|
| ① | Use the inverse operation on both sides of the equation. | $n + (-2) - (-2) = 11 - (-2)$ | $n - 6 + 6 = -36 + 6$ |
| ② | Simplify. | $n = 13$ | $n = -30$ |
| ③ | Check. | $n + (-2) = 11$ <br> $13 + (-2) \stackrel{?}{=} 11$ <br> $11 = 11$ ✔ | $n - 6 = -36$ <br> $-30 - 6 \stackrel{?}{=} -36$ <br> $-36 = -36$ ✔ |

---

**Solve each equation. Check each answer.**

**1.** $n + 6 = 8$

$n + 6 - 6 = 8 -$ _____

$n =$ _____

**2.** $n - 3 = 20$

$n - 3 +$ _____ $= 20 + 3$

$n =$ _____

**3.** $n - (-3) = -1$

$n - (-3) +$ _____ $= -1 +$ _____

$n =$ _____

**4.** $-2 = n + 5$

$-2 -$ _____ $= n + 5 -$ _____

_____ $= n$

**5.** $n - (-4) = -2$

$n - (-4) +$ _____ $= -2 +$ _____

$n =$ _____

**6.** $n - 16 = -23$

$n - 16 +$ _____ $= -23 +$ _____

$n =$ _____

**Use a calculator, pencil and paper, or mental math. Solve each equation.**

**7.** $n + 1 = 17$

_____

**8.** $n - (-6) = 7$

_____

**9.** $n - 8 = -12$

_____

**10.** $n - 19 = 34$

_____

**11.** $61 = n + 29$

_____

**12.** $n + 84 = 131$

_____

**13.** $-13 = n + 9$

_____

**14.** $-18 = n - (-5)$

_____

**15.** In track practice Jesse ran a mile in 7 minutes. His mile time was $2\frac{1}{2}$ minutes faster than Michael's time. Write and solve an equation to calculate Michael's mile time.

_____

# Practice 2-3

**Solve each equation. Check your answer.**

**1.** $n + 2 = 5$

**2.** $x - 1 = -3$

**3.** $7 = a + 2$

**4.** $p + 2 = -6$

**5.** $-9 = -4 + a$

**6.** $-2 = c + 2$

**7.** $x - (-3) = 7$

**8.** $a + (-6) = 5$

**9.** $10 = r - 5$

**10.** $x + 10 = 2$

**11.** $-5 + c = -1$

**12.** $-12 = 7 + h$

**13.** $16 + s = 6$

**14.** $p + (-2) = 19$

**15.** $r - 7 = -13$

**16.** $25 = a - (-3)$

**Use a calculator, paper and pencil, or mental math. Solve each equation.**

**17.** $t + 43 = 28$

**18.** $-19 = r + 6$

**19.** $25 = r + 7$

**20.** $13 = 24 + c$

**21.** $d - 19 = -46$

**22.** $b + 27 = -18$

**23.** $46 = f - 19$

**24.** $z - 74 = -19$

**25.** The odometer on your family car reads 20,186.7 after going 62.3 miles. Write and solve an equation to determine how many miles were on the odometer before going 62.3 miles.

_____

**26.** Michael bought a $25.00 gift for a friend. After he bought the gift, Michael had $176.89. Write and solve an equation to calculate how much money Michael had before he bought the gift.

_____

**27.** This spring it rained a total of 11.5 inches. This was 3 inches less than last spring. Write and solve an equation to find the amount of rain last season.

_____

# Reteaching 2-4

**Solving Equations by Multiplying or Dividing**

**Follow these steps to solve equations.**

Solve: $\frac{t}{5} = -7$         Solve: $-2x = 8$

① Use the inverse operation on both sides of the equation.

$(5)\frac{t}{5} = (5)(-7)$         $\frac{-2x}{-2} = \frac{8}{-2}$

② Simplify.

$t = -35$         $x = -4$

③ Check.

$\frac{t}{5} = -7$         $-2x = 8$

$\frac{-35}{5} \overset{?}{=} -7$         $-2(-4) \overset{?}{=} 8$

$-7 = -7$ ✔         $8 = 8$ ✔

---

**Solve and check each equation.**

**1.** $-5n = 30$

$\frac{-5n}{\boxed{\phantom{x}}} = \frac{30}{\boxed{\phantom{x}}}$

$n = $ _____

**2.** $\frac{a}{2} = -16$

$(\boxed{\phantom{x}})\frac{a}{2} = (\boxed{\phantom{x}})(-16)$

$a = $ _____

**3.** $-2w = -4$

$\frac{-2w}{\boxed{\phantom{x}}} = \frac{-4}{\boxed{\phantom{x}}}$

$w = $ _____

**4.** $8t = 32$

$\frac{8t}{\boxed{\phantom{x}}} = \frac{32}{\boxed{\phantom{x}}}$

$t = $ _____

**5.** $5 = \frac{g}{6}$

$(\boxed{\phantom{x}})(5) = (\boxed{\phantom{x}})\frac{g}{6}$

_____ $= g$

**6.** $\frac{n}{-3} = -5$

$(\boxed{\phantom{x}})\frac{n}{-3} = (\boxed{\phantom{x}})(-5)$

$n = $ _____

**Use a calculator, pencil and paper, or mental math. Solve each equation.**

**7.** $\frac{x}{4} = -1$

_____

**8.** $-5w = 125$

_____

**9.** $\frac{m}{-8} = 10$

_____

**10.** $-2 = \frac{x}{-4}$

_____

**11.** $3y = 12$

_____

**12.** $-4t = -64$

_____

**13.** $9w = -81$

_____

**14.** $21 = -3z$

_____

**15.** $\frac{a}{-4} = 12$

_____

**16.** $-6b = 42$

_____

**17.** $-3 = \frac{c}{-8}$

_____

**18.** $5 = \frac{d}{7}$

_____

**19.** $2t = 38$

_____

**20.** $-9 = 9q$

_____

**21.** $n \div 6 = -3$

_____

**22.** $-8k = -40$

_____

# Practice 2-4

**Solving Equations by Multiplying or Dividing**

## Use a calculator, paper and pencil, or mental math. Solve each equation.

**1.** $9n = 126$

**2.** $\frac{d}{3} = -81$

**3.** $-2t = 56$

**4.** $\frac{k}{-3} = 6$

**5.** $-18 = \frac{y}{-2}$

**6.** $\frac{y}{16} = 3$

**7.** $-56 = 8r$

**8.** $9w = -63$

**9.** $-3v = -48$

**10.** $13 = \frac{x}{-4}$

**11.** $28 = -4a$

**12.** $\frac{t}{-42} = 3$

**13.** $-19 = \frac{f}{6}$

**14.** $75 = -5s$

**15.** $\frac{q}{4} = 56$

**16.** $18w = -36$

**17.** $24 = \frac{f}{-4}$

**18.** $15 = -3j$

**19.** $102k = 408$

**20.** $\frac{b}{-96} = -3$

## Solve and check each equation.

**21.** $\frac{x}{19} = -21$

**22.** $\frac{x}{-22} = -63$

**23.** $-41x = 164$

**24.** $-100r = 1,200$

**25.** $\frac{x}{91} = -98$

**26.** $452 = -4x$

**27.** $50x = -2,500$

**28.** $79x = -6,320$

## Write and solve an equation to represent each situation.

**29.** One of the largest flowers, the Rafflesia, weighs about 15 lb. How many Rafflesia flowers can be placed in a container that can hold a maximum of 240 lb?

_____

**30.** "Heavy water" is a name given to a compound used in some nuclear reactors. Heavy water costs about $1,500 per gallon. If a nuclear plant spent $10,500 on heavy water, how many gallons of heavy water were bought?

_____

# Reteaching 2-5

**Exploring Two-Step Problems**

You can change a word expression into an algebraic expression by converting the words to variables, numbers, and operation symbols.

To write a two-step algebraic expression for *seven more than three times a number,* follow these steps.

① Define the variable.

Let $n$ represent the number.

② Ask yourself are there any key words?

"More than" means add and "times" means multiply.

③ Write an algebraic expression.

$7 + 3 \cdot n$

④ Simplify.

$7 + 3n$

---

**Define a variable and write an algebraic expression for each phrase.**

1. 3 inches more than 4 times your height _____

2. 4 less than 6 times the weight of a turkey _____

3. 8 more than one-half the number of miles run last week _____

4. twice the cost plus 30 _____

**Solve.**

5. Three friends pay $4 per hour to rent a paddleboat plus $5 for snacks. Write an expression for the total cost of rental and snacks. Then evaluate the expression for 2 hours.

_____

6. A lawn care service charges $10 plus $15 per hour to mow and fertilize lawns. Write an expression for the total cost of having your lawn mowed and fertilized. Then evaluate the expression for 4 hours.

_____

**Solve each equation using number sense.**

7. $2s + 6 = 12$

8. $\frac{f}{10} - 1 = 2$

9. $4r - 7 = 9$

_____ _____ _____

10. $4x - 10 = 30$

11. $2n - 7 = 13$

12. $\frac{s}{3} + 2 = 4$

_____ _____ _____

# Practice 2-5

**Define a variable and write an algebraic expression for each phrase.**

1. six times the price of gas minus 20

_____

2. one-half the distance from Boston to New York minus 25

_____

3. two fewer than five times the number of eggs needed in the recipe

_____

4. 10 megabytes less than the number of megabytes in a computer, divided by 6

_____

**Solve each equation using number sense.**

5. $10 + 5h = 25$

_____

6. $8s - 8 = 64$

_____

7. $3y + 78 = 81$

_____

8. $2g + 4 = 12$

_____

9. $5j + 5 = 15$

_____

10. $3w + 8 = 20$

_____

11. $\frac{h}{2} + 1 = 4$

_____

12. $\frac{g}{8} + 12 = 16$

_____

13. $2 + \frac{b}{7} = 3$

_____

14. For a walk-a-thon a sponsor committed to give you a flat fee of $5 plus $2 for every mile you walk. Write an expression for the total amount you will collect from your sponsor at the end of the walk-a-thon. Then evaluate your expression for 20 miles walked.

_____

15. To win the neighborhood tomato-growing contest Johnny needs for his tomato plants to produce 8 tomatoes per week. He needs 30 tomatoes to win the contest. He already has 6 tomatoes. Write and solve an equation to find the number of weeks he needs to produce 30 tomatoes.

_____

# Reteaching 2-6

The marbles and boxes represent this equation.

$$2x + 3 = 7$$

The variable $x$ stands for the number of marbles (unseen) in each box.

To solve the equation, follow these steps.

### Step 1

Subtract the extra marbles from both sides.

$$2x + 3 - 3 = 7 - 3$$
$$2x = 4$$

### Step 2

Divide the number of marbles by 2, the number of boxes.

$$\frac{2x}{2} = \frac{4}{2}$$
$$x = 2$$

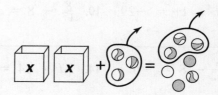

**There are the same number of marbles on each side and the same number of marbles in each box.**

---

**Write and solve an equation for each situation.**

**1.**

_____ + _____ = _____

$x =$ _____

**2.**

_____ + _____ = _____

$x =$ _____

**Complete to solve each equation.**

**3.** $5x + 7 = 2$

$5x + 7 -$ _____ $= 2 -$ _____

$\dfrac{5x}{\boxed{\phantom{0}}} = \dfrac{-5}{\boxed{\phantom{0}}}$

$x =$ _____

**4.** $2x - 1 = 9$

$2x - 1 +$ _____ $= 9 +$ _____

$\dfrac{2x}{\boxed{\phantom{0}}} = \dfrac{10}{\boxed{\phantom{0}}}$

$x =$ _____

**Solve each equation.**

**5.** $4x + 7 = 15$ _____

**6.** $3b - 5 = 13$ _____

**7.** $5t - 2 = -17$ _____

**8.** $3z + 1 = 16$ _____

**9.** $7h - 9 = -2$ _____

**10.** $2k + 12 = -2$ _____

# Practice 2-6

**Solve each equation. Then check your answer.**

1. $7m + 8 = 71$    2. $\frac{y}{7} + 6 = 11$    3. $12y + 2 = 146$    4. $\frac{m}{9} - 17 = 21$

_____    _____    _____    _____

5. $\frac{y}{-12} + 1 = 6$    6. $2a - 1 = 19$    7. $\frac{c}{9} - 8 = 17$    8. $-4t + 16 = 24$

_____    _____    _____    _____

9. $4f + 11 = -29$    10. $\frac{g}{17} - 8 = -6$    11. $13n - 9 = 17$    12. $5v - 42 = 73$

_____    _____    _____    _____

13. $\frac{b}{-2} - 8 = -6$    14. $3d + 14 = 11$    15. $\frac{z}{17} - 1 = 8$    16. $\frac{e}{5} - 14 = 21$

_____    _____    _____    _____

17. $\frac{f}{-9} + 4 = 2$    18. $-2y + 16 = 10$    19. $4w - 26 = 82$    20. $\frac{j}{19} - 2 = -5$

_____    _____    _____    _____

**Solve each equation.**

21. $3n - 8 = 4$    22. $\frac{n}{5} - 4 = 11$

_____    _____

23. $2n - 3 = 9$    24. $1 + \frac{n}{4} = 9$

_____    _____

**Match each sentence with a two-step equation.**

25. Half a dollar minus five dollars equals fifteen dollars.    **A.** $4n - 8 = -5$

_____

**B.** $3n - 2 = 12$

26. Five hours more than one half of an hour equals fifteen hours.    **C.** $\frac{n}{2} + 5 = 15$

_____

**D.** $3n + 2 = 12$

27. Two less than three times the number of feet of fencing    **E.** $\frac{n}{2} - 5 = 15$
required equals twelve feet.

**F.** $\frac{n}{4} - 8 = -5$

_____

28. Eight less than the quotient of Dave's gold score and four
equals negative five.    _____

29. Three times Gail's age increased by two years equals twelve years.    _____

30. Eight fewer than four times the elevation of a city equals negative five.    _____

# Reteaching 2-7

**Problem Solving: Write an Equation**

The cost for a car and driver on a car ferry is $15. Each additional passenger is $2. If Brett pays a toll of $21, how many additional passengers does he have?

**Read and Understand**

What information are you given? *You know the cost for the car and driver, the cost for each passenger and the total toll paid.* What are you asked to find? *You want to find the number of additional passengers.*

**Plan and Solve**

You are given a relationship between numbers. So, an equation may help solve the problem. The toll is $15 for the car and driver plus $2 for each passenger ($p$).

$$15 + 2p = \text{toll}$$
$$15 + 2p = 21$$

Solve the equation for $p$.

$$15 + 2p = 21$$
$$15 - 15 + 2p = 21 - 15 \quad \leftarrow \textbf{Subtract 15.}$$
$$2p = 6 \quad \leftarrow \textbf{Simplify.}$$
$$\frac{2p}{2} = \frac{6}{2} \quad \leftarrow \textbf{Divide by 2.}$$
$$p = 3 \quad \leftarrow \textbf{Simplify.}$$

There are 3 passengers.

**Look Back and Check**

$15 for car + $2 × 3 additional passengers = $21.

---

**Solve each problem by writing an equation.**

1. A jacket costs $28 more than twice the cost of a pair of slacks. If the jacket costs $152, how much do the slacks cost?

2. Jennifer has $22.75 in her bank. She saves quarters and half dollars. She has $10.50 in half dollars. How many quarters does she have?

3. The monthly fee for cable is $25 plus $4.50 per movie channel. Eugene paid $56.50 in May for his cable bill. How many movie channels does he get?

4. Eric and Wyatt collect football cards. Eric has seven cards more than four times as many as Wyatt. Wyatt has 20 cards. How many cards does Eric have?

# Practice 2-7

**Solve each problem by writing an equation.**

1. In order to make a teaspoon of honey, a honeybee must make 154 trips. If a honeybee made 924 trips, how many teaspoons of honey could it make?

   _____

2. Eight travelers sleeping in a hostel are snoring. The hostel has 15 sleeping travelers. How many travelers are not snoring?

   _____

3. On a trip, a family drove an average of 250 mi each day. If the family drove a total of 3,000 mi on their trip, how many days were they gone?

   _____

4. Juanita has completed typing 6 pages of her term paper. If her term paper is 18 pages long, how many more pages does she have to type?

   _____

5. You plan to read 500 pages of a book in one week. You have read 142 pages so far this week. How many more pages must you read?

   _____

6. After withdrawing $58, Mark had $200 left in his savings account. How much money was in the account before the withdrawal?

   _____

**Solve using any strategy.**

7. In a pet store the number of fish is 120 more than three times the number of reptiles. If the pet store has 210 fish, how many reptiles does it have?

   _____

8. On a farm, there are 20 fewer cows than twice the number of pigs. If there are 50 cows, how many pigs are there?

   _____

9. A garage charged $248 in parts and $30/h in labor for work on a car. How many hours did the garage spend working on the car if the total bill was $572?

   _____

10. For a campfire, Brian brought 7 more logs than Max. If Max brought 24 logs, how many logs did Brian bring?

   _____

# Reteaching 2-8

**Graphing and Writing Inequalities**

Two expressions separated by an inequality sign form an **inequality.**
An inequality shows that the two expressions *are not* equal. Unlike
the equations you have worked with, an inequality has many
solutions.

The **solutions of an inequality** are the values that make the inequality
true. They can be graphed on a number line. Use a closed circle (●)
for ≤ and ≥ and an open circle (○) for > and <. For example:

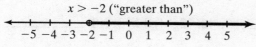

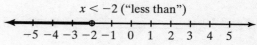

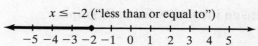

**Graph the inequality $x > 4$.**

The inequality is read as "$x$ is greater than 4." Since all numbers to
the right of 4 are greater than 4, you can draw an arrow from 4 to the
right. Since 4 is not greater than itself, use an open circle on 4.

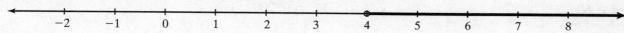

1. **Graph the inequality $x \leq -3$.**

   **a.** Write the inequality in words. _____

   **b.** Will the circle at −3 be open or closed? _____

   **c.** Graph the solution.
   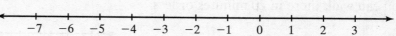

2. **Graph the inequality $x \geq -1$.**

   **a.** Write the inequality in words. _____

   **b.** Will the circle at −1 be open or closed? _____

   **c.** Graph the solution.
   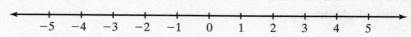

3. **Graph the inequality $x < 3$.**

   **a.** Write the inequality in words. _____

   **b.** Will the circle at 3 be open or closed? _____

   **c.** Graph the solution.
   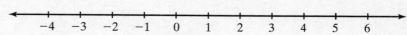

# Practice 2-8

**Graph the solution of each inequality on a number line.**

**1.** $x \leq 3$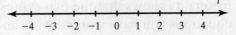

**2.** $t > 1$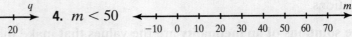

**3.** $q \geq -10$

**4.** $m < 50$

**For each inequality, tell whether the number in bold is a solution.**

**5.** $x < 7; \textbf{7}$ _____

**6.** $p > -3; \textbf{3}$ _____

**7.** $k \geq 5; \textbf{0}$ _____

**8.** $3z \leq 12; \textbf{4}$ _____

**9.** $n - 5 > 3; \textbf{6}$ _____

**10.** $2g + 8 \geq 3; \textbf{-1}$ _____

**Write an inequality for each graph.**

**11.** _____

**12.** _____

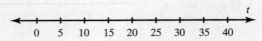

**Write a real-world statement for each inequality.**

**13.** $d \geq 60$

**14.** $p < 200$

_____  _____

_____  _____

**Write an inequality for each statement. Graph each solution on the number line shown.**

**15.** You can walk there in 20 minutes or less.

_____

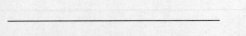

**16.** Each prize is worth over $150.

_____

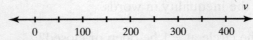

**17.** A species of catfish, *malapterurus electricus,* can generate up to 350 volts of electricity.

    **a.** Write an inequality to represent the amount of electricity generated by the catfish.

        _____

    **b.** Draw a graph of the inequality you wrote in **a.**

# Reteaching 2-9

**Solving Inequalities by Adding or Subtracting**

To solve an inequality you can add the same number to or subtract it from each side of the inequality.

Solve $x + 5 \geq 9$.    Graph the solution.

$x + 5 \geq 9$
$x + 5 - 5 \geq 9 - 5$    Subtract 5 from each side.
$\quad\quad x \geq 4$    Simplify.

Solve $y - 3 < 2$.    Graph the solution.

$y - 3 < 2$
$y - 3 + 3 < 2 + 3$    Add 3 to each side.
$\quad\quad y < 5$    Simplify.

Graph:

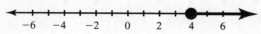

Graph:

---

**Solve each inequality. Graph the solution.**

**1.** $2 + a > 6$    _____

**2.** $-4 + w \leq 0$    _____

**3.** $3 + a \geq 8$    _____

**4.** $w + 1 \leq 4$    _____

**5.** $y + 3 < 5$    _____

**6.** $6 + g \geq 12$    _____

**7.** $2 + x > 7$    _____

**8.** $2 + r < 8$    _____

# Practice 2-9

**Solve each inequality. Graph each solution.**

**1.** $w + 4 < -2$

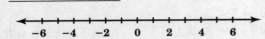

**2.** $a - 4 \geq 0$

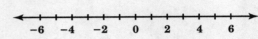

**3.** $a + 19 > 13$

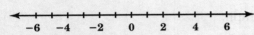

**4.** $x + 7 \leq 12$

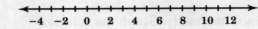

**5.** $a + 2 > -3$

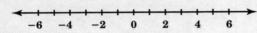

**6.** $t - 6 < 3$

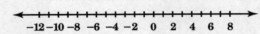

**7.** $f - 5 \leq -5$

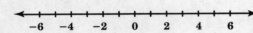

**8.** $a + 4 \geq -6$

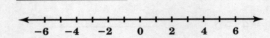

**9.** $-14 + w \geq -12$

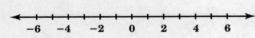

**10.** $r - 16 > -20$

**11.** $r - 3.4 \leq 2.6$

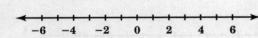

**12.** $a + 5.7 \geq -2.3$

**13.** $h - 4.9 > -0.9$

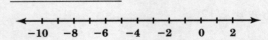

**14.** $y + 3.4 < -4.6$

**Write an inequality for each problem. Solve the inequality.**

**15.** The school record for the most points scored in a football season is 85. Lawrence has 44 points so far this season. How many more points does he need to break the record?

_____

_____

**16.** The maximum weight limit for a fully loaded truck is 16,000 pounds. The truck you are loading currently weighs 12,500 pounds. How much more weight can be added and not exceed the weight limit?

_____

_____

_____

# Reteaching 2-10

To solve an inequality you can multiply or divide each side by the same number. However, if the number is negative, you must also reverse the direction of the inequality sign.

Solve $-4y \geq 16$. Graph the solution.

$-4y \geq 16$

$\dfrac{-4y}{-4} \leq \dfrac{16}{-4}$    Divide each side by $-4$.
                 Reverse the direction
                 of the inequality symbol.
$y \leq -4$    Simplify.

Solve $\dfrac{w}{3} > 2$. Graph the solution.

$\dfrac{w}{3} > 2$

$(3)\dfrac{w}{3} > 2(3)$    Multiply each side by 3.
$w > 6$         Simplify.

Graph:

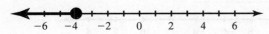

Graph:

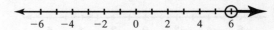

---

**Solve each inequality. Graph the solution.**

**1.** $2a > 10$     _____

**2.** $-4w < 16$   _____

**3.** $\dfrac{r}{2} \geq -2$    _____

**4.** $18 \leq 9a$    _____

**5.** $\dfrac{a}{3} < 1$    _____

**6.** $6g < 6$    _____

**7.** $-3x \geq -6$   _____

**8.** $\dfrac{m}{-2} > 0$   _____

Name _____ Class _____ Date _____

# Practice 2-10

**Solve each inequality. Graph each solution.**

**1.** $6w \leq 36$

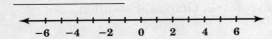

**2.** $10a \geq 40$

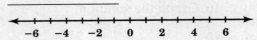

**3.** $\frac{f}{3} \leq -2$

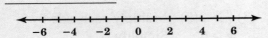

**4.** $\frac{v}{4} > 2$

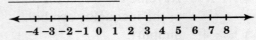

**5.** $7a > -28$

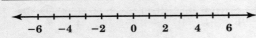

**6.** $\frac{c}{-3} \geq 3$

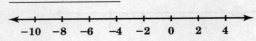

**7.** $\frac{f}{2} > -1$

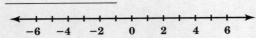

**8.** $9a \leq 63$

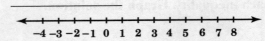

**9.** $4w \geq -12$

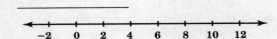

**10.** $\frac{h}{-2} \geq -5$

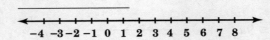

**11.** $\frac{p}{5} \leq 0$

**12.** $8a \geq 56$

**Write an inequality to solve each problem. Then solve the inequality.**

**13.** Marcus wants to buy 5 baseballs. He has $35. What is the most each baseball can cost?

_____

_____

**14.** Melinda charges $4 per hour for babysitting. Mrs. Garden does not want to spend more than $25 for babysitting. What is the maximum number of hours that she can have Melinda babysit?

_____

_____

_____

# Reteaching 3-1

**Exponents and Order of Operations**

You can use a shortcut to indicate repeated multiplication. The **exponent** tells how many times the **base** is used as a factor.

$5^4$ is called an **exponential expression** and 625 is the **value of the expression.**

$$5 \times 5 \times 5 \times 5 = 5^4 = 625$$

exponent

base

You can use this sentence to remember the order of operations for expressions with exponents. ⟶ **P**lease **E**xcuse **M**y **D**ear **A**unt **S**ally.

$2^2 + 4(7 - 3) + 6 = 2^2 + 4(4) + 6$

| | |
|---|---|
| **P** | Do all operations within **P**arentheses first. |

$= 4 + 4(4) + 6$

| | |
|---|---|
| **E** | Evaluate any terms with **E**xponents. |

$= 4 + 16 + 6$

| | |
|---|---|
| **M-D** | **M**ultiply and **D**ivide in order from left to right. |

$= 26$

| | |
|---|---|
| **A-S** | **A**dd and **S**ubtract in order from left to right. |

---

**Write each expression using exponents.**

**1.** $6 \times 6 \times 6 \times 6 \times 6$ _____

**2.** $0.2 \times 0.2 \times 0.2$ _____

**3.** $9 \times 9 \times 9 \times 9$ _____

**4.** $12 \times 12 \times 12 \times 12 \times 12$ _____

**Write each expression as a product of its factors. Then evaluate each expression.**

**5.** $12^2$

**6.** $8^3$

**7.** $(0.4)^3$

**8.** $5^5$

**9.** $3^6$

**10.** $1.4^2$

**Simplify each expression.**

**11.** $7^2 + 3^3$

**12.** $8 + 4^2$

**13.** $5(0.2 + 0.8)^{10}$

**14.** $(9 - 7)^2$

**15.** $(8^2 + 16) \div 2$

**16.** $5^3 + 100$

**17.** $(4 + 7)^2 - 8$

**18.** $(9 - 3)^2 + 6 \times 2$

Name _____ Class _____ Date _____

# Practice 3-1

**Write using exponents.**

1. $3 \times 3 \times 3 \times 3 \times 3$ _____

2. $2.7 \times 2.7 \times 2.7$ _____

3. $11.6 \times 11.6 \times 11.6 \times 11.6$ _____

4. $2 \times 2 \times 2 \times 2 \times 2 \times 2$ _____

5. $8.3 \times 8.3 \times 8.3 \times 8.3 \times 8.3$ _____

6. $4 \times 4 \times 4 \times 4 \times 4 \times 4 \times 4 \times 4$ _____

**Write as the product of repeated factors. Then simplify.**

7. $(0.5)^3$ _____

8. $(-4)^5$ _____

9. $(2.7)^2$ _____

10. $2^3$ _____

11. $(-5)^6$ _____

12. $(8.1)^3$ _____

**Simplify. Use a calculator, paper and pencil, or mental math.**

13. $-4^3$

14. $8^3 + 9$

15. $11 + (-6^3)$

16. $14 + 16^2$

_____  _____  _____  _____

17. $8 + 6^4$

18. $2^5 + 2^3$

19. $3^2 \cdot 5^4$

20. $6^2 - 2^4$

_____  _____  _____  _____

21. $4(0.9 + 1.3)^3$

22. $-3(1.5 - 0.2)^3$

23. $35 - (4^2 + 5)$

24. $(3^3 + 6) - 7$

_____  _____  _____  _____

25. $5(0.3 \cdot 1.2)^2$

26. $-18 \div (1.4 - 0.4)^2$

27. $5(4 + 2)^2$

28. $(8 - 6.7)^3$

_____  _____  _____  _____

29. The volume of an aquarium is approximately $4.3^3$ ft³. Find the volume of the aquarium.

_____

30. Lana is $2^3$ in. taller than her little sister. How many inches taller is Lana than her sister?

_____

# Reteaching 3-2

**Scientific notation** is an efficient way to write very large numbers. A number is written as the product of a number between 1 and 10 and a power of 10.

Write 4,000,000,000 in scientific notation.

① Count the number of places that you need to move the decimal point to the left to get a factor between 1 and 10.

$$4,000,000,000 \rightarrow 4.000\ 000\ 000$$

**9 places**

② Use the number of places as the exponent of 10.

$$4,000,000,000 = 4 \times 10^9$$

To change a number from scientific notation to standard form, undo the steps at the left.

Write $3.5 \times 10^8$ in standard form.

① Note the exponent of 10. (Here it is 8.)

② Move the decimal point to the right the number of places that is equal to the exponent.

$$3.5 \times 10^8 \rightarrow 350,000,000$$

**8 places**

$$3.5 \times 10^8 = 350,000,000$$

**Write in scientific notation.**

1. 3,500

   Move the decimal point _____ places

   to the _____.

   3,500 = _____ × _____

2. 1,400,000

   Move the decimal point _____ places

   to the _____.

   1,400,000 = _____ × _____

3. 93,000,000 _____

4. 1,200,000 _____

5. 17,000 _____

6. 750,000 _____

7. 2,400 _____

8. 6,532,000 _____

9. 560,000,000,000 _____

10. 34,800,000 _____

**Write in standard form.**

11. $2.58 \times 10^3$ _____

12. $8 \times 10^6$ _____

13. $4.816 \times 10^5$ _____

14. $8.11 \times 10^2$ _____

15. $1.85 \times 10^7$ _____

16. $3.7509 \times 10^3$ _____

17. $8.003 \times 10^1$ _____

18. $5.66 \times 10^9$ _____

19. $4.23 \times 10^2$ _____

20. $9.992 \times 10^{10}$ _____

# Practice 3-2

**Write each number in scientific notation.**

1. 73,000,000

2. 4,300

3. 510

4. 56,870

_____  _____  _____  _____

5. 68,900

6. 98,000,000,000

7. 4,890,000

8. 38

_____  _____  _____  _____

9. 120,000

10. 543,000

11. 27

12. 54,000

_____  _____  _____  _____

**Write in standard form.**

13. $5.7 \times 10^6$

14. $2.45 \times 10^8$

15. $4.706 \times 10^{11}$

_____  _____  _____

16. $8 \times 10^1$

17. $7.2 \times 10^3$

18. $1.63 \times 10^{12}$

_____  _____  _____

19. $8.03 \times 10^{14}$

20. $3.26 \times 10^4$

21. $5.179 \times 10^5$

_____  _____  _____

**Write each number in scientific notation.**

22. One type of roundworm can lay 200,000 eggs each day.

_____

23. The nose of a German shepherd dog has about 220 million cells that are used in picking out smells.

_____

24. In a given day, a total of 15,000 tons of potatoes are consumed by the people of Britain.

_____

25. Personal computers are often equipped with 572,000 bytes of RAM (random access memory.).

_____

26. The brain contains about 100 trillion nerve connections.

_____

27. During an average life span, the human heart will beat about 2,800,000,000 times.

_____

28. The volume of the water behind the Grand Coulee Dam is about 10.6 million cubic yards.

_____

29. A second has been defined as the time it takes for an atom of a particular metal to vibrate 9,192,631,770 times.

_____

# Reteaching 3-3

**Divisibility Tests**

One integer is **divisible** by another if the remainder is 0 when you divide the larger number by the smaller number.

**Divisibility Tests for 2, 3, 4, 5, 8, 9, and 10.**

An integer is divisible by
- 2 if it ends in 0, 2, 4, 6, or 8.
- 3 if the sum of its digits is divisible by 3.
- 4 if the number formed by the last two digits is divisible by 4.
- 5 if it ends in 0 or 5.
- 8 if the number formed by the last three digits is divisible by 8.
- 9 if the sum of its digits is divisible by 9.
- 10 if it ends in zero.

Is the first number divisible by the second?

| | | |
|---|---|---|
| **a.** 1,256 by 2 | Yes, 1,256 is even. | |
| **b.** 287 by 3 | No, $2 + 8 + 7 = 17$, which is not divisible by 3. | |
| **c.** 1,536 by 4 | Yes, 36 is divisible by 4. | |
| **d.** 922 by 5 | No, 922 does not end in 5 or 0. | |
| **e.** 30,780 by 8 | No, 780 is not divisible by 8. | |
| **f.** 4,518 by 9 | Yes, $4 + 5 + 1 + 8 = 18$, which is divisible by 9. | |
| **g.** 541 by 10 | No, 541 does not end in zero. | |

---

**Is the first number divisible by the second? Explain.**

**1.** 2,336 by 8

**2.** 580 by 10

**3.** 722 by 5

_____

_____

_____

**4.** 2,505 by 3

**5.** 225,325 by 9

**6.** 421 by 4

_____

_____

_____

**Tell whether each number is divisible by 2, 3, 4, 5, 8, 9, or 10. Some numbers may be divisible by more than one number.**

**7.** 526

**8.** 1,325

**9.** 888

_____

**10.** 981

**11.** 62,810

**12.** 565,852

_____

# Practice 3-3

**Is the first number divisible by the second? Explain.**

**1.** 390 by 3

_____

_____

**2.** 4,310 by 5

_____

_____

**3.** 471 by 2

_____

_____

**4.** 1,255 by 10

_____

_____

**5.** 2,648 by 4

_____

_____

**6.** 531 by 9

_____

_____

**7.** 364,824 by 8

_____

_____

**8.** 312,544 by 2

_____

_____

**9.** 1,541,231 by 3

_____

_____

**10.** 2,553 by 5

_____

_____

**11.** 82,544 by 9

_____

_____

**12.** 650 by 4

_____

_____

**Tell whether each number is divisible by 2, 3, 4, 5, 8, 9, or 10. Some numbers may be divisible by more than one number.**

**13.** 410

_____

**14.** 450

_____

**15.** 432

_____

**16.** 265

_____

**17.** 72,424

_____

**18.** 8,304

_____

**19.** 2,235

_____

**20.** 6,168

_____

**21.** 810

_____

**22.** 3,864

_____

**23.** 2,421

_____

**24.** 875

_____

**Write the missing digit to make each number divisible by 3.**

**25.** 1,3☐1

**26.** 1,843,☐89

**27.** 1☐5,687

**Write the missing digit to make each number divisible by 8.**

**28.** 2,4☐2

**29.** 744,7☐8

**30.** 1,325,☐84

# Reteaching 3-4

A **prime number** has exactly
two factors, 1 and itself.
2 and 7 are prime numbers.
2 is the smallest prime number.

$$2 \times 1 = 2 \qquad 7 \times 1 = 7$$

Every **composite number** can be
written as a product of two or more
prime numbers. This is called the
**prime factorization** of the number.

$$60 = 2 \cdot 2 \cdot 3 \cdot 5 = 2^2 \cdot 3 \cdot 5$$
$$40 = 2 \cdot 2 \cdot 2 \cdot 5 = 2^3 \cdot 5$$

You can use a *factor tree* and division to find the prime factorization
of a number.

① Divide by a factor other than 1 and
   the number itself. Record the divisor
   and the quotient in the factor tree.

② Continue dividing until all the
   factors are prime numbers.

③ Use exponents to write the
   prime factorization.

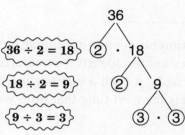

$$36 = 2^2 \cdot 3^2$$

---

**Complete each factor tree. Then write the prime factorization using
exponents where possible.**

**1.**

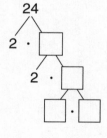

_____

**2.**

_____

**3.**

_____

**Write the prime factorization of each number. Use exponents where
possible.**

**4.** 20 = _____

**5.** 54 = _____

**6.** 40 = _____

**7.** 48 = _____

**8.** 56 = _____

**9.** 150 = _____

# Practice 3-4

**Find the LCM of each pair of numbers.**

**1.** 11, 5 _____      **2.** 5, 12 _____      **3.** 12, 7 _____

**4.** 5, 9 _____       **5.** 5, 18 _____      **6.** 5, 20 _____

**7.** 7, 10 _____      **8.** 17, 13 _____     **9.** 14, 8 _____

**10.** 11, 23 _____    **11.** 14, 5 _____     **12.** 16, 9 _____

**13.** Cameron is making bead necklaces. He has 90 green beads and 108 blue beads. What is the greatest number of identical necklaces he can make if he wants to use all of the beads?

_____

**14.** One radio station broadcasts a weather forecast every 18 minutes and another station broadcasts a commercial every 15 minutes. If the stations broadcast both a weather forecast and a commercial at noon, when is the next time that both will be broadcast at the same time?

_____

**Tell whether each number is prime or composite.**

**15.** 97 _____   **16.** 63 _____   **17.** 29 _____   **18.** 120 _____

**Write the prime factorization. Use exponents where possible.**

**19.** 42 _____          **20.** 130 _____

**21.** 78 _____          **22.** 126 _____

**23.** 125 _____         **24.** 90 _____

**25.** 92 _____          **26.** 180 _____

**Find the GCF of each pair of numbers.**

**27.** 45, 60 _____   **28.** 18, 42 _____   **29.** 32, 80 _____

**30.** 20, 65 _____   **31.** 24, 90 _____   **32.** 17, 34 _____

**33.** 14, 35 _____   **34.** 51, 27 _____   **35.** 42, 63 _____

# Reteaching 3-5

A fraction is in **simplest form** when the numerator and denominator have no common factors other than 1.

To write $\frac{18}{24}$ in the simplest form:

① Divide the numerator and denominator by a common factor.  $\frac{18 \div 2}{24 \div 2} = \frac{9}{12}$

② Continue dividing by common factors until the only common factor is 1.  $\frac{9 \div 3}{12 \div 3} = \frac{3}{4}$  The only factor common to 3 and 4 is 1.

In simplest form $\frac{18}{24}$ is $\frac{3}{4}$.

You can use the greatest common factor (GCF) to write a fraction in simplest form. Divide the numerator and the denominator by the GCF.

The GCF of 18 and 24 is 6.

$$\frac{18}{24} = \frac{18 \div 6}{24 \div 6} = \frac{3}{4}$$

---

**Complete to write each fraction in simplest form.**

1. $\frac{10}{20} = \frac{10 \div}{20 \div 2} = \frac{\phantom{0}\div}{10 \div} = $ _____

2. $\frac{24}{60} = \frac{24 \div 6}{60 \div} = \frac{\phantom{0}\div}{10 \div} = $ _____

**Find the GCF of the numerator and denominator of each fraction.**
**Then write each fraction in simplest form.**

3. $\frac{12}{14} = $ _____
   GCF = _____

4. $\frac{9}{15} = $ _____
   GCF = _____

5. $\frac{35}{42} = $ _____
   GCF = _____

6. $\frac{40}{50} = $ _____
   GCF = _____

**Write each fraction in simplest form.**

7. $\frac{42}{60} = $ _____

8. $\frac{20}{36} = $ _____

9. $\frac{18}{20} = $ _____

10. $\frac{9}{27} = $ _____

11. $\frac{42}{56} = $ _____

12. $\frac{16}{72} = $ _____

13. $\frac{24}{40} = $ _____

14. $\frac{18}{32} = $ _____

15. $\frac{25}{75} = $ _____

16. $\frac{65}{75} = $ _____

17. $\frac{40}{60} = $ _____

18. $\frac{50}{95} = $ _____

# Practice 3-5

**Write each fraction in simplest form.**

1. $\frac{8}{12}$ _____

2. $\frac{9}{15}$ _____

3. $\frac{16}{20}$ _____

4. $\frac{20}{25}$ _____

5. $\frac{15}{18}$ _____

6. $\frac{14}{30}$ _____

7. $\frac{11}{44}$ _____

8. $\frac{24}{36}$ _____

9. $\frac{12}{16}$ _____

10. $\frac{34}{68}$ _____

11. $\frac{28}{42}$ _____

12. $\frac{30}{65}$ _____

**Write each fraction in simplest form. Give the GCF of the numerator and denominator.**

13. $\frac{18}{45}$ ____ GCF = ____

14. $\frac{66}{121}$ ____ GCF = ____

15. $\frac{36}{102}$ ____ GCF = ____

16. $\frac{125}{200}$ ____ GCF = ____

17. $\frac{36}{64}$ ____ GCF = ____

18. $\frac{65}{90}$ ____ GCF = ____

19. $\frac{45}{72}$ ____ GCF = ____

20. $\frac{35}{85}$ ____ GCF = ____

21. $\frac{30}{42}$ ____ GCF = ____

**Solve.**

22. Emily exercised from 4:05 P.M. to 4:32 P.M. For what part of an hour did Emily exercise? Write the fraction in simplest form.

_____

23. Luis rode his bike after school for 48 min. For what part of an hour did he ride his bike? Write the fraction in simplest form.

_____

24. Philip played video games for 55 min before dinner. For what part of an hour did he play?

_____

25. What part of an hour is your school lunch time?

_____

26. Survey 12 people to find their favorite kind of pizza from the following choices. Write the results in fraction form. Then shade the pizza shapes using different colors to indicate their choices.

**Pizza Favorites**

Cheese _____

Green Pepper _____

Olive _____

Mushroom _____

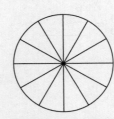

# Reteaching 3-6

**Follow these steps to** *compare* $\frac{2}{5}$ **and** $\frac{3}{10}$ **(unlike denominators).**

① Find the **least common denominator** (LCD).

The denominators are 5 and 10. The LCD of 5 and 10 is their least common multiple.

② Write the equivalent fractions using the LCD.

$\frac{2}{5} = \frac{4}{10}$ and $\frac{3}{10} = \frac{3}{10}$

③ Compare the numerators.

$4 > 3$

So, $\frac{4}{10} > \frac{3}{10}$ and $\frac{2}{5} > \frac{3}{10}$.

**Follow these steps to** *order* **the fractions** $\frac{1}{2}, \frac{3}{5},$ **and** $\frac{2}{3}$.

① Find the LCD.

The LCD of 2, 5, and 3 is 30.

② Write equivalent fractions using the LCD.

$\frac{1}{2} = \frac{1 \cdot 15}{2 \cdot 15} = \frac{15}{30}$

$\frac{3}{5} = \frac{3 \cdot 6}{5 \cdot 6} = \frac{18}{30}$

$\frac{2}{3} = \frac{2 \cdot 10}{3 \cdot 10} = \frac{20}{30}$

③ Order the fractions using their numerators.

$\frac{15}{30} < \frac{18}{30} < \frac{20}{30}$

So, $\frac{1}{2} < \frac{3}{5} < \frac{2}{3}$.

---

**Find each missing number. Then compare the fractions. Use <, >, or =.**

1. $\frac{2}{3}$ and $\frac{3}{5}$

   a. $\frac{2}{3} = \frac{\boxed{\phantom{0}}}{15}, \frac{3}{5} = \frac{\boxed{\phantom{0}}}{15}$

   b. $\frac{2}{3} \boxed{\phantom{0}} \frac{3}{5}$

2. $\frac{1}{2}$ and $\frac{5}{8}$

   a. $\frac{1}{2} = \frac{\boxed{\phantom{0}}}{8}, \frac{5}{8} = \frac{\boxed{\phantom{0}}}{8}$

   b. $\frac{1}{2} \boxed{\phantom{0}} \frac{5}{8}$

3. $\frac{3}{4}$ and $\frac{9}{12}$

   a. $\frac{3}{4} = \frac{\boxed{\phantom{0}}}{12}, \frac{9}{12} = \frac{\boxed{\phantom{0}}}{12}$

   b. $\frac{3}{4} \boxed{\phantom{0}} \frac{9}{12}$

**Compare each pair of fractions. Use <, >, or =.**

4. $\frac{3}{5} \boxed{\phantom{0}} \frac{4}{5}$

5. $\frac{3}{4} \boxed{\phantom{0}} \frac{7}{8}$

6. $\frac{8}{12} \boxed{\phantom{0}} \frac{2}{3}$

7. $\frac{1}{2} \boxed{\phantom{0}} \frac{9}{16}$

8. $\frac{2}{3} \boxed{\phantom{0}} \frac{1}{2}$

9. $\frac{5}{9} \boxed{\phantom{0}} \frac{10}{18}$

10. $\frac{6}{7} \boxed{\phantom{0}} \frac{5}{6}$

11. $\frac{3}{8} \boxed{\phantom{0}} \frac{3}{5}$

**Order from least to greatest.**

12. $\frac{1}{2}, \frac{4}{5}, \frac{1}{4}$ _____

13. $\frac{2}{3}, \frac{3}{8}, \frac{1}{2}$ _____

14. $\frac{5}{6}, \frac{7}{8}, \frac{1}{4}$ _____

15. $\frac{1}{2}, \frac{5}{8}, \frac{5}{6}$ _____

16. $\frac{7}{10}, \frac{2}{3}, \frac{1}{5}$ _____

17. $\frac{2}{3}, \frac{1}{4}, \frac{11}{12}$ _____

# Practice 3-6

**Comparing and Ordering Fractions**

**Write the two fractions for these models and compare them with <, >, or =.**

1. [model] 2. [model] 3. [model]

_____ _____ _____

**Find the LCD of each pair of fractions.**

4. $\frac{5}{8}, \frac{5}{6}$ _____

5. $\frac{5}{12}, \frac{7}{8}$ _____

6. $\frac{9}{10}, \frac{1}{2}$ _____

7. $\frac{2}{3}, \frac{3}{4}$ _____

8. $\frac{1}{6}, \frac{3}{10}$ _____

9. $\frac{1}{4}, \frac{2}{15}$ _____

10. $\frac{5}{6}, \frac{8}{15}$ _____

11. $\frac{7}{12}, \frac{9}{20}$ _____

**Compare each pair of fractions. Use <, >, or =.**

12. $\frac{7}{8} \square \frac{3}{10}$

13. $\frac{4}{5} \square \frac{1}{2}$

14. $\frac{6}{12} \square \frac{4}{8}$

15. $\frac{7}{15} \square \frac{11}{15}$

16. $\frac{4}{5} \square \frac{6}{10}$

17. $\frac{7}{12} \square \frac{2}{3}$

18. $\frac{8}{15} \square \frac{1}{2}$

19. $\frac{10}{15} \square \frac{8}{12}$

20. $\frac{4}{9} \square \frac{7}{9}$

21. $\frac{2}{5} \square \frac{3}{8}$

22. $\frac{1}{2} \square \frac{11}{20}$

23. $\frac{7}{16} \square \frac{1}{2}$

**Order from least to greatest.**

24. $\frac{1}{4}, \frac{1}{3}, \frac{1}{6}$ _____

25. $\frac{1}{2}, \frac{5}{6}, \frac{7}{8}$ _____

26. $\frac{1}{4}, \frac{2}{5}, \frac{3}{8}$ _____

27. $\frac{7}{8}, \frac{5}{9}, \frac{2}{3}$ _____

28. $\frac{3}{8}, \frac{5}{6}, \frac{1}{2}$ _____

29. $\frac{9}{10}, \frac{11}{12}, \frac{15}{16}$ _____

30. $\frac{3}{4}, \frac{1}{2}, \frac{7}{8}$ _____

31. $\frac{5}{9}, \frac{2}{3}, \frac{7}{12}$ _____

32. $\frac{15}{16}, \frac{7}{8}, \frac{1}{2}$ _____

**Solve.**

33. A pattern requires a seam of at least $\frac{5}{8}$ in. Rachel sewed a seam $\frac{1}{2}$ in. wide. Did she sew the seam wide enough? Explain.

_____

34. Marc needs $\frac{3}{4}$ cup of milk for a recipe. He has $\frac{2}{3}$ cup. Does he have enough? Explain.

_____

35. Monica is growing three bean plants as part of a science experiment. Plant A is $\frac{1}{2}$ in. tall. Plant B is $\frac{3}{4}$ in. tall. Plant C is $\frac{3}{8}$ in. tall. Order the plants from shortest to tallest.

_____

36. During a rainstorm Willow received $\frac{7}{16}$ in. of rain and Riverton received $\frac{5}{8}$ in. of rain. Which community received more rain?

_____

# Reteaching 3-7

**Problem Solving: Solve a Simpler Problem and Look for a Pattern**

When solving a problem it may be helpful to look for a pattern.

Look at the three drawings of boxes. How many boxes should there be in the next drawing?

**Read and Understand** Think about the information you are given. You know there are 2 boxes in the first drawing, 4 boxes in the second, and 8 boxes in the third.

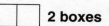

2 boxes

4 boxes

8 boxes

**Plan and Solve** You know the number of boxes in each drawing. It makes sense to look for a pattern. There is a pattern. The number of boxes doubles each time. The next drawing should have 16 boxes.

**Look Back and Check** Is there another pattern possible?

---

**For Exercises 1–2, describe each pattern and draw the next arrangement of boxes.**

1.

   Pattern: _____

2. How many diagonals can you draw in a 12-sided regular polygon?

   _____

3. Look for a pattern to find the value of $(-1)^{100}$.

   **a.** $(-1)^1 =$ _____

   **b.** $(-1)^2 =$ _____

   **c.** $(-1)^3 =$ _____

   **d.** $(-1)^4 =$ _____

   **e.** $(-1)^{100} =$ _____

4. Describe the pattern you used in Exercise 3.

   _____

5. A winter coat is on sale. Look for a pattern in the prices to predict the price of the coat on the tenth day.

   _____

   | Winter Coat Sale Price | |
   |---|---|
   | Day 1—$129.00 | Day 2—$124.50 |
   | Day 3—$120.00 | Day 4—$115.50 |

# Practice 3-7

**Problem Solving: Solve a Simpler Problem and Look for a Pattern**

**Solve each problem by solving a simpler problem and then looking for a pattern.**

1. Find a pattern for the ones digit of the powers of 6. What is the ones digit of $6^6$?

_____

_____

2. Find the sum of the two hundred even numbers from 0 to 398.

_____

3. The figures at the right represent the first three *rectangular numbers*. Describe the pattern. Find the value of the eighth rectangular number.

_____

_____

4. The same cube is shown from three different angles. What color is on the bottom in the first position? (HINT: Cut out a model.)

_____

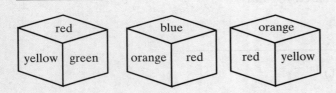

5. A school's gym lockers are numbered from 1 to 125. How many locker numbers contain the digit 4?

_____

6. How many diagonals can you draw in an 8-sided regular polygon?

_____

7. Sixty-four players signed up for a tennis tournament. A player is eliminated upon losing a match. How many matches must be scheduled to determine the tournament champion?

_____

8. Study the dot patterns. How many dots will the 12th pattern have?

_____

# Reteaching 3-8

**Mixed Numbers and Improper Fractions**

An **improper fraction** is greater than or equal to 1. Its numerator is greater than or equal to its denominator.

Improper fractions

$\frac{6}{4}$  $\frac{8}{8}$  $\frac{10}{8}$  $\frac{7}{2}$

A mixed number is the sum of a whole number and a fraction.

Mixed numbers

$1\frac{2}{3}$  $5\frac{4}{9}$  $3\frac{1}{2}$

To write a mixed number as an improper fraction:

① Write the mixed number as a sum.

② Write both numbers as fractions.

③ Add the fractions.

$3\frac{1}{2} = 3 + \frac{1}{2}$

$= \frac{6}{2} + \frac{1}{2}$

$= \frac{7}{2}$

To write an improper fraction as a mixed number:

① Divide the numerator by the denominator.

② Write the whole number, then the remainder over the divisor.

$\frac{7}{2}$ $\overbrace{\text{Think: } 7 \div 2}$

$\begin{array}{r} 3 \\ 2\overline{)7} \\ -6 \\ \hline 1 \end{array}$

$\frac{7}{2} = 3\frac{1}{2}$

---

**Write each mixed number as an improper fraction.**

**1.** $3\frac{1}{4} =$ _____

**2.** $2\frac{2}{3} =$ _____

**3.** $1\frac{3}{8} =$ _____

**4.** $5\frac{2}{7} =$ _____

**5.** $6\frac{3}{4} =$ _____

**6.** $1\frac{1}{9} =$ _____

**7.** $4\frac{1}{2} =$ _____

**8.** $3\frac{4}{5} =$ _____

**9.** $5\frac{1}{6} =$ _____

**10.** $3\frac{1}{3} =$ _____

**11.** $5\frac{7}{8} =$ _____

**12.** $4\frac{1}{8} =$ _____

**Write each improper fraction as a mixed number in simplest form.**

**13.** $\frac{14}{4} =$ _____

**14.** $\frac{12}{2} =$ _____

**15.** $\frac{22}{5} =$ _____

**16.** $\frac{16}{3} =$ _____

**17.** $\frac{47}{8} =$ _____

**18.** $\frac{56}{7} =$ _____

**19.** $\frac{17}{4} =$ _____

**20.** $\frac{21}{6} =$ _____

**21.** $\frac{13}{5} =$ _____

**22.** $\frac{23}{4} =$ _____

**23.** $\frac{13}{9} =$ _____

**24.** $\frac{14}{2} =$ _____

# Practice 3-8

1. Write a mixed number and an improper fraction for the model below.

    _____

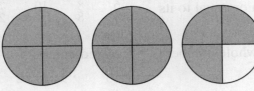

**Write each mixed number as an improper fraction.**

2. $2\frac{3}{8}$ _____

3. $5\frac{1}{3}$ _____

4. $1\frac{7}{10}$ _____

5. $3\frac{4}{9}$ _____

6. $4\frac{5}{8}$ _____

7. $3\frac{5}{12}$ _____

8. $1\frac{15}{16}$ _____

9. $2\frac{3}{10}$ _____

**Write each improper fraction as a mixed number in simplest form.**

10. $\frac{25}{3}$ _____

11. $\frac{42}{7}$ _____

12. $\frac{18}{4}$ _____

13. $\frac{28}{6}$ _____

14. $\frac{27}{12}$ _____

15. $\frac{11}{6}$ _____

16. $\frac{20}{3}$ _____

17. $\frac{34}{8}$ _____

18. $\frac{125}{5}$ _____

19. $\frac{34}{7}$ _____

20. $\frac{40}{6}$ _____

21. $\frac{84}{12}$ _____

**The distance around the inside of a shopping mall is $\frac{12}{16}$ mi.**

22. Juan jogged around the mall 4 times. How far did he jog?

    _____

23. Aaron walked around the mall 3 times. How far did he walk?

    _____

**The distance around an indoor running track is $\frac{1}{6}$ mile.**

24. Aruna jogged around the track 16 times. How far did she jog?

    _____

25. Theresa walked around the track 22 times.  How far did she walk?

    _____

26. Shade the figures below to represent $3\frac{5}{8}$. How many eighths are shaded?

    _____

  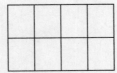 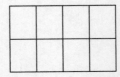

# Reteaching 3-9

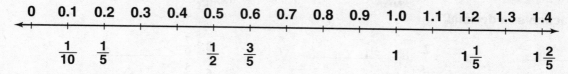

To change a fraction to a decimal, divide the numerator by the denominator.

$\frac{3}{5}$ ⟨ Think: 3 ÷ 5 ⟩

$$5\overline{)3.0} \quad \begin{array}{r} 0.6 \\ \underline{-30} \\ 0 \end{array}$$

$\frac{3}{5} = 0.6$

To change a decimal to a fraction:

① Read the decimal to find the denominator. Write the decimal digits over 10, 100, or 1,000.

0.65 is 65 *hundredths* → $\frac{65}{100}$

② Use the GCF to write the fraction in simplest form.

The GCF of 65 and 100 is 5.

$\frac{65}{100} = \frac{65 \div 5}{100 \div 5} = \frac{13}{20}$

---

**Write each fraction as a decimal.**

**1.** $\frac{4}{5} =$ _____    **2.** $\frac{3}{4} =$ _____    **3.** $\frac{1}{6} =$ _____

**4.** $\frac{1}{4} =$ _____    **5.** $\frac{2}{3} =$ _____    **6.** $\frac{7}{10} =$ _____

**7.** $\frac{5}{9} =$ _____    **8.** $\frac{1}{5} =$ _____    **9.** $\frac{3}{8} =$ _____

**Write each decimal as a mixed number or fraction in simplest form.**

**10.** $0.4 =$ _____    **11.** $0.75 =$ _____    **12.** $1.5 =$ _____

**13.** $0.35 =$ _____    **14.** $2.7 =$ _____    **15.** $1.8 =$ _____

**16.** $0.625 =$ _____    **17.** $0.78 =$ _____    **18.** $0.88 =$ _____

**Order from least to greatest.**

**19.** $2.\overline{6}, \frac{13}{6}, 2\frac{5}{6}$    **20.** $2.\overline{02}, 2\frac{1}{200}, 2.0202$    **21.** $\frac{5}{4}, 1\frac{4}{5}, 1.\overline{4}$

_____    _____    _____

# Practice 3-9

**Write each fraction as a decimal.**

1. $\frac{3}{5}$ _____

2. $\frac{7}{8}$ _____

3. $\frac{7}{9}$ _____

4. $\frac{5}{16}$ _____

5. $\frac{1}{6}$ _____

6. $\frac{5}{8}$ _____

7. $\frac{1}{3}$ _____

8. $\frac{2}{3}$ _____

9. $\frac{9}{10}$ _____

10. $\frac{7}{11}$ _____

11. $\frac{9}{20}$ _____

12. $\frac{3}{4}$ _____

13. $\frac{4}{9}$ _____

14. $\frac{9}{11}$ _____

15. $\frac{11}{20}$ _____

16. $\frac{9}{2}$ _____

17. $\frac{5}{4}$ _____

18. $\frac{11}{8}$ _____

19. $\frac{11}{12}$ _____

20. $\frac{8}{15}$ _____

**Write each decimal as a mixed number or fraction in simplest form.**

21. 0.6 _____

22. 0.45 _____

23. 0.62 _____

24. 0.8 _____

25. 0.325 _____

26. 0.725 _____

27. 4.75 _____

28. 0.33 _____

29. 0.925 _____

30. 3.8 _____

31. 4.7 _____

32. 0.05 _____

33. 0.65 _____

34. 0.855 _____

35. 0.104 _____

36. 0.47 _____

37. 0.894 _____

38. 0.276 _____

39. 1.84 _____

40. 2.59 _____

**Order from least to greatest.**

41. $0.\overline{2}, \frac{1}{5}, 0.02$

42. $1.\overline{1}, 1\frac{1}{10}, 1.101$

_____

_____

43. $\frac{6}{5}, 1\frac{5}{6}, 1.\overline{3}$

44. $4.\overline{3}, \frac{9}{2}, 4\frac{3}{7}$

_____

_____

45. $0.\overline{13}, \frac{2}{75}, 1.3$

46. $\frac{1}{8}, \frac{1}{4}, 0.12$

_____

_____

47. A group of gymnasts was asked to name their favorite piece of equipment. 0.33 of the gymnasts chose the vault, $\frac{4}{9}$ chose the beam, and $\frac{1}{7}$ chose the uneven parallel bars. List their choices in order of preference from greatest to least.

_____

# Reteaching 3-10

A **rational number** is a number that can be written as a quotient of two integers, where the divisor is not zero.

A negative rational number can be written in three different ways.

$$-\frac{2}{3} = \frac{-2}{3} = \frac{2}{-3}$$

**Comparing Negative Rational Numbers**

Compare $-\frac{2}{3}$ and $-\frac{1}{4}$.

**Method 1** Use a number line. Graph both points on a number line and see which is farther to the left.

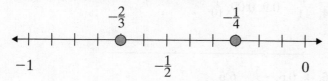

Since $-\frac{2}{3}$ is farther to the left, $-\frac{2}{3} < -\frac{1}{4}$.

**Method 2** Use the lowest common denominator.

$$-\frac{2}{3} = \frac{-2}{3} = \frac{-2 \times 4}{3 \times 4} = \frac{-8}{12} \qquad -\frac{1}{4} = \frac{-1}{4} = \frac{-1 \times 3}{4 \times 3} = \frac{-3}{12}$$

Since $\frac{-8}{12} < \frac{-3}{12}$, then $-\frac{2}{3} < -\frac{1}{4}$.

---

**Compare. Use <, >, or =.**

1. $-\frac{4}{9}$ ☐ $-\frac{2}{3}$

2. $-1$ ☐ $-\frac{4}{5}$

3. $-\frac{7}{8}$ ☐ $-\frac{1}{8}$

4. $-\frac{1}{3}$ ☐ $-\frac{5}{6}$

5. $-\frac{2}{5}$ ☐ $-\frac{1}{10}$

6. $-\frac{2}{8}$ ☐ $-\frac{1}{4}$

**Order from least to greatest.**

7. $-\frac{1}{3}, 0.3, -0.35, -\frac{3}{10}$

8. $\frac{1}{5}, -0.25, 0.21, \frac{3}{10}$

_____

9. $-6.25, 2\frac{8}{9}, \frac{-5}{12}, 2.1$

10. $\frac{-9}{11}, -0.5\overline{5}, \frac{-3}{4}, \frac{-12}{25}$

_____

11. You and your brother invested an equal amount of money in a college savings plan. In the last quarter your investment was worth $1\frac{5}{6}$ of its original value. Your brother's investment was worth 1.85 of its original value. Whose investment is worth more?

_____

# Practice 3-10

**Compare. Use <, >, or =.**

1. $-\frac{2}{9}$ ☐ $-\frac{4}{9}$

2. $-\frac{1}{6}$ ☐ $-\frac{2}{3}$

3. $-\frac{5}{12}$ ☐ $-\frac{3}{4}$

4. $-1$ ☐ $-\frac{1}{3}$

5. $-\frac{5}{6}$ ☐ $-\frac{10}{12}$

6. $-\frac{1}{8}$ ☐ $-\frac{1}{2}$

7. $-1.2$ ☐ $-2.1$

8. $-0.6$ ☐ $-0.52$

9. $-1.23$ ☐ $-1.25$

10. $-5.3$ ☐ $-5.\overline{3}$

11. $-3\frac{1}{4}$ ☐ $-3.25$

12. $-4\frac{2}{5}$ ☐ $-4.12$

**Order from least to greatest.**

13. $\frac{5}{4}, 1.5, -\frac{3}{2}, -0.5$

14. $\frac{1}{11}, -0.9, 0.09, \frac{1}{10}$

_____

_____

15. $0.1\overline{2}, -\frac{11}{12}, -\frac{1}{6}, -0.1$

16. $\frac{2}{3}, 0.6, -\frac{5}{6}, -6.6$

_____

_____

17. $1.312, 1\frac{3}{8}, -1\frac{3}{10}, -1.33$

18. $1, \frac{4}{5}, -\frac{8}{9}, -1$

_____

_____

**Evaluate. Write in simplest form.**

19. $\frac{y}{z}$, for $y = -6$ and $z = -20$ _____

20. $\frac{2y}{-z}$, for $y = -5$ and $z = -12$ _____

21. $\frac{y + z}{2z}$, for $y = -4$ and $z = 8$ _____

22. $\frac{-2y + 1}{-z}$, for $y = 3$ and $z = 10$ _____

**Compare.**

23. The temperature at 3:00 A.M. was $-17.3°$F. By noon the
temperature was $-17.8°$F. At what time was it the coldest?

_____

24. Samuel is $\frac{5}{8}$ in. taller than Jackie. Shelly is 0.7 in. taller than
Jackie. Who is the tallest?

_____

# Reteaching 4-1

**Estimating With Fractions and Mixed Numbers**

You can estimate sums, differences, and products by using benchmarks.
A *benchmark* is a value that can be used as a reference point.

- You can use the benchmarks to estimate fractions.

- Round mixed numbers to the nearest whole number.

**Estimate the sum:**

$\frac{5}{6} + \frac{7}{12}$

$1 + \frac{1}{2} = 1\frac{1}{2}$

**Estimate the difference:**

$3\frac{5}{6} - 2\frac{1}{3}$

$4 - 2 = 2$

**Estimate the product:**

$4\frac{1}{3} \times 2\frac{2}{3}$

$4 \times 3 = 12$

You can estimate a quotient by using compatible numbers.

**Estimate:** $15\frac{3}{8} \div 4\frac{1}{8}$

**Think:** $15\frac{3}{8}$ is close to 16.

16 is divisible by 4.

$15\frac{3}{8} \div 4\frac{1}{8} \approx 16 \div 4 = 4$

---

**Circle the better estimate.**

1. $\frac{1}{2} + \frac{3}{8}$    1 or $\frac{1}{2}$

2. $\frac{9}{10} - \frac{7}{8}$    0 or $\frac{1}{2}$

3. $\frac{5}{8} + \frac{3}{7}$    $\frac{1}{2}$ or 1

4. $\frac{8}{9} - \frac{1}{9}$    $\frac{1}{2}$ or 1

5. $\frac{5}{8} + \frac{8}{9}$    1 or $1\frac{1}{2}$

6. $\frac{5}{6} + \frac{11}{12}$    $1\frac{1}{2}$ or 2

**Estimate each sum or difference.**

7. $\frac{1}{2} + \frac{3}{7}$ _____

8. $\frac{5}{9} - \frac{3}{7}$ _____

9. $4\frac{2}{3} - \frac{1}{2}$ _____

10. $6\frac{7}{8} + 4\frac{4}{9}$ _____

11. $5\frac{8}{9} + 3\frac{1}{3}$ _____

12. $11\frac{1}{5} - 4\frac{1}{12}$ _____

**Circle the better choice to estimate each product or quotient.**

13. $5\frac{1}{4} \cdot 2\frac{1}{8}$

    $5 \cdot 2$ or $5 \cdot 3$

14. $13\frac{1}{4} \div 3\frac{7}{8}$

    $12 \div 4$ or $15 \div 3$

15. $6\frac{3}{4} \cdot 8\frac{7}{8}$

    $7 \cdot 8$ or $7 \cdot 9$

16. $21\frac{1}{2} \div 4\frac{1}{4}$

    $20 \div 4$ or $24 \div 4$

17. $4\frac{13}{15} \cdot 7\frac{2}{9}$

    $5 \cdot 7$ or $4 \cdot 8$

18. $38\frac{5}{6} \div 5\frac{1}{3}$

    $35 \div 5$ or $40 \div 5$

**Estimate each product or quotient.**

19. $6\frac{1}{4} \cdot 3\frac{5}{6}$ _____

20. $9\frac{1}{2} \div 2\frac{5}{8}$ _____

21. $2\frac{1}{7} \cdot 3\frac{5}{7}$ _____

22. $9\frac{4}{5} \cdot 4\frac{5}{6}$ _____

23. $15\frac{1}{2} \div 3\frac{5}{7}$ _____

24. $11\frac{1}{9} \cdot 2\frac{7}{8}$ _____

# Practice 4-1

**Estimating With Fractions and Mixed Numbers**

## Estimate each sum or difference.

1. $\frac{1}{6} + \frac{5}{8}$ _____

2. $\frac{7}{8} - \frac{1}{16}$ _____

3. $\frac{9}{10} + \frac{7}{8}$ _____

4. $\frac{1}{12} + \frac{9}{10}$ _____

5. $\frac{1}{10} + \frac{5}{6}$ _____

6. $\frac{4}{5} - \frac{1}{6}$ _____

7. $\frac{11}{12} - \frac{5}{16}$ _____

8. $\frac{15}{16} + \frac{11}{12}$ _____

9. $2\frac{1}{6} + 7\frac{1}{9}$ _____

10. $4\frac{9}{10} - 3\frac{5}{8}$ _____

11. $4\frac{7}{8} + 8\frac{1}{5}$ _____

12. $14\frac{7}{9} - 9\frac{1}{8}$ _____

13. $14\frac{3}{4} + 9\frac{7}{8}$ _____

14. $7\frac{11}{15} - 6\frac{7}{16}$ _____

15. $3\frac{11}{15} - 2\frac{9}{10}$ _____

16. $8\frac{7}{8} - \frac{11}{12}$ _____

## Estimate each product or quotient.

17. $13\frac{1}{8} \div 6\frac{1}{5}$ _____

18. $5\frac{1}{6} \cdot 8\frac{4}{5}$ _____

19. $8\frac{1}{6} \div 1\frac{9}{10}$ _____

20. $1\frac{9}{10} \cdot 4\frac{7}{8}$ _____

21. $27\frac{6}{7} \div 3\frac{2}{3}$ _____

22. $20\frac{4}{5} \cdot 2\frac{2}{7}$ _____

23. $9\frac{1}{3} \div 2\frac{7}{8}$ _____

24. $16\frac{1}{9} \cdot 2\frac{1}{8}$ _____

25. $19\frac{4}{5} \div 4\frac{5}{8}$ _____

26. $9\frac{2}{13} \div 3\frac{1}{18}$ _____

27. $42\frac{1}{6} \div 6\frac{1}{16}$ _____

28. $3\frac{9}{10} \cdot 8\frac{7}{8}$ _____

29. $15\frac{1}{20} \cdot 3\frac{1}{10}$ _____

30. $72\frac{2}{15} \div 8\frac{3}{4}$ _____

31. $3\frac{5}{6} \cdot 10\frac{1}{12}$ _____

32. $36\frac{1}{4} \div 5\frac{15}{16}$ _____

## Solve each problem.

33. Each dress for a wedding party requires $7\frac{1}{8}$ yd of material. Estimate the amount of material you would need to make 6 dresses.

_____

34. A fabric store has $80\frac{3}{8}$ yd of a particular fabric. About how many pairs of curtains could be made from this fabric if each pair requires $4\frac{1}{8}$ yd of fabric?

_____

35. Adam's car can hold $16\frac{1}{10}$ gal of gasoline. About how many gallons are left if he started with a full tank and has used $11\frac{9}{10}$ gal?

_____

36. Julia bought stock at $\$28\frac{1}{8}$ per share. The value of each stock increased by $\$6\frac{5}{8}$. About how much is each share of stock now worth?

_____

## Estimate each answer.

37. $6\frac{2}{9} - 2\frac{7}{8}$ _____

38. $\frac{1}{8} + \frac{9}{10}$ _____

39. $8\frac{2}{9} \cdot 10\frac{4}{9}$ _____

40. $6\frac{1}{4} \div 2\frac{3}{11}$ _____

41. $5\frac{1}{11} \cdot 8\frac{13}{15}$ _____

42. $\frac{21}{40} - \frac{5}{89}$ _____

43. $\frac{81}{100} - \frac{1}{2}$ _____

44. $11\frac{5}{9} \div 2\frac{1}{2}$ _____

45. $\frac{3}{5} + \frac{7}{8}$ _____

# Reteaching 4-2

Follow these steps to add or subtract fractions with different denominators.

Add: $\frac{1}{3} + \frac{1}{6}$    Subtract: $\frac{11}{12} - \frac{1}{6}$

① Write the fractions with the same denominator.

$\frac{2}{6} + \frac{1}{6}$    $\frac{11}{12} - \frac{2}{12}$

② Add or subtract the numerators.

$\frac{2}{6} + \frac{1}{6} = \frac{3}{6}$    $\frac{11}{12} - \frac{2}{12} = \frac{9}{12}$

③ Simplify the fraction.

$\frac{3}{6} = \frac{1}{2}$    $\frac{9}{12} = \frac{3}{4}$

**Complete to find each sum or difference.**

1. $\frac{3}{10} + \frac{2}{5}$

$\frac{3}{10} + \frac{\square}{10} = \frac{\square}{\square}$

2. $\frac{1}{4} + \frac{3}{6}$

$\frac{\square}{12} + \frac{\square}{12} = \frac{\square}{\square} = \frac{\square}{\square}$

3. $\frac{5}{8} + \frac{1}{4}$

$\frac{5}{8} + \frac{\square}{8} = \frac{\square}{\square}$

4. $\frac{3}{4} - \frac{1}{2}$

$\frac{3}{4} - \frac{\square}{4} = \frac{\square}{\square}$

5. $\frac{5}{9} - \frac{1}{3}$

$\frac{5}{9} - \frac{\square}{9} = \frac{\square}{\square}$

6. $\frac{3}{5} - \frac{1}{3}$

$\frac{\square}{15} - \frac{\square}{15} = \frac{\square}{\square}$

**Find each sum or difference. Write it in simplest form.**

7. $\frac{4}{5} + \frac{4}{5}$

8. $\frac{7}{8} - \frac{5}{8}$

9. $\frac{5}{6} - \frac{2}{3}$

10. $\frac{5}{12} - \frac{1}{4}$

11. $\frac{7}{8} + \frac{1}{4}$

12. $\frac{3}{4} - \frac{1}{8}$

13. $\frac{2}{5} + \frac{1}{10}$

14. $\frac{7}{12} - \frac{1}{3}$

15. $\frac{3}{5} + \frac{7}{15}$

16. $\frac{1}{2} + \frac{9}{10}$

17. $\frac{5}{6} - \frac{1}{4}$

18. $\frac{9}{10} - \frac{1}{2}$

19. $\frac{5}{8} + \frac{1}{2}$

20. $\frac{2}{5} - \frac{3}{10}$

21. $\frac{5}{6} - \frac{7}{12}$

Name _____ Class _____ Date _____

# Practice 4-2

Adding and Subtracting Fractions

**Write a number statement for each model.**

1.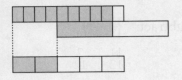

2.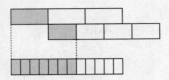

3.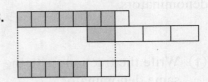

_____    _____    _____

**Find each sum or difference.**

4. $\frac{1}{6} + \frac{7}{8}$ _____

5. $\frac{9}{10} - \frac{1}{6}$ _____

6. $\frac{4}{5} + \frac{9}{10}$ _____

7. $\frac{1}{6} + \frac{1}{6}$ _____

8. $\frac{1}{10} + \frac{2}{5}$ _____

9. $\frac{8}{9} - \frac{2}{9}$ _____

10. $\frac{5}{6} + \frac{1}{12}$ _____

11. $\frac{2}{3} - \frac{1}{2}$ _____

12. $\frac{3}{10} + \frac{3}{10}$ _____

13. $\frac{7}{9} - \frac{1}{3}$ _____

14. $\frac{3}{4} - \frac{1}{4}$ _____

15. $\frac{3}{8} + \frac{5}{12}$ _____

16. $\frac{1}{5} + \frac{3}{4}$ _____

17. $\frac{1}{3} + \frac{1}{2}$ _____

18. $\frac{11}{12} - \frac{3}{4}$ _____

19. $\frac{1}{8} + \frac{1}{12}$ _____

20. $\frac{7}{10} - \frac{1}{3}$ _____

21. $\frac{5}{8} + \frac{1}{4}$ _____

**Use the table at the right for Exercises 22–27. Tell which two snacks combine to make each amount.**

22. $\frac{5}{6}$ c _____

23. $\frac{1}{2}$ c _____

24. $\frac{3}{4}$ c _____

25. $\frac{11}{12}$ c _____

26. 1 c _____

27. $\frac{19}{24}$ c _____

| Snack | Serving Amount |
| --- | --- |
| Raisins | $\frac{1}{4}$ c |
| Walnuts | $\frac{3}{8}$ c |
| Almonds | $\frac{1}{8}$ c |
| Sesame sticks | $\frac{2}{3}$ c |
| Mini pretzels | $\frac{5}{8}$ c |
| Dried apricots | $\frac{1}{6}$ c |

**Solve each equation.**

28. $\frac{4}{10} + x = \frac{9}{10}$ _____

29. $\frac{2}{3} + x = \frac{4}{6}$ _____

30. $s - \frac{1}{5} = \frac{2}{10}$ _____

31. $y + \frac{2}{9} = \frac{6}{18}$ _____

32. $b - \frac{4}{12} = \frac{8}{12}$ _____

33. $c + \frac{1}{6} = \frac{5}{12}$ _____

34. $\frac{4}{7} + k = \frac{20}{21}$ _____

35. $\frac{3}{8} + d = \frac{7}{8}$ _____

36. $f - \frac{1}{10} = \frac{2}{5}$ _____

# Reteaching 4-3

**Adding and Subtracting Mixed Numbers**

Follow these steps to add or subtract mixed numbers with different denominators.

|  | Add: | $2\frac{2}{5} + 1\frac{3}{4}$ | Subtract: | $4\frac{1}{3} - 2\frac{5}{6}$ |
|---|---|---|---|---|

① Write the equivalent fractions with the LCD.

$$2\frac{8}{20} + 1\frac{15}{20} \qquad\qquad 4\frac{2}{6} - 2\frac{5}{6}$$

② Rename, if necessary.

$$4\frac{2}{6} = 3 + 1\frac{2}{6} = 3\frac{8}{6}$$

③ Add or subtract the whole numbers. Add or subtract the fractions.

$$2\frac{8}{20} + 1\frac{15}{20} = 3\frac{23}{20} \qquad\qquad 3\frac{8}{6} - 2\frac{5}{6} = 1\frac{3}{6}$$

④ Simplify.

$$3\frac{23}{20} = 4\frac{3}{20} \qquad\qquad 1\frac{3}{6} = 1\frac{1}{2}$$

---

**Complete to find each sum or difference.**

1. $4\frac{3}{4} - 2\frac{3}{8}$

$$4\frac{\square}{8} - 2\frac{\square}{8} = \square\frac{\square}{\square}$$

2. $4\frac{7}{12} + 2\frac{5}{6}$

$$4\frac{\square}{12} + 2\frac{\square}{12} = \square\frac{\square}{\square}$$

$$= \square\frac{\square}{\square}$$

3. $4\frac{1}{3} - 1\frac{3}{5}$

$$4\frac{\square}{15} - 1\frac{\square}{15}$$

$$= \square\frac{\square}{\square} - \square\frac{\square}{\square}$$

$$= \square\frac{\square}{\square}$$

**Find each sum or difference. Write it in simplest form.**

4. $2\frac{3}{5} + 1\frac{1}{10}$ _____

5. $2\frac{5}{6} + 3\frac{4}{9}$ _____

6. $5 - 3\frac{7}{10}$ _____

7. $3\frac{1}{6} - 2\frac{1}{3}$ _____

8. $4\frac{3}{4} - 1\frac{2}{3}$ _____

9. $3\frac{1}{2} + 4\frac{1}{3}$ _____

10. $3\frac{3}{10} + 1\frac{3}{5}$ _____

11. $6\frac{1}{3} + 7\frac{1}{4}$ _____

12. $4\frac{3}{5} + 6\frac{7}{10}$ _____

13. $7\frac{15}{16} - 2\frac{3}{8}$ _____

14. $4 - 2\frac{3}{10}$ _____

15. $5\frac{1}{4} - 1\frac{3}{8}$ _____

16. $2\frac{1}{2} + 5\frac{3}{5}$ _____

17. $7\frac{1}{4} - 3\frac{3}{5}$ _____

18. $5 - 2\frac{5}{8}$ _____

19. $9\frac{3}{5} + 1\frac{7}{10}$ _____

20. $6 - 5\frac{5}{6}$ _____

21. $4\frac{7}{10} + 4\frac{1}{2}$ _____

22. Shea cut $2\frac{1}{8}$ in. material off of the bottom of a $21\frac{1}{4}$ in. skirt. How long is the skirt now?

_____

Name _____ Class _____ Date _____

# Practice 4-3

**Find each sum.**

1. $5\frac{1}{3} + 3\frac{2}{3}$ 
_____

2. $7\frac{1}{4} + 4\frac{3}{8}$ 
_____

3. $2\frac{1}{8} + 6\frac{5}{8}$ 
_____

4. $8\frac{1}{5} + 4\frac{3}{10}$ 
_____

5. $9\frac{1}{6} + 6\frac{1}{4}$ 
_____

6. $3\frac{2}{3} + 10\frac{5}{6}$ 
_____

**Find each difference.**

7. $6\frac{11}{12} - 4\frac{5}{12}$ 
_____

8. $12 - 5\frac{3}{10}$ 
_____

9. $14\frac{1}{2} - 7\frac{1}{5}$ 
_____

10. $9 - 5\frac{5}{6}$ 
_____

11. $13\frac{3}{4} - 10\frac{1}{2}$ 
_____

12. $15\frac{1}{6} - 6\frac{5}{12}$ 
_____

**Find each sum or difference.**

13. $1\frac{1}{6} - \frac{3}{4}$ 
_____

14. $4\frac{1}{2} - 2\frac{7}{8}$ 
_____

15. $9\frac{3}{4} + 7\frac{7}{8}$ 
_____

16. $5\frac{1}{6} - 4\frac{7}{12}$ 
_____

17. $9\frac{8}{15} + 11\frac{5}{12}$ 
_____

18. $\frac{14}{15} - \frac{1}{2}$ 
_____

19. $\frac{7}{12} + \frac{5}{6}$ 
_____

20. $1\frac{4}{9} + 3\frac{1}{6}$ 
_____

21. $3\frac{1}{2} - 2\frac{1}{4}$ 
_____

**Write a mixed number for each time period. Be sure each fraction is in lowest terms.**

22. 8:00 A.M. to 9:20 A.M. 
_____

23. 9:00 A.M. to 2:45 P.M. 
_____

24. 11:00 A.M. to 3:55 P.M. 
_____

25. 8:30 A.M. to 10:40 P.M. 
_____

26. 5:30 P.M. to 10:45 P.M. 
_____

27. 7:20 A.M. to 11:00 A.M. 
_____

# Reteaching 4-4

**Multiplying Fractions and Mixed Numbers**

Follow these steps to multiply fractions and mixed numbers.

Multiply: $\frac{3}{4} \cdot \frac{2}{5}$　　　Multiply: $2\frac{2}{3} \cdot 1\frac{5}{8}$

① Write the mixed numbers as improper fractions if necessary.

$$\frac{8}{3} \cdot \frac{13}{8}$$

② Multiply numerators. Multiply denominators.

$$\frac{3 \cdot 2}{4 \cdot 5} = \frac{6}{20} \qquad \frac{8 \cdot 13}{3 \cdot 8} = \frac{104}{24}$$

③ Simplify, if necessary.

$$\frac{6}{20} = \frac{3}{10} \qquad \frac{104}{24} = 4\frac{1}{3}$$

**Complete to find each product.**

1. $\frac{1}{5} \cdot \frac{2}{3}$

$$\frac{1 \cdot 2}{5 \cdot 3} = \frac{\boxed{\phantom{0}}}{\boxed{\phantom{0}}}$$

Product _____

2. $\frac{1}{4} \cdot 4\frac{1}{8}$

$$\frac{1}{4} \cdot \frac{\boxed{\phantom{0}}}{8} = \frac{\boxed{\phantom{0}}}{32}$$

Product _____

3. $2\frac{3}{4} \cdot 1\frac{2}{3}$

$$\frac{\boxed{\phantom{0}}}{4} \cdot \frac{\boxed{\phantom{0}}}{3} = \frac{\boxed{\phantom{0}}}{12}$$

Product _____

**Find each product. Write the product in simplest form.**

4. $\frac{5}{8} \cdot \frac{2}{5}$ _____

5. $\frac{2}{3} \cdot 9$ _____

6. $\frac{5}{12} \cdot \frac{3}{10}$ _____

7. $\frac{3}{4} \cdot 1\frac{4}{5}$ _____

8. $\frac{1}{2} \cdot 5\frac{1}{6}$ _____

9. $3\frac{4}{5} \cdot \frac{1}{6}$ _____

10. $1\frac{2}{3} \cdot 5$ _____

11. $1\frac{3}{4} \cdot 3\frac{1}{7}$ _____

12. $2\frac{3}{5} \cdot \frac{1}{4}$ _____

13. $2\frac{3}{5} \cdot \frac{7}{8}$ _____

14. $4\frac{1}{5} \cdot \frac{5}{7}$ _____

15. $\frac{1}{2} \cdot 2\frac{1}{8}$ _____

16. $3\frac{5}{6} \cdot 2\frac{1}{4}$ _____

17. $2\frac{5}{7} \cdot 1\frac{1}{3}$ _____

18. $7\frac{2}{3} \cdot 2\frac{1}{7}$ _____

19. $5\frac{1}{2} \cdot 2\frac{2}{3}$ _____

20. $\frac{5}{6} \cdot 3\frac{3}{5}$ _____

21. $7\frac{3}{4} \cdot 2$ _____

# Practice 4-4

**Multiplying Fractions and Mixed Numbers**

**Find each product.**

1. $\frac{5}{6} \cdot \frac{3}{5}$ _____

2. $\frac{7}{8} \cdot \frac{4}{5}$ _____

3. $\frac{9}{10} \cdot \frac{5}{12}$ _____

4. $\frac{5}{8} \cdot \frac{3}{5}$ _____

5. $\frac{1}{6}$ of 36 _____

6. $\frac{2}{3}$ of 36 _____

7. $\frac{5}{9} \cdot 36$ _____

8. $\frac{3}{4} \cdot 36$ _____

9. $5 \cdot \frac{3}{4}$ _____

10. $2 \cdot \frac{9}{10}$ _____

11. $8 \cdot \frac{9}{10}$ _____

12. $4 \cdot \frac{7}{12}$ _____

13. $\frac{1}{3} \cdot 3\frac{1}{3}$ _____

14. $\frac{5}{6}$ of $1\frac{3}{5}$ _____

15. $\frac{4}{5} \cdot 2\frac{5}{6}$ _____

16. $\frac{1}{8}$ of $1\frac{4}{5}$ _____

17. $3 \cdot 4\frac{1}{2}$ _____

18. $4 \cdot 2\frac{2}{3}$ _____

19. $5 \cdot 2\frac{1}{4}$ _____

20. $3 \cdot 2\frac{2}{3}$ _____

21. $4\frac{1}{2} \cdot 1\frac{1}{6}$ _____

22. $3\frac{2}{3} \cdot 1\frac{1}{2}$ _____

23. $4\frac{1}{6} \cdot 2\frac{2}{5}$ _____

24. $3\frac{1}{4} \cdot 2\frac{1}{6}$ _____

**Solve.**

25. A sheet of plywood is $\frac{5}{8}$ in. thick. How tall is a stack of 21 sheets of plywood?

_____

26. A poster measures 38 cm across. If a photocopy machine is used to make a copy that is $\frac{3}{5}$ of the original size, what is the width of the copy?

_____

27. A one-kilogram object weighs about $2\frac{1}{5}$ pounds. Find the weight, in pounds, of a computer monitor with mass $7\frac{3}{8}$ kilograms.

_____

28. The population of Sweden is about $1\frac{11}{16}$ times as great as the population of Denmark. Find the population of Sweden if the population of Denmark is about 5,190,000.

_____

# Reteaching 4-5

**Dividing Fractions and Mixed Numbers**

To find the **reciprocal** of a fraction, interchange the numerator and the denominator.

Examples: The reciprocal of $\frac{1}{4}$ is $\frac{4}{1}$. The reciprocal of $\frac{7}{5}$ is $\frac{5}{7}$.

Follow these steps to divide fractions and mixed numbers.

|  | Divide: $\frac{2}{3} \div \frac{1}{4}$ | Divide: $3\frac{3}{4} \div 1\frac{2}{5}$ |
|---|---|---|
| ① Rewrite mixed numbers as improper fractions as needed. |  | $\frac{15}{4} \div \frac{7}{5}$ |
| ② Multiply by the reciprocal of the divisor. | $\frac{2}{3} \cdot \frac{4}{1}$ | $\frac{15}{4} \cdot \frac{5}{7}$ |
| ③ Multiply numerators. Multiply denominators. | $\frac{2 \cdot 4}{3 \cdot 1} = \frac{8}{3}$ | $\frac{15 \cdot 5}{4 \cdot 7} = \frac{75}{28}$ |
| ④ Simplify. | $\frac{8}{3} = 2\frac{2}{3}$ | $\frac{75}{28} = 2\frac{19}{28}$ |

**Find the reciprocal of each number.**

1. $\frac{7}{8}$ _____

2. $\frac{1}{6}$ _____

3. $\frac{8}{3}$ _____

4. $\frac{9}{10}$ _____

**Write each mixed number as an improper fraction. Then find the reciprocal.**

5. $1\frac{1}{2}$ _____

6. $2\frac{1}{3}$ _____

7. $1\frac{4}{5}$ _____

8. $2\frac{3}{4}$ _____

**Complete to find each quotient. Write the quotient in simplest form.**

9. $\frac{2}{3} \div \frac{3}{8}$

$\frac{2}{3} \cdot \frac{\square}{3} = \frac{\square}{9}$

Quotient _____ $= \frac{\square}{7}$

10. $10 \div \frac{7}{8}$

$\frac{\square}{1} \div \frac{7}{8} = \frac{\square}{1} \cdot \frac{\square}{\square}$

$= \frac{\square}{7}$

Quotient _____

11. $3\frac{3}{5} \div 1\frac{1}{5}$

$\frac{\square}{5} \div \frac{\square}{5} = \frac{\square}{5} \cdot \frac{\square}{\square}$

$= \frac{\square}{30}$

Quotient _____

12. $\frac{1}{5} \div \frac{1}{2}$ _____

13. $\frac{3}{8} \div \frac{2}{3}$ _____

14. $8 \div \frac{4}{5}$ _____

15. $6 \div \frac{3}{4}$ _____

16. $1\frac{1}{8} \div 2\frac{2}{5}$ _____

17. $3\frac{1}{5} \div 2\frac{2}{3}$ _____

# Practice 4-5

**Find the reciprocal of each number.**

1. $\frac{1}{2}$ _____

2. $\frac{3}{4}$ _____

3. $\frac{7}{8}$ _____

4. $\frac{9}{16}$ _____

5. $\frac{4}{5}$ _____

6. $1\frac{1}{4}$ _____

7. $2\frac{1}{3}$ _____

8. $3\frac{2}{5}$ _____

9. $2\frac{9}{10}$ _____

10. $3\frac{1}{6}$ _____

**Find each quotient.**

11. $\frac{3}{4} \div \frac{1}{4}$ _____

12. $\frac{7}{8} \div \frac{1}{4}$ _____

13. $\frac{5}{6} \div \frac{1}{12}$ _____

14. $\frac{1}{12} \div \frac{5}{6}$ _____

15. $4 \div \frac{1}{3}$ _____

16. $6 \div \frac{3}{4}$ _____

17. $5 \div \frac{9}{10}$ _____

18. $8 \div \frac{2}{3}$ _____

19. $\frac{4}{5} \div 2$ _____

20. $\frac{7}{8} \div 3$ _____

21. $\frac{5}{6} \div 5$ _____

22. $\frac{4}{9} \div 8$ _____

23. $1\frac{1}{2} \div \frac{2}{3}$ _____

24. $1\frac{1}{2} \div \frac{3}{2}$ _____

25. $\frac{3}{4} \div 1\frac{1}{3}$ _____

26. $2\frac{1}{2} \div 1\frac{1}{4}$ _____

27. $2\frac{1}{2} \div 2\frac{1}{4}$ _____

28. $1\frac{3}{4} \div \frac{3}{4}$ _____

29. $1\frac{7}{10} \div \frac{1}{2}$ _____

30. $3\frac{1}{4} \div 1\frac{1}{3}$ _____

31. $4\frac{1}{2} \div 2\frac{1}{2}$ _____

32. $6 \div 3\frac{4}{5}$ _____

33. $4\frac{3}{4} \div \frac{7}{8}$ _____

34. $5\frac{5}{6} \div 1\frac{1}{3}$ _____

35. $3\frac{3}{8} \div 1\frac{1}{4}$ _____

36. $6\frac{1}{2} \div 1\frac{1}{2}$ _____

37. $2\frac{9}{10} \div 1\frac{3}{4}$ _____

**Solve each problem.**

38. Rosa makes $2\frac{1}{2}$ c of pudding. How many $\frac{1}{3}$ c servings can she get from the pudding?

_____

39. One type of lightning bug glows once every $1\frac{1}{2}$ s. How many times can it glow in 1 min?

_____

40. Bea can run $\frac{1}{6}$ mi in 2 min. How long should it take her to run 2 mi?

_____

41. Joe drives 20 mi in $\frac{1}{2}$ h. How long will it take him to drive 50 mi?

_____

# Reteaching 4-6

To solve equations, remember to use inverse operations.

$$n + 4\tfrac{1}{4} = 5\tfrac{3}{4} \qquad \leftarrow \quad \textbf{Addition equation: use subtraction to solve.}$$
$$n + 4\tfrac{1}{4} - 4\tfrac{1}{4} = 5\tfrac{3}{4} - 4\tfrac{1}{4} \qquad \leftarrow \quad \textbf{Subtract } 4\tfrac{1}{4} \textbf{ from each side.}$$
$$n = 1\tfrac{2}{4} = 1\tfrac{1}{2} \qquad \leftarrow \quad \textbf{Simplify.}$$

$$n - 1\tfrac{3}{4} = \tfrac{1}{2} \qquad \leftarrow \quad \textbf{Subtraction equation: use addition to solve.}$$
$$n - 1\tfrac{3}{4} + 1\tfrac{3}{4} = \tfrac{1}{2} + 1\tfrac{3}{4} \qquad \leftarrow \quad \textbf{Add } 1\tfrac{3}{4} \textbf{ to each side.}$$
$$n = \tfrac{2}{4} + 1\tfrac{3}{4} \qquad \leftarrow \quad \textbf{Find a common denominator.}$$
$$n = 1\tfrac{5}{4} = 2\tfrac{1}{4} \qquad \leftarrow \quad \textbf{Simplify.}$$

**Complete to solve each equation.**

**1.** $x + \tfrac{1}{5} = \tfrac{3}{5}$

$x + \tfrac{1}{5} - \underline{\quad} = \tfrac{3}{5} - \underline{\quad}$

$x = \underline{\quad}$

**2.** $\tfrac{1}{4} + t = 1\tfrac{3}{4}$

$\tfrac{1}{4} - \underline{\quad} + t = 1\tfrac{3}{4} - \underline{\quad}$

$t = \underline{\quad} = \underline{\quad}$

**3.** $\tfrac{7}{8} = w - \tfrac{3}{8}$

$\tfrac{7}{8} + \underline{\quad} = w - \tfrac{3}{8} + \underline{\quad}$

$\underline{\quad} = \underline{\quad} = w$

**4.** $h - 2\tfrac{1}{3} = \tfrac{2}{3}$

$h - 2\tfrac{1}{3} + \underline{\quad} = \tfrac{2}{3} + \underline{\quad}$

$h = \underline{\quad}$

**Solve each equation.**

**5.** $a + 1\tfrac{2}{5} = 4\tfrac{4}{5}$ _____

**6.** $2\tfrac{3}{4} = f - \tfrac{1}{4}$ _____

**7.** $\tfrac{5}{9} + k = 1\tfrac{7}{9}$ _____

**8.** $z - \tfrac{3}{5} = \tfrac{9}{10}$ _____

**9.** $4\tfrac{2}{3} + s = 6$ _____

**10.** $\tfrac{5}{8} = b - \tfrac{1}{8}$ _____

**11.** $3\tfrac{5}{6} + m = 10\tfrac{2}{3}$ _____

**12.** $n - 1\tfrac{1}{3} = \tfrac{1}{2}$ _____

**13.** $\tfrac{3}{5} = t + \tfrac{1}{3}$ _____

**14.** $z + 1\tfrac{2}{7} = 2\tfrac{5}{7}$ _____

**15.** $r - 3\tfrac{1}{2} = 4\tfrac{3}{8}$ _____

**16.** $x + \tfrac{7}{9} = 2\tfrac{2}{3}$ _____

**17.** $3\tfrac{5}{9} = r + 2\tfrac{1}{6}$ _____

**18.** $k - 2\tfrac{3}{10} = \tfrac{4}{5}$ _____

**19.** $2\tfrac{1}{4} = m + 1\tfrac{1}{6}$ _____

**20.** $\tfrac{6}{7} = a + \tfrac{2}{3}$ _____

# Practice 4-6

**Solve each equation.**

1. $m + \frac{7}{8} = 1\frac{1}{2}$ _____

2. $j - \frac{1}{4} = \frac{7}{8}$ _____

3. $t + \frac{9}{10} = 1\frac{4}{5}$ _____

4. $k - \frac{5}{6} = \frac{11}{12}$ _____

5. $\frac{7}{8} = n + \frac{1}{4}$ _____

6. $\frac{1}{5} = a - \frac{9}{10}$ _____

7. $b + \frac{7}{10} = 1\frac{1}{2}$ _____

8. $c - \frac{7}{8} = \frac{5}{8}$ _____

9. $w + 2\frac{1}{4} = 5\frac{5}{8}$ _____

10. $x - 1\frac{3}{5} = 2\frac{7}{10}$ _____

11. $\frac{2}{9} = z - \frac{2}{3}$ _____

12. $\frac{1}{2} = d + \frac{1}{6}$ _____

13. $4y = 9$ _____

14. $\frac{d}{9} = 16$ _____

15. $\frac{1}{5}a = 47$ _____

16. $51m = 3$ _____

17. $\frac{x}{9} = 4$ _____

18. $5j = 50$ _____

19. $16b = 2$ _____

20. $\frac{1}{4}c = 9$ _____

21. $\frac{z}{12} = 8$ _____

22. $11e = 15$ _____

23. $50p = 75$ _____

24. $19 = \frac{1}{6}q$ _____

25. $\frac{2}{3}x + 4 = 8$ _____

26. $\frac{z}{4} - 2 = 10$ _____

27. $\frac{m}{3} + 4 = 6$ _____

28. $\frac{5}{6}n - 2 = 8$ _____

29. $3 + \frac{7}{8}z = 24$ _____

30. $\frac{j}{7} - 10 = 32$ _____

**Solve each problem by writing and solving an equation. Equations may vary.**

31. Lacey had a ribbon $5\frac{7}{8}$ yd long. She used $1\frac{1}{2}$ yd for a belt for a dress. What length of the ribbon remains?

_____

32. The depth of a river at one spot is normally $16\frac{3}{4}$ ft deep. The water rose $5\frac{1}{2}$ ft during a flood. What was the depth of the river at that spot during the flood?

_____

33. Katrina rode her bicycle $6\frac{3}{4}$ mi before she realized she forgot her lock. She rode $2\frac{1}{2}$ mi toward home before she met Magda. How far does Katrina need to ride before she is home?

_____

34. A shoreline is washing away at a rate of $1\frac{7}{10}$ ft each year. A house is $225\frac{9}{10}$ ft from the water. If erosion continues at the same rate, how far from the water will the house be next year?

_____

35. If $\frac{1}{3}$ of a number is 21, what is the number?

_____

36. If 8 times a number is 15, what is the number?

_____

# Reteaching 4-7

**Problem Solving: Try, Check, and Revise and Work Backward**

Ramón began his shopping trip by cashing his paycheck. While shopping, he noted what he spent. At the end of the day, he had $49.50 left. What was the amount of his paycheck?

| Videotape | $13.95 |
|-----------|--------|
| Sweater | 45.99 |
| Shirt | 17.99 |
| Pants | 32.45 |

**Read and Understand**     What information are you given? *You know how much Ramón had left and how much he spent.*

**Plan and Solve**     It makes sense to *work backward* to find the amount Ramón began with.

Add the amount spent to the amount left. Ramón's paycheck was for $159.88.

| Amount left | $49.50 |
|-------------|--------|
| Amount spent | 32.45 |
| | 17.99 |
| | 45.99 |
| | 13.95 |
| | $159.88 |

**Look Back and Check**     You can check your answer by *working forward*. Begin with $159.88. Subtract each amount Ramón spent.

---

**Solve each problem by using either of the methods in the lesson. Check each answer in the original problem.**

1. Madeline took her month's allowance to the amusement park. She had $1.50 left at the end of the day. She made a list of her expenses.

   | Rides | $3.50 |
   |-------|-------|
   | Food | 2.50 |
   | Admission | 1.50 |
   | Toss-a-ring | 2.00 |

   How much was her allowance?

   Allowance: _____

2. Dana left nuts out for the chipmunks. She kept track of how many each chipmunk took.

   | Curlytail | 15 |
   |-----------|-----|
   | Whitefoot | 22 |
   | Squeaker | 19 |
   | Stripes | 32 |

   If there were 12 nuts left, how many did she start with?

   Total nuts: _____

3. Suzy multiplied her age by 2, subtracted 5, divided by 3, and added 9. The result was 20. How old is she?

   _____

4. Each time a ball bounces it returns to a height $\frac{2}{3}$ the height of the previous bounce. After the third bounce, the ball returns to a height of 4 ft. From what height was it dropped?

# Practice 4-7

**Problem Solving: Try, Check, and Revise and Work Backward**

**Solve each problem by using either of the methods in the lesson.
Check each answer in the original problem.**

1. A fast-growing mushroom doubled in size every day. After 30 days, it measured 6 in. tall. On which day did it measure $1\frac{1}{2}$ in. tall?

   _____

2. If you start with a number, subtract 14, then divide by 12, the result is 248. What was the original number?

   _____

3. Mrs. Wainright is in a car pool. It takes her 20 min to pick up her passengers. From her last stop, it takes her 45 min to drive to the office. The group likes to arrive 10 min before office hours begin. If office hours start at 8:30 A.M., what time should Mrs. Wainright leave her apartment?

   _____

**Use any strategy to solve each problem. Show your work.**

4. James went shopping one Saturday afternoon. He spent $\frac{1}{2}$ of the money he had on a new stereo system. He spent half of the money he had left on a new suit. Half of what remained, he spent on a new sweater. Half of what remained, he spent on a new CD. If he went home with $15, how much money did he have to begin with?

   _____

5. At a middle school, half the students leave immediately after school because they walk home. After 5 min, $\frac{1}{4}$ of the students remaining are gone, riding home on their bicycles. After another 5 min, $\frac{3}{4}$ of those remaining depart on buses. At this time, 51 students remain for after-school activities. How many students attend the middle school?

   _____

6. Trish spent a fourth of her money on a new book. She paid a friend $3.50 that she had borrowed. Later she spent $4.75 on a pair of earrings. When she arrived home, she had $18.00. How much money did she have to start with?

   _____

7. During one day, Howard wrote checks for $125.00, $98.57, and $23.46. He made a deposit of $475.00. If his account now has $472.96, how much was in the account at the start of the day?

   _____

# Reteaching 4-8

**Changing Units in the Customary System**

| Length | Weight | Capacity |
|---|---|---|
| 12 inches (in.) = 1 foot (ft) | 16 ounces (oz) = 1 pound (lb) | 8 fluid ounces (fl oz) = 1 cup (c) |
| 3 ft = 1 yard (yd) | 2,000 lb = 1 ton (t) | 2 c = 1 pint (pt) |
| 5,280 ft = 1 mile (mi) | | 2 pt = 1 quart (qt) |
| | | 4 qt = 1 gallon (gal) |

To change to a *larger* unit, divide.

66 in. = __?__

1 ft is larger than 1 in.
12 in. = 1 ft

$66 \div 12 = \frac{66}{12} = 5\frac{6}{12} = 5\frac{1}{2}$

66 in. = $5\frac{1}{2}$ ft

To change to a *smaller* unit, multiply.

$3\frac{1}{2}$ qt = __?__ pt

1 pt is smaller than 1 qt.
1 qt = 2 pt

$3\frac{1}{2} \cdot 2 = \frac{7}{2} \cdot \frac{2}{1} = \frac{14}{2} = 7$

$3\frac{1}{2}$ qt = 7 pt

**Multiply to change to a smaller unit. Write the fact you used.**

1. $3\frac{1}{2}$ ft = _____

2. $1\frac{1}{2}$ c = _____

3. 5 lb = _____

4. $5\frac{1}{2}$ qt = _____

5. $3\frac{1}{4}$ gal = _____

6. 4 pt = _____

7. 2 mi = _____

8. 6 qt = _____

9. $1\frac{1}{2}$ t = _____

**Divide to change to a larger unit. Write the fact you used.**

10. 24 oz = _____

11. 32 oz = _____

12. 10 qt = _____

13. 3 c = _____

14. 4,000 lb = _____

15. 17 oz = _____

16. 7 pt = _____

17. 27 ft = _____

18. 30 in. = _____

19. The Missouri River is 4,470,400 yards long. Express this measurement in miles. _____

# Practice 4-8

**Tell whether you would multiply or divide to change from one unit of measure to the other.**

**1.** tons to pounds

_____

**2.** pints to quarts

_____

**3.** feet to yards

_____

**4.** gallons to pints

_____

**5.** cups to quarts

_____

**6.** pounds to ounces

_____

**Complete.**

**7.** 9 qt = _____ gal

**8.** $2\frac{1}{4}$ t = _____ lb

**9.** $3\frac{1}{2}$ yd = _____ in.

**10.** 4 yd = _____ ft

**11.** 60 c = _____ qt

**12.** $1\frac{3}{4}$ gal = _____ pt

**13.** 246 in. = _____ ft

**14.** 1,750 oz = _____ lb

**15.** $\frac{3}{4}$ t = _____ oz

**16.** 84 ft = _____ yd

**17.** 198 in. = _____ yd

**18.** 11,880 ft = _____ mi

**19.** 480 fl oz = _____ pt

**20.** $\frac{1}{4}$ gal = _____ fl oz

**21.** $1\frac{1}{2}$ pt = _____ fl oz

**22.** $\frac{1}{2}$ mi = _____ ft

**23.** $\frac{1}{10}$ mi = _____ in.

**24.** 3 mi = _____ yd

**25.** 2 lb 6 oz = _____ lb

**26.** 2 qt 8 fl oz = _____ qt

**27.** 4 yd 2 ft = _____ yd

**Solve.**

**28.** United States farms produced 2,460,000,000 bushels of soybeans in 1994. How many quarts is this? (A bushel is 32 quarts.)

_____

**29.** In 1994, Brian Berg built an 81-story "house" using playing cards. The house was $15\frac{2}{3}$ ft tall. How many inches is this?

_____

**Choose an appropriate customary unit of measure.**

**30.** capacity of a mug

_____

**31.** length of a family room

_____

**32.** distance between two capital cities

_____

**32.** capacity of a shampoo bottle

_____

# Reteaching 4-9

The precision of a measurement refers to its degree of exactness. The smaller the unit of measure, the more precise the measurement. If the same unit is used in two measurements, then the measurement to the smallest decimal place is more precise.

Determine which measurement in each set is more precise.

**a.** 3 yd, 110 in.

Since the units of measure are different, the measurement with the smaller unit of measure is more precise. An inch is smaller than a yard, so 110 in. is more precise than 3 yd.

**b.** 45.12 cm, 45.2 cm

Since the units of measure are the same, the measurement with the smaller decimal place is more precise. Since 45.12 has the smaller decimal place, 45.12 cm is more precise than 45.2 cm.

---

**Write the more precise measurement.**

**1.** 1.6 mi, 8,448 ft

_____

**2.** 8.9 km, 8.87 km

_____

**3.** 2 ft, 13 in.

_____

**4.** 5.64 cm, 56.2 cm

_____

**5.** 4.3 yd, 2 mi

_____

**6.** 17.33 mm, 17 mm

_____

**7.** 100 ft, 56.5 ft

_____

**8.** 6.2 km, 3.25 km

_____

**Compute. Round your answer appropriately.**

**9.** 2,100 cm − 418 cm

_____

**10.** 41.3 in. × 84 in.

_____

**11.** 2.3 in. + 6.31 in.

_____

**12.** 17.2 cm × 5 cm

_____

**13.** 4 cm × 7.70 cm

_____

**14.** 19.65 ft − 4.3 ft

_____

**15.** 24 mm − 16.1 mm

_____

**16.** 2.25 yd × 6 yd

_____

# Practice 4-9

**Underline the more precise measurement.**

1. 23 oz, 20.7 oz

2. 1,830 g, 2.5 kg

3. 160 qt, 137 qt

4. 63.7 L, 63.70 L

5. 3.7 t, 5,610 lb

6. 47 qt, 83 pt

7. 58.3 cm, 4.6 m

8. 12 L, 1,735 mL

9. 61 lb, 63.7 lb

10. 3,008 pt, 0.95 pt

11. 7.3 min, 516 sec

12. 2.7 mL, 12 mL

13. 26.4 cm, 8.39 cm

14. 216 ft, 3,106 in.

15. 4.1 lb, 6.123 lb

**Find each sum or difference. Round your answer to match the less precise measurement.**

16. 6.35 oz + 4.2 oz

17. 83 g − 1.8 g

18. 6.25 in. + 15.85 in.

19. 4.20 yd + 8.64 yd

20. 21 cm + 5360 cm

21. 8,137 hr − 500 hr

22. 5.382 m + 8 m

23. 6.4 ft + 4300 ft

24. 30 mi + 16.5 mi

25. 2.713 mL + 8.4 mL

26. 50 lb − 4.6 lb

27. 6.83 km + 10.3 km

28. Boundary Peak in Nevada is 13,000 ft high. Guadalupe Peak in Texas is 8,749 ft high. How much higher than Guadalupe Peak is Boundary Peak? Round your answer to match the less precise measurement.

29. You measure the area of your garden as 9 yd wide by 11 yd long. Your brother measures the garden as $27\frac{1}{2}$ ft wide by $32\frac{3}{4}$ ft long. Whose measurement is more precise? Why?

# Reteaching 5-1

**Ratios**

A ratio is a comparison of two numbers by division. You can write a ratio three ways.

Compare the number of red tulips to the number of yellow tulips.

**red tulips**   **yellow tulips**   **orange mums**   **white mums**

6 to 2, 6 : 2, or $\frac{6}{2}$

To find equal ratios, multiply or divide each part of the ratio by the same nonzero number.

$\frac{6}{2} = \frac{6 \times 2}{2 \times 2} = \frac{12}{4}$   ← **Multiply by 2.**

The ratio $\frac{3}{1}$ is in **simplest form.**

$\frac{6}{2} = \frac{6 \div 2}{2 \div 2} = \frac{3}{1}$   ← **Divide by 2.**

---

**Use the drawings at the top of the page. Write each ratio in three ways.**

1. yellow tulips to red tulips

   _____

2. white mums to orange mums

   _____

3. red tulips to orange mums

   _____

4. yellow tulips to white mums

   _____

5. red tulips to all flowers

   _____

6. orange mums to all flowers

   _____

7. tulips to mums

   _____

8. white mums to tulips

   _____

9. yellow tulips to all flowers

   _____

10. yellow tulips to orange mums

   _____

**Write two ratios equal to the given ratio.**

11. $\frac{5}{10}$ _____

12. 2:5 _____

13. 18 to 30 _____

**Write each ratio in simplest form.**

14. $\frac{8}{16}$ _____

15. 8 to 2 _____

16. 10 : 15 _____

17. $\frac{48}{24}$ _____

18. $\frac{6}{100}$ _____

19. 8 : 18 _____

# Practice 5-1

**Write a ratio for each situation in three ways.**

1. Ten years ago in Louisiana, schools averaged 182 pupils for every 10 teachers.

_____

2. In a recent year, 41 out of 250 people in the labor force belonged to a union.

_____

3. Between 1899–1900, 284 out of 1,000 people in the United States were 5–17 years old.

_____

4. In a recent year, 7 out of 10 people with Japanese heritage who lived in the United States lived in either Hawaii or California.

_____

**Use the chart below for Exercises 5–6.**

The seventh-grade classes were asked whether they wanted chicken or pasta served at their awards banquet.

| Room Number | Chicken | Pasta |
| --- | --- | --- |
| 201 | 10 | 12 |
| 202 | 8 | 17 |
| 203 | 16 | 10 |

5. In room 201, what is the ratio of students who prefer chicken to students who prefer pasta?

_____

6. Combine the totals for all three rooms. What is the ratio of the number of students who prefer pasta to the number of students who prefer chicken?

_____

**Write each ratio in simplest form.**

7. $\frac{2}{6}$ _____

8. 3 : 21 _____

9. 16 to 20 _____

10. $\frac{3}{30}$ _____

11. 12 to 18 _____

12. 81 : 27 _____

13. $\frac{6}{28}$ _____

14. 49 to 14 _____

15. A bag contains green, yellow, and orange marbles. The ratio of green marbles to yellow marbles is 2 : 5. The ratio of yellow marbles to orange marbles is 3 : 4. What is the ratio of green marbles to orange marbles?

_____

# Reteaching 5-2

**Unit Rates and Proportional Reasoning**

A **rate** is a ratio that compares two quantities measured in different units.

The cost for 10 copies is $1.50.

The rate is $1.50/10 copies ($1.50 per 10 copies).

A **unit rate** is a rate that has a denominator of 1. You can compare using unit rates.

To find the unit rate for 10 copies:

$$\$1.50/10 \text{ copies} = \frac{\$1.50}{10}$$
$$= \frac{\$1.50 \div 10}{10 \div 10}$$
$$= \frac{\$.15}{1}$$

The unit rate is $.15 per copy. This is also the *unit price*.

| COPY CENTER Color Copies | |
| --- | --- |
| 1 copy | $.25 |
| 10 copies | $1.50 |
| 25 copies | $2.50 |
| 50 copies | $4.50 |
| 100 copies | $6.00 |

For the better buy, compare unit rates.

The unit price for 10 copies is $.15/copy.

The unit price for 1 copy is $.25/copy.

Since $.15 < $.25, the 10-copy price is the better buy.

---

**Use the Copy Center chart. Find the unit rate.**

1. 25 copies
   $$\frac{\$2.50}{25} = \frac{\$2.50 \div \boxed{\phantom{0}}}{25 \div \boxed{\phantom{0}}} =$$
   _____

2. 100 copies
   $$\frac{\$6.00}{100} = \frac{\$6.00 \div \boxed{\phantom{0}}}{100 \div \boxed{\phantom{0}}} =$$

3. 50 copies
   $$\frac{\$4.50}{50} = \frac{\$4.50 \div \boxed{\phantom{0}}}{50 \div \boxed{\phantom{0}}} =$$

**Write the unit rate for each situation.**

4. drive 1,800 mi in 30 h
   _____

5. 390 mi on 15 gal of gasoline _____

6. jog 4,000 m in 12 min
   _____

7. $25.50 for 17 tickets
   _____

8. 456 mi on 12 gal of gasoline _____

9. 54 c of flour for 12 cakes _____

**Find each unit price. Then determine the better buy.**

10. juice: 18 oz for $1.26
    8 oz for $.70

    _____

11. cloth: 2 yd for $3.15
    6 yd for $7.78

    _____

12. socks: 2 pairs for $3.50
    6 pairs for $9.00

    _____

13. pecans: 1 lb for $4.80
    2 oz for $1.00

    _____

# Practice 5-2

**Unit Rates and Proportional Reasoning**

**Write the unit rate for each situation.**

1. travel 250 mi in 5 h

2. earn $75.20 in 8 h

3. read 80 pages in 2 h

4. type 8,580 words in 2 h 45 min

5. manufacture 2,488 parts in 8 h

6. 50 copies of a book on 2 shelves

7. $30 for 6 books

8. 24 points in 3 games

**Find each unit price. Then determine the better buy.**

9. paper: 100 sheets for $.99
   500 sheets for $4.29

10. peanuts: 1 lb for $1.29
    12 oz for $.95

11. crackers: 15 oz for $1.79
    12 oz for $1.49

12. apples: 3 lb for $1.89
    5 lb for $2.49

13. mechanical pencils: 4 for $1.25
    25 for $5.69

14. bagels: 4 for $.89
    6 for $1.39

15. a. Yolanda and Yoko ran in a 100-yd dash. When Yolanda crossed the finish line, Yoko was 10 yd behind her. The girls then repeated the race, with Yolanda starting 10 yd behind the starting line. If each girl ran at the same rate as before, who won the race? By how many yards?

    b. Assuming the girls run at the same rate as before, how far behind the starting line should Yolanda be in order for the two to finish in a tie?

# Reteaching 5-3

**Problem Solving: Draw a Diagram and Solve a Simpler Problem**

If a problem has large numbers or many steps, try to solve a similar, but simpler, problem or drawing a diagram.

**Read and Understand**  The coach needs 24 jump ropes for his physical education students. He has a rope long enough to be cut into 24 jump ropes. How many cuts are needed?

**What are you asked to do?**  *Find out how many cuts are needed to make a rope into 24 jump ropes.*

**Plan and Solve**  Try solving a similar problem, but with simpler numbers.

A rope is long enough to be cut into 2 jump ropes.  1 cut
A rope is long enough to be cut into 3 jump ropes.  2 cuts
A rope is long enough to be cut into 4 jump ropes.  3 cuts

**What pattern do you see?**  *The number of cuts is 1 less than the number of pieces. So, it would take 24 − 1, or 23 cuts to create 24 jump ropes.*

**Look Back**  How could you check your answer? *Try solving the problem another way. You can draw a diagram.*

---

**Solve each problem by either drawing a diagram or solving a simpler problem.**

1. You are hand-numbering the pages of a report. If there are 238 numbered pages, how many digits will you write?

_____

2. A square flower garden is enclosed with 7 posts on each side. How many posts are there in all?

_____

3. Martin is planning to bike 160 miles in a road race. On the first day he biked $\frac{1}{2}$ of the distance. On the next day he biked $\frac{1}{4}$ of the remaining distance. How far did he have left to go?

_____

4. A landscape design company is planning a large outdoor display. They planted 60 plants in the first row, 62 plants in the second row, 64 in the third row, and 66 in the fourth row. At this rate, how many plants will be planted in the sixteenth row?

_____

5. The county closes a section of road to repair the road and replace a bridge. The detour is west for 4 miles, south for 6 miles, east for 2 miles, north for 2 miles and east for 2 miles. How many miles long is the closed section of road?

_____

# Practice 5-3

**Problem Solving: Draw a Diagram and Solve a Simpler Problem**

**Solve each problem by either drawing a diagram or solving a simpler problem.**

1. The six members of the Chess Club have a tournament in which every player plays a game against every other player. How many games are there in the tournament?

_____

2. Seventy-two teams signed up for a soccer tournament. A team is eliminated upon losing a match. How many games must be scheduled to determine the tournament winner?

_____

3. Katrina took a train trip to visit her aunt. By 1:15 the train had traveled 40 miles. By 1:30 the train had traveled an additional 20 miles. Katrina is now halfway to her aunt's. At what time will she reach her aunt's town if the train's speed is constant?

_____

4. A school's first floor lockers are numbered from 1 to 130. How many locker numbers contain the digit 5?

_____

5. Roberto is building a square pasture. He has decided to use 12 posts on each side. How many posts will he need to purchase?

_____

6. Nicholas' cat Smokey loves to climb trees. From the bottom of a tree, Smokey climbs 3 feet up, then backs down 2 feet. Then Smokey climbs up 4 feet and backs down 2 feet. In two more climbs of 3 feet and 5 feet each, Smokey reaches a big branch. How many feet above the ground is this branch?

_____

7. In how many pieces can you cut a board with 15 cuts?

_____

Name _____ Class _____ Date _____

# Reteaching 5-4

· · · · · · · · · · · · · · · · · · · · · · · · · · · · · · · · · · · · · · · · ·

A **proportion** is an equation stating that two ratios are equal.

Consider $\frac{2}{10}$ and $\frac{5}{25}$.

$\frac{2}{10} = \frac{2 \div 2}{10 \div 2} = \frac{1}{5}$

$\frac{5}{25} = \frac{5 \div 5}{25 \div 5} = \frac{1}{5}$

Both ratios are equal to $\frac{1}{5}$, so the ratios are proportional.

If two ratios form a proportion, the **cross products** are equal.

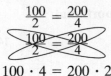

$\frac{100}{2} = \frac{200}{4}$

$100 \cdot 4 = 200 \cdot 2$

$400 = 400$

─────────────────────────────────────────────

**Complete the cross products to determine which pairs of ratios could form a proportion. Then write *yes* or *no*.**

**1.** $\frac{3}{10} \overset{?}{=} \frac{6}{20}$

$3 \cdot 20 =$ _____

$10 \cdot 6 =$ _____

_____

**2.** $\frac{12}{24} \overset{?}{=} \frac{2}{4}$

$12 \cdot 4 =$ _____

$24 \cdot \boxed{\phantom{0}} =$ _____

_____

**3.** $\frac{8}{5} \overset{?}{=} \frac{16}{8}$

$8 \cdot \boxed{\phantom{0}} =$ _____

$5 \cdot \boxed{\phantom{0}} =$ _____

_____

**Can the pair of ratios form a proportion? Write *yes* or *no*.**

**4.** $\frac{7}{5}, \frac{21}{15}$

_____

**5.** $\frac{16}{3}, \frac{5}{1}$

_____

**6.** $\frac{12}{9}, \frac{4}{3}$

_____

**7.** $\frac{4}{24}, \frac{2}{6}$

_____

**8.** $\frac{15}{5}, \frac{6}{2}$

_____

**9.** $\frac{9}{3}, \frac{27}{9}$

_____

**Determine if the ratios in each pair are proportional.**

**10.** $\frac{25}{35}, \frac{5}{7}$

_____

**11.** $\frac{15}{3}, \frac{10}{2}$

_____

**12.** $\frac{9}{3}, \frac{12}{4}$

_____

**13.** $\frac{2}{5}, \frac{6}{15}$

_____

**14.** $\frac{3.6}{200}, \frac{1.8}{100}$

_____

**15.** $\frac{6}{12}, \frac{4}{8}$

_____

**16.** $\frac{16}{11}, \frac{96}{24}$

_____

**17.** $\frac{3}{7}, \frac{2}{5}$

_____

**18.** $\frac{2}{22}, \frac{1}{11}$

_____

· · · · · · · · · · · · · · · · · · · · · · · · · · · · · · · · · · · · · · · · ·

# Practice 5-4

**Determine if the ratios in each pair are proportional.**

1. $\frac{12}{16}, \frac{30}{40}$ _____

2. $\frac{8}{12}, \frac{15}{21}$ _____

3. $\frac{27}{21}, \frac{81}{56}$ _____

4. $\frac{45}{24}, \frac{75}{40}$ _____

5. $\frac{5}{9}, \frac{80}{117}$ _____

6. $\frac{15}{25}, \frac{75}{125}$ _____

7. $\frac{2}{14}, \frac{20}{35}$ _____

8. $\frac{9}{6}, \frac{21}{14}$ _____

9. $\frac{24}{15}, \frac{16}{10}$ _____

10. $\frac{3}{4}, \frac{8}{10}$ _____

11. $\frac{20}{4}, \frac{17}{3}$ _____

12. $\frac{25}{6}, \frac{9}{8}$ _____

**Decide if each pair of ratios is proportional.**

13. $\frac{14}{10} \overset{?}{=} \frac{9}{7}$

14. $\frac{18}{8} \overset{?}{=} \frac{36}{16}$

15. $\frac{6}{10} \overset{?}{=} \frac{15}{25}$

16. $\frac{7}{16} \overset{?}{=} \frac{4}{9}$

17. $\frac{6}{4} \overset{?}{=} \frac{12}{8}$

18. $\frac{19}{3} \overset{?}{=} \frac{114}{8}$

19. $\frac{5}{14} \overset{?}{=} \frac{6}{15}$

20. $\frac{6}{27} \overset{?}{=} \frac{8}{36}$

21. $\frac{27}{15} \overset{?}{=} \frac{45}{25}$

22. $\frac{3}{18} \overset{?}{=} \frac{4}{20}$

23. $\frac{5}{2} \overset{?}{=} \frac{15}{6}$

24. $\frac{20}{15} \overset{?}{=} \frac{4}{3}$

**Solve.**

25. During the breaststroke competitions of the 1992 Olympics, Nelson Diebel swam 100 meters in 62 seconds, and Mike Bowerman swam 200 meters in 130 seconds. Are the rates proportional? _____

26. During a vacation, the Vasquez family traveled 174 miles in 3 hours on Monday, and 290 miles in 5 hours on Tuesday. Are the rates proportional? _____

# Reteaching 5-5

**Using Proportional Reasoning**

•••••••••••••••••••••••••••••••••••••••••••••••••••••••••••••

*Solving* a proportion means finding a missing part of the proportion. You can use unit rates to solve a proportion. First find the unit rate. Then multiply to solve the proportion.

Shawn filled 8 bags of leaves in 2 hours. At this rate, how many bags would he fill in 6 hours?

① Find a unit rate for the number of bags per hour. Divide by the denominator.

$\frac{8 \text{ bags}}{2 \text{ hours}} = \frac{8 \text{ bags} \div 2}{2 \text{ hours} \div 2} = \frac{4 \text{ bags}}{1 \text{ hour}}$   The unit rate is 4 bags per hour.

② Multiply the unit rate by 6 to find the number of bags he will fill in 6 hours.

Unit rate   Number of hours   Total
↓          ↓                ↓
4    ×     6       =        24

At this rate, Shawn can fill 24 bags in 6 hours.

If two ratios form a proportion, the **cross products** are equal.

Solve.   $\frac{5}{15} = \frac{n}{3}$

① Write the cross products.          $5 \cdot 3 = 15 \cdot n$

② Simplify.                          $15 = 15n$

③ Solve the equation.                $n = 1$

─────────────────────────────────────────────────────

**Solve.**

1. The bookstore advertises 5 notebooks for $7.75. At this rate, how

   much will 7 notebooks cost? _____

2. Leroy can lay 144 bricks in 3 hours. At this rate, how many

   bricks can he lay in 7 hours? _____

**Solve each proportion using cross products.**

3. $\frac{4}{24} = \frac{n}{6}$          4. $\frac{30}{5} = \frac{6}{n}$          5. $\frac{n}{6} = \frac{27}{9}$

   $4 \cdot$ _____ $= 24 \cdot$ _____        _____ $=$ _____        _____ $=$ _____

   $n =$ _____                 $n =$ _____              $n =$ _____

**Solve each proportion.**

6. $\frac{50}{70} = \frac{n}{7}$ _____   7. $\frac{14}{7} = \frac{6}{n}$ _____   8. $\frac{n}{15} = \frac{2}{5}$ _____

9. $\frac{4}{10} = \frac{n}{15}$ _____   10. $\frac{4}{200} = \frac{n}{100}$ _____   11. $\frac{6}{n} = \frac{5}{10}$ _____

12. $\frac{32}{22} = \frac{96}{n}$ _____   13. $\frac{6}{3} = \frac{n}{5}$ _____   14. $\frac{2}{n} = \frac{4}{10}$ _____

•••••••••••••••••••••••••••••••••••••••••••••••••••••••••••••

# Practice 5-5

**Use mental math to solve for each value of *n*.**

1. $\frac{n}{14} = \frac{20}{35}$ _____

2. $\frac{9}{6} = \frac{21}{n}$ _____

3. $\frac{24}{n} = \frac{16}{10}$ _____

4. $\frac{3}{4} = \frac{n}{10}$ _____

5. $\frac{n}{4} = \frac{17}{3}$ _____

6. $\frac{25}{n} = \frac{9}{8}$ _____

**Solve each proportion using cross products.**

7. $\frac{k}{8} = \frac{14}{4}$

   $k =$ _____

8. $\frac{u}{3} = \frac{10}{5}$

   $u =$ _____

9. $\frac{14}{6} = \frac{d}{15}$

   $d =$ _____

10. $\frac{5}{1} = \frac{m}{4}$

    $m =$ _____

11. $\frac{36}{32} = \frac{n}{8}$

    $n =$ _____

12. $\frac{5}{30} = \frac{1}{x}$

    $x =$ _____

13. $\frac{t}{4} = \frac{5}{10}$

    $t =$ _____

14. $\frac{9}{2} = \frac{v}{4}$

    $v =$ _____

15. $\frac{x}{10} = \frac{6}{4}$

    $x =$ _____

16. $\frac{8}{12} = \frac{2}{b}$

    $b =$ _____

17. $\frac{v}{15} = \frac{4}{6}$

    $v =$ _____

18. $\frac{3}{18} = \frac{2}{s}$

    $s =$ _____

**Solve.**

19. A contractor estimates it will cost $2,400 to build a deck to a customer's specifications. How much would it cost to build five similar decks?

    _____

20. A recipe requires 3 c of flour to make 27 dinner rolls. How much flour is needed to make 9 rolls?

    _____

**Solve using a calculator, paper and pencil, or mental math.**

21. Mandy runs 4 km in 18 min. She plans to run in a 15 km race. How long will it take her to complete the race?

    _____

22. Ken's new car can go 26 miles per gallon of gasoline. The car's gasoline tank holds 14 gal. How far will he be able to go on a full tank?

    _____

23. Eleanor can complete two skirts in 15 days. How long will it take her to complete eight skirts?

    _____

24. Three eggs are required to make two dozen muffins. How many eggs are needed to make 12 dozen muffins?

    _____

Name _____ Class _____ Date _____

# Reteaching 5-6 ...................................

**Using Similar Figures**

Two polygons are **similar,** if

- corresponding angles have the same measure, and

- the lengths of corresponding sides are proportional.

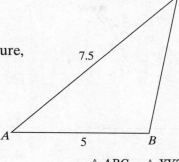
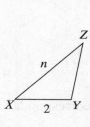

$\triangle ABC \sim \triangle XYZ$

You can use proportions to find missing lengths in similar ($\sim$) figures.

① Find corresponding sides.

$\overline{AB}$ corresponds to $\overline{XY}$.
$\overline{AC}$ corresponds to $\overline{XZ}$.
$\overline{BC}$ corresponds to $\overline{YZ}$.

② Write ratios of their lengths in a proportion.

$\dfrac{AB}{XY} = \dfrac{AC}{XZ}$

③ Substitute the information you know.

$\dfrac{5}{2} = \dfrac{7.5}{n}$

④ Write cross products. Solve for $n$.

$5n = 2 \cdot 7.5$

$n = 3$

The length of $\overline{XZ}$ is 3 units.

---

**The figures are similar. Find the corresponding sides.
Then complete the proportion and solve for $n$.**

**1.** $\overline{AB}$ corresponds to _____.

$\overline{BC}$ corresponds to _____.

$\overline{CA}$ corresponds to _____.

**2.** $\dfrac{CA}{SQ} = \dfrac{\boxed{\phantom{xx}}}{\overline{RS}}$

$\dfrac{8}{20} = \dfrac{\boxed{\phantom{xx}}}{\boxed{\phantom{xx}}}$

$n = $ _____

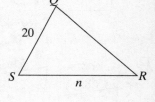

**The pairs of figures below are similar. Find the value of each variable.**

**3.** _____

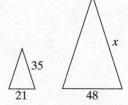

**4.** _____

# Practice 5-6

$\triangle$ *MNO* ~ $\triangle$ *JKL*. Complete each statement.

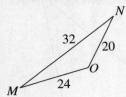

1. $\angle M$ corresponds to _____.

2. $\angle L$ corresponds to _____.

3. $\overline{ON}$ corresponds to _____.

4. $\angle K$ corresponds to _____.

5. $\overline{JL}$ corresponds to _____.

6. $\overline{MN}$ corresponds to _____.

7. What is the ratio of the lengths of the corresponding sides? _____

**The pairs of figures below are similar. Find the value of each variable.**

8.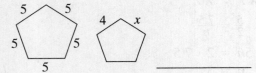

_____

9.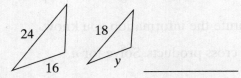

_____

10.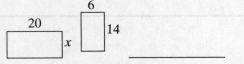

_____

11.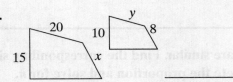

_____

12.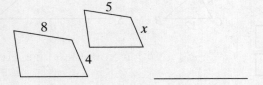

_____

13.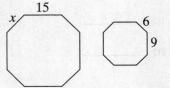

_____

14. On a sunny day, if a 36-inch yardstick casts a 21-inch shadow, how tall is a building whose shadow is 168 ft?

_____

15. Oregon is about 400 miles from west to east, and 300 miles from north to south. If a map of Oregon is 15 inches tall (from north to south), about how wide is the map?

_____

# Reteaching 5-7

A **scale drawing** is an enlarged or reduced drawing of an object. A map is a scale drawing. On this map, the pool is 3 cm from the horse corral. What is the actual distance from the corral to the pool?

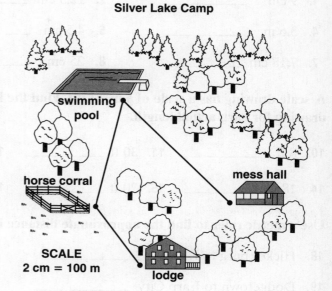

**Silver Lake Camp**

**SCALE**
**2 cm = 100 m**

① Use the scale. Write a ratio of distance on the map to actual distance.

$$\frac{\text{map (cm)}}{\text{actual (m)}} = \frac{2}{100}$$

② Write a proportion using the scale.

$$\frac{\text{map (cm)}}{\text{actual (m)}} = \frac{2}{100} = \frac{3}{n}$$

③ Use cross products. Solve for $n$.

$$2n = 100 \cdot 3$$
$$n = 150 \text{ m}$$

The pool is 150 m from the corral.

---

**Use the information on the map. Write and solve a proportion to find the distance.**

1. On the map, the mess hall is 4 cm from the pool. What is the actual distance from the pool to the mess hall?

   $$\frac{\text{map}}{\text{actual}} = \frac{\boxed{\phantom{x}}}{100} = \frac{\boxed{\phantom{x}}}{n}$$

   $$n = \underline{\hspace{2cm}}$$

2. The lodge is 2 cm from the horse corral on the map. What is the actual distance from the corral to the lodge?

   $$\frac{\text{map}}{\text{actual}} = \frac{\boxed{\phantom{x}}}{100} = \frac{\boxed{\phantom{x}}}{n}$$

   $$n = \underline{\hspace{2cm}}$$

3. The pool is actually 225 m from the lodge. How far would the pool be from the lodge on the map?

   $$\frac{\text{map}}{\text{actual}} = \frac{\boxed{\phantom{x}}}{100} = \frac{\boxed{\phantom{x}}}{n}$$

   $$n = \underline{\hspace{2cm}}$$

4. The mess hall is 150 m from the lodge. How far would the mess hall be from the lodge on the map?

   $$\frac{\text{map}}{\text{actual}} = \frac{\boxed{\phantom{x}}}{100} = \frac{\boxed{\phantom{x}}}{n}$$

   $$n = \underline{\hspace{2cm}}$$

5. A volleyball court will be built 175 m from the lodge. How far would the volleyball court be from the lodge on the map?

   _____

# Practice 5-7

**The scale of a map is 2 cm : 21 km. Find the actual distances for the following map distances.**

**1.** 9 cm _____  **2.** 12.5 cm _____  **3.** 14 mm _____

**4.** 3.6 m _____  **5.** 4.5 cm _____  **6.** 7.1 cm _____

**7.** 7.18 cm _____  **8.** 25 cm _____  **9.** 1 cm _____

**A scale drawing has a scale of $\frac{1}{4}$ in. : 12 ft. Find the length on the drawing for each actual length.**

**10.** 8 ft _____  **11.** 30 ft _____  **12.** 15 ft _____  **13.** 56 ft _____

**14.** 18 ft _____  **15.** 20 ft _____  **16.** 40 ft _____  **17.** 80 ft _____

**Use a metric ruler to find the approximate distance between the towns.**

**18.** Hickokburg to Kidville _____

**19.** Dodgetown to Earp City _____

**20.** Dodgetown to Kidville _____

**21.** Kidville to Earp City _____

**22.** Dodgetown to Hickokburg _____

**23.** Earp City to Hickokburg _____

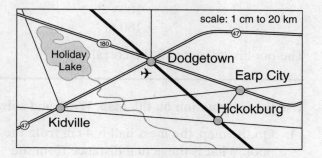

**Solve.**

**24.** The scale drawing shows a two-bedroom apartment. The master bedroom is 9 ft × 12 ft. Use an inch ruler to measure the drawing.

    **a.** The scale is _____.

    **b.** Write the actual dimensions in place of the scale dimensions.

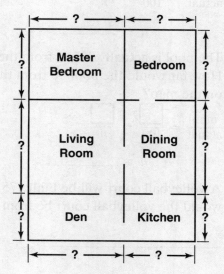

# Reteaching 6-1

A **percent** is a ratio that compares a number to 100. The figure at the right contains 25 squares.

$\frac{9}{25}$ of the squares are shaded.

To write $\frac{9}{25}$ as a percent, follow these steps.

① Write a ratio with a denominator of 100 that is equal to $\frac{9}{25}$.

$$\frac{9}{25} = \frac{9 \cdot 4}{25 \cdot 4} = \frac{36}{100}$$

② Write the ratio as a percent.

$$\frac{36}{100} = 36\%$$

36% of the squares are shaded.

**Write a percent for each shaded figure.**

**1.**
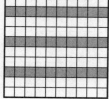
_____

**2.**
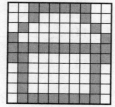
_____

**3.**
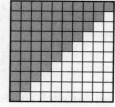
_____

**4.**
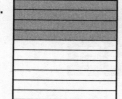
_____

**5.**
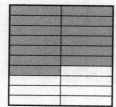
_____

**6.**
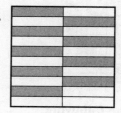
_____

**Write each ratio as a percent.**

**7.** $\frac{3}{5}$ _____

**8.** $\frac{17}{100}$ _____

**9.** $\frac{18}{25}$ _____

**10.** $\frac{13}{20}$ _____

**11.** $\frac{8}{10}$ _____

**12.** $\frac{1}{4}$ _____

**13.** $\frac{17}{50}$ _____

**14.** $\frac{11}{25}$ _____

**15.** $\frac{7}{20}$ _____

**16.** $\frac{21}{25}$ _____

**17.** $\frac{3}{10}$ _____

**18.** $\frac{16}{25}$ _____

**19.** $\frac{2}{5}$ _____

**20.** $\frac{99}{100}$ _____

**21.** $\frac{11}{20}$ _____

**22.** $\frac{13}{25}$ _____

**23.** $\frac{1}{10}$ _____

**24.** $\frac{39}{50}$ _____

**25.** $\frac{19}{20}$ _____

**26.** $\frac{6}{25}$ _____

# Practice 6-1

**Shade each grid to represent each of the following percents.**

**1.** 53%

**2.** 23%

**3.** 71%

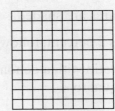

**Write each ratio as a percent.**

**4.** $\frac{4}{5}$ _____

**5.** $\frac{3}{5}$ _____

**6.** $\frac{9}{10}$ _____

**7.** $\frac{3}{10}$ _____

**8.** $\frac{6}{25}$ _____

**9.** $\frac{7}{100}$ _____

**10.** $\frac{9}{50}$ _____

**11.** $\frac{9}{25}$ _____

**12.** $\frac{2}{5}$ _____

**13.** $\frac{7}{10}$ _____

**14.** $\frac{4}{25}$ _____

**15.** $\frac{16}{25}$ _____

**16.** $\frac{11}{20}$ _____

**17.** $\frac{19}{20}$ _____

**18.** $\frac{27}{50}$ _____

**19.** 41 : 50 _____

**Write a percent for each shaded figure.**

**20.**

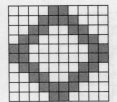

**21.**

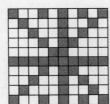

**22.**

**Complete the following.**

Ancient Egyptians did not write the fraction $\frac{4}{5}$ as "$\frac{4}{5}$". Instead, they used *unit fractions*. The numerator of a unit fraction is always 1. No denominator used to represent a given fraction can be repeated. For this reason, Egyptians would have written $\frac{4}{5}$ as $\frac{1}{2} + \frac{1}{5} + \frac{1}{10}$ and not as $\frac{1}{2} + \frac{1}{10} + \frac{1}{10} + \frac{1}{10}$. Write each of the following as a sum of unit fractions.

**23.** $\frac{3}{4}$ _____

**24.** $\frac{5}{8}$ _____

**25.** $\frac{9}{10}$ _____

**26.** $\frac{7}{12}$ _____

**27.** $\frac{11}{12}$ _____

**28.** $\frac{11}{15}$ _____

# Reteaching 6-2

To write a percent as a fraction, write a fraction with 100 as the denominator.

$45\% = \dfrac{45}{100}$      ← **Denominator 100**

     $= \dfrac{45 \div 5}{100 \div 5} = \dfrac{9}{20}$ ← **Simplify.**

$45\% = \dfrac{9}{20}$

---

To write a decimal as a percent, multiply by 100.

Write 0.85 as a percent.

$0.85 \cdot 100 = 85$

     $0.85 = 85\%$

To write a percent as a decimal, divide by 100.

Write 46% as a decimal.

$46 \div 100 = 0.46$

     $46\% = 0.46$

---

**Write each fraction as a percent.**

**1.** $\dfrac{3}{4}$            **2.** $\dfrac{12}{25}$           **3.** $\dfrac{4}{5}$           **4.** $\dfrac{23}{4}$

_____     _____     _____     _____

**Write each percent as a fraction in simplest form.**

**5.** 45%          **6.** 60%          **7.** 16%          **8.** 25%

_____     _____     _____     _____

**9.** 37.5%        **10.** 99%         **11.** 40%         **12.** 86%

_____     _____     _____     _____

**Write each percent as a decimal or each decimal as a percent.**

**13.** 35%         **14.** 48%         **15.** 116%       **16.** 8%

_____     _____     _____     _____

**17.** 12%         **18.** 5.5%       **19.** 400%       **20.** 0.6%

_____     _____     _____     _____

**21.** 0.39        **22.** 0.735      **23.** 0.86        **24** 0.34

_____     _____     _____     _____

**25.** 0.4         **26.** 0.6         **27.** 0.004      **28.** 6

_____     _____     _____     _____

Name _____ Class _____ Date _____

# Practice 6-2

**Write each percent as a fraction in simplest form and as a decimal.**

**1.** 65% _____   **2.** 37.5% _____   **3.** 80% _____   **4.** 25% _____

**5.** 18% _____   **6.** 46% _____   **7.** 87% _____   **8.** 8% _____

**9.** 43% _____   **10.** 55% _____   **11.** 94% _____   **12.** 36% _____

**Write each number as a percent. Round to the nearest tenth of a
percent where necessary.**

**13.** $\frac{7}{10}$ _____   **14.** 0.635 _____   **15.** 0.037 _____   **16.** $\frac{8}{15}$ _____

**17.** $\frac{7}{50}$ _____   **18.** 0.56 _____   **19.** 0.0413 _____   **20.** $\frac{3}{8}$ _____

**21.** $\frac{7}{12}$ _____   **22.** 0.387 _____   **23.** 0.283 _____   **24.** $\frac{2}{9}$ _____

**Write each number as a percent. Place the number into the puzzle
without using the percent sign or decimal point.**

**25.**

**Across**

1. 0.134

3. $\frac{53}{100}$

5. 0.565

7. $1\frac{7}{50}$

9. 0.456

10. 0.63

11. $\frac{11}{200}$

13. 0.58

14. $\frac{191}{200}$

16. 0.605

**Down**

2. 0.346

4. 0.324

5. $\frac{1}{2}$

6. 0.515

8. $\frac{33}{200}$

9. 0.4385

10. $\frac{659}{1,000}$

12. $\frac{1,087}{20,000}$

15. $\frac{14}{25}$

# Reteaching 6-3

You can express a percent that is less than 1% or greater than 100% as a decimal and as a fraction. A percent that is less than 1% is a quantity that is less than $\frac{1}{100}$. A percent that is greater than 100% is a quantity that is greater than 1.

- Write 0.5% as a decimal and as a fraction.

Move the decimal point two places to the left to write a percent as a decimal. Add zeros as needed.

$$00.5\% = 0.005$$

Since percent means per 100, you can write the percent as a fraction with a denominator of 100.

$$0.5\% = \frac{0.5}{100}$$

Then rewrite the numerator as a whole number. Since $10 \times 0.5 = 5$, multiply the numerator and the denominator by 10. Then simplify.

$$\frac{0.5}{100} = \frac{0.5 \times 10}{100 \times 10} = \frac{5}{1,000} = \frac{1}{200}$$

So, $0.5\% = 0.005 = \frac{1}{200}$.

- Write 125% as a decimal and as a fraction.

Move the decimal point two places to the left to write a percent as a decimal. Add zeros as needed.

$$125\% = 1.25.$$

Since percent means per 100, you can write the percent as a fraction with a denominator of 100.

$$125\% = \frac{125}{100}$$

Then simplify.

$$\frac{125}{100} = \frac{125 \div 25}{100 \div 25} = \frac{5}{4} = 1\frac{1}{4}$$

So, $125\% = 1.25 = 1\frac{1}{4}$.

---

**Write each percent as a fraction and a decimal.**

**1.** 0.01%

**2.** 0.45%

**3.** 0.2%

**4.** 0.67%

**5.** 150%

**6.** 225%

**7.** 186%

**8.** 201%

# Practice 6-3

**Percents Greater Than 100 or Less Than 1**

**Classify each of the following as: (A) less than 1%, (B) greater than 100%, or (C) between 1% and 100%.**

1. $\frac{1}{2}$ _____

2. $\frac{4}{3}$ _____

3. $\frac{2}{300}$ _____

4. $\frac{3}{10}$ _____

5. 10.8 _____

6. 0.7 _____

7. 1.4 _____

8. 0.06 _____

9. 1.03 _____

10. 0.009 _____

11. 0.635 _____

12. 0.0053 _____

**Use > , < , or = to compare the numbers in each pair.**

13. $\frac{1}{4}$ ☐ 20%

14. $\frac{1}{2}$% ☐ 50

15. 0.008 ☐ 8%

16. 35% ☐ $\frac{3}{8}$

17. 150% ☐ $\frac{5}{4}$

18. 3 ☐ 300%

19. $\frac{7}{250}$ ☐ 0.3%

20. 650% ☐ 7

**Write each fraction or decimal as a percent. Round to the nearest tenth of a percent if necessary.**

21. $\frac{7}{5}$ _____

22. $\frac{137}{100}$ _____

23. $\frac{0.8}{100}$ _____

24. $\frac{21}{4}$ _____

25. $\frac{17}{10}$ _____

26. $\frac{65}{40}$ _____

27. $\frac{37}{20}$ _____

28. $\frac{7}{500}$ _____

29. $\frac{9}{8}$ _____

**Write each decimal as a percent.**

30. 0.003 _____

31. 1.8 _____

32. 0.0025 _____

33. 5.3 _____

34. 0.0041 _____

35. 0.083 _____

36. 0.0009 _____

37. 0.83 _____

38. 20 _____

**Write each percent as a decimal and as a fraction in simplest form.**

39. 175% _____

40. 120% _____

41. $\frac{2}{5}$% _____

42. $\frac{5}{8}$% _____

43. 750% _____

44. $8\frac{1}{4}$% _____

45. In 1990, the population of Kansas was 2,477,574, which included 21,965 Native Americans. What percent of the people living in Kansas were Native Americans?

_____

46. The mass of Earth is $\frac{1}{318}$ of the mass of Jupiter. What percent is this?

_____

# Reteaching 6-4

| | | Find 12% of 50. | Find 150% of 90. |
|---|---|---|---|
| ① | Write the percent as a decimal. | 0.12 | 1.5 |
| ② | Multiply. | $0.12 \cdot 50 = 6$ | $1.5 \cdot 90 = 135$ |
| | | 12% of 50 is 6. | 150% of 90 is 135. |

## Complete to find each answer.

**1.** 15% of 80

15% = _____

_____ · 80 = _____

**2.** 4% of 70

4% = _____

_____ · 70 = _____

**3.** 70% of 20

70% = _____

_____ · 20 = _____

## Find each answer.

**4.** 10% of 80

_____

**5.** 20% of 80

_____

**6.** 50% of 80

_____

**7.** 75% of 80

_____

**8.** 9% of 70

_____

**9.** 2% of 66

_____

**10.** 28% of 50

_____

**11.** 75% of 20

_____

**12.** 16% of 35

_____

**13.** 94% of 22

_____

**14.** 33% of 50

_____

**15.** 40% of 45

_____

**16.** 120% of 30

_____

**17.** 110% of 70

_____

**18.** 160% of 200

_____

**19.** 180% of 250

_____

**20.** 145% of 78

_____

**21.** 187% of 40

_____

**22.** 164% of 350

_____

**23.** 125% of 230

_____

## Solve.

**24.** Pablo's weekly salary is $105. Each week he saves 60% of his salary. How much does he save each week?

_____

**25.** The sixth-grade class is selling magazine subscriptions to raise money for charity. They will give 55% of the money they raise to the homeless. If they raise $2,670, how much do they give to the homeless?

_____

# Practice 6-4

**Find each answer.**

**1.** 20% of 560

_____

**2.** 42% of 200

_____

**3.** 9% of 50

_____

**4.** 40% of 70

_____

**5.** 25% of 80

_____

**6.** 50% of 80

_____

**7.** 40% of 200

_____

**8.** 5% of 80

_____

**9.** 75% of 200

_____

**Find each answer using mental math.**

**10.** 14% of 120

_____

**11.** 30% of 180

_____

**12.** 62.5% of 24

_____

**13.** 34% of 50

_____

**14.** 25% of 240

_____

**15.** 85.5% of 23

_____

**16.** 120% of 56

_____

**17.** 80% of 90

_____

**18.** 42% of 120

_____

**Solve.**

**19.** A farmer raised a watermelon that weighed 20 lb. From his
experience with raising watermelons, he estimated that 95% of
the watermelon's weight is water.

**a.** How much of the watermelon is water? _____

**b.** How much of the watermelon is not water? _____

**c.** The watermelon was shipped off to market. There it sat,
until it had dehydrated (lost water). If the watermelon
is still 90% water, what percent of it is not water? _____

**d.** The solid part of the watermelon still weighs the same.
What was the weight of the watermelon at this point? _____

**20.** A bicycle goes on sale at 75% of its original price of $160.
What is its sale price?

_____

# Reteaching 6-5

**Solving Percent Problems Using Proportions**

You can use proportions to solve percent problems. Remember, the percent is compared to 100.

| Finding the part: | Finding the whole: | Finding the percent: |
|---|---|---|
| 10% of 40 is __?__. | 20% of __?__ is 8. | __?__ % of 25 is 20. |
| $\frac{10}{100} = \frac{n}{40}$ | $\frac{20}{100} = \frac{8}{n}$ | $\frac{n}{100} = \frac{20}{25}$ |
| $100 \cdot n = 10 \cdot 40$ | $20 \cdot n = 100 \cdot 8$ | $25 \cdot n = 100 \cdot 20$ |
| $n = 4$ | $n = 40$ | $n = 80$ |
| 10% of 40 is 4. | 20% of 40 is 8. | 80% of 25 is 20. |

**Complete to solve for n.**

**1.** 75% of __?__ is 12.

$$\frac{75}{100} = \frac{12}{n}$$

$75 \cdot \text{\_\_\_\_\_} = 100 \cdot \text{\_\_\_\_\_}$

$n = \text{\_\_\_\_\_}$

**2.** 20% of __?__ is 82.

$$\frac{20}{100} = \frac{82}{\boxed{\phantom{n}}}$$

$75 \cdot \text{\_\_\_\_\_} = 100 \cdot \text{\_\_\_\_\_}$

$n = \text{\_\_\_\_\_}$

**3.** 5% of __?__ is 9.

$$\frac{5}{100} = \frac{\boxed{\phantom{n}}}{n}$$

$\text{\_\_\_\_\_} = \text{\_\_\_\_\_}$

$n = \text{\_\_\_\_\_}$

**4.** 60 is 5% of n.

$$\frac{5}{100} = \frac{\boxed{\phantom{n}}}{n}$$

$5n = 100 \cdot \text{\_\_\_\_\_}$

$n = \text{\_\_\_\_\_}$

**5.** 6% of n is 4.8.

$$\frac{6}{\boxed{\phantom{n}}} = \frac{\boxed{\phantom{n}}}{n}$$

$6n = \text{\_\_\_\_\_} \cdot 4.8$

$n = \text{\_\_\_\_\_}$

**6.** 51 is 170% of n.

$$\frac{\boxed{\phantom{n}}}{100} = \frac{\boxed{\phantom{n}}}{n}$$

$\text{\_\_\_\_\_} = \text{\_\_\_\_\_}$

$n = \text{\_\_\_\_\_}$

**Use a proportion to solve.**

**7.** 12% of n is 9.

_____

**8.** 49% of n is 26.95.

_____

**9.** 18% of n is 27.

_____

**10.** What is 210% of 44?

_____

**11.** What is 30% of 200?

_____

**12.** 64 is what percent of 80?

_____

# Practice 6-5

**Solving Percent Problems Using Proportions**

**Use a proportion to solve.**

1. 48 is 60% of what number?

   _____

2. What is 175% of 85?

   _____

3. What percent of 90 is 50?

   _____

4. 76 is 80% of what number?

   _____

5. What is 50% of 42.88?

   _____

6. 96 is 160% of what number?

   _____

7. What percent of 24 is 72?

   _____

8. What is 85% of 120?

   _____

9. What is 80% of 12?

   _____

10. 56 is 75% of what number?

    _____

11. What percent of 80 is 50?

    _____

12. 85 is what percent of 200?

    _____

**Solve.**

13. The sale price of a bicycle is $120. This is 75% of the original
    price. Find the original price.

    _____

14. The attendance at a family reunion was 160 people. This was
    125% of last year's attendance. How many people attended the
    reunion last year?

    _____

15. A company has 875 employees. On "Half-Price Wednesday," 64%
    of the employees eat lunch at the company cafeteria. How many
    employees eat lunch at the cafeteria on Wednesdays?

    _____

16. There are 1,295 students attending a small university. There are
    714 women enrolled. What percentage of students are women?

    _____

Name _____ Class _____ Date _____

# Reteaching 6-6

**Solving Percent Problems Using Equations**

You can write equations to solve percent problems by substituting amounts into the statement: "_____% of _____ is _____?"

- 64% of 50 is what number?

  ① Choose a variable for the unknown amount.          Let $n$ = unknown number.

  ② Reword the statement, _____% of _____ is _____.          64% of 50 is $n$

  ③ Write an equation.          $64\% \cdot 50 = n$

  ④ Write the percent as a decimal.          $0.64 \cdot 50 = n$

  ⑤ Multiply to solve for $n$.          $32 = n$

  ⑥ So, 64% of 50 is 32.

- What percent of 36 is 18?

  ① Choose a variable for the unknown amount.          Let $p$ = unknown percent.

  ② Reword the statement, _____% of _____ is _____.          $p\%$ of 36 is 18.

  ③ Write an equation.          $36 \cdot p = 18$

  ④ Divide each side by 36.          $36 \cdot \frac{p}{36} = \frac{18}{36}$

  ⑤ Simplify and write the decimal as a percent.          $p = 0.5 = 50\%$

  ⑥ So, 18 is 50% of 36.

---

**Answer each question.**

1. Write an equation for: 9% of 150 is what number. _____ · _____ = $n$

2. Solve the equation to find 9% of 150 is what number? _____

3. 48% of 250 is what number? _____

4. 82% of 75 is what number? _____

5. 16% of 50 is what number? _____

6. 32% of 800 is what number? _____

7. Reword the statement: What percent of 75 is 12? _____ % of _____ is _____

8. Use the statement to find what percent of 75 is 12. _____

9. What percent of 60 is 18? _____

10. What percent of 50 is 35? _____

# Practice 6-6

**Write and solve an equation. Round answers to the nearest tenth.**

**1.** What percent of 64 is 48?

_____

**2.** 16% of 130 is what number?

_____

**3.** 25% of what number is 24?

_____

**4.** What percent of 18 is 12?

_____

**5.** 48% of 83 is what number?

_____

**6.** 40% of what number is 136?

_____

**7.** What percent of 530 is 107?

_____

**8.** 74% of 643 is what number?

_____

**9.** 62% of what number is 84?

_____

**10.** What percent of 84 is 50?

_____

**11.** 37% of 245 is what number?

_____

**12.** 12% of what number is 105?

_____

**13.** What percent of 42 is 7.5?

_____

**14.** 98% of 880 is what number?

_____

**15.** 7% of what number is 63?

_____

**16.** What percent of 95 is 74?

_____

**Solve.**

**17.** A cafe offers senior citizens a 15% discount off its regular price
of $8.95 for the dinner buffet.

   **a.** What percent of the regular price is the price for senior citizens? _____

   **b.** What is the price for senior citizens? _____

**18.** In 1990, 12.5% of the people in Oregon did not have health
insurance. If the population of Oregon was 2,880,000,
how many people were uninsured?

_____

# Reteaching 6-7

**Finding Sales Tax**

sales tax = percent of tax · purchase price

Find the amount of sales tax on a television that costs $350 with an 8% sales tax.

sales tax = 8% · $350
sales tax = 0.08 · 350
sales tax = 28

The sales tax is $28.

How much does the television cost with sales tax?

$350 + $28 = $378

**Finding a Commission**

commission = commission rate · sales

Find the commission earned with a 3% commission rate on $3,000 in sales.

commission = 3% · $3,000
commission = 0.03 · 3,000
commission = 90

The commission earned is $90.

How much do you earn if you have a base salary of $500 plus 3% commission on sales of $3,000?

$90 + $500 = $590

**Find each payment.**

1. $10.00 with a 4% sales tax

   _____

2. $8.75 with a 5.25% sales tax

   _____

3. $61.00 with an 7% sales tax

   _____

4. $320.00 with a 6.5% sales tax

   _____

5. $6.30 with a 8% sales tax

   _____

6. $26.75 with a 7.5% sales tax

   _____

**Find each commission.**

7. 6% on $3,000 in sales

   _____

8. 1.5% on $400,000 in sales

   _____

9. 8% on $1,200 in sales

   _____

10. 5.5% on $2,400 in sales

   _____

# Practice 6-7

**Find each payment.**

**1.** $17.50 with a 7% sales tax

**2.** $21.95 with a 4.25% sales tax

_____

**3.** $52.25 with an 8% sales tax

**4.** $206.88 with a 5.75% sales tax

_____

**5.** The price of a pair of shoes is $85.99 before sales tax.
The sales tax is 7.5%. Find the total cost of the shoes. _____

**Calculate a 15% tip for each amount.**

**6.** $12.68

**7.** $18.25

**8.** $15.00

_____

**Find the total payment, given the cost, tax rate, and tip rate.**

**9.** $28.60, 6.5% tax, 15% tip

**10.** $85.24, 5% tax, 20% tip

_____

**Find each commission.**

**11.** 2% on $1,500 in sales

**12.** 8% on $80,000 in sales

_____

**13.** 5% on $600 in sales

**14.** 12% on $3,200 in sales

_____

**Find the total earnings, given the salary, commission rate, and sales.**

**15.** $1,000 plus 6% on sales of $2,000

**16.** $500 plus 10% on sales of $1,400

_____

# Reteaching 6-8

**Finding Percent of Change**

**Percent of change** is the percent something increases or decreases from its original amount.

|  | Find the percent of increase from 12 to 18. | Find the percent of decrease from 20 to 12. |
|---|---|---|
| ① Subtract to find the amount of change. | $18 - 12 = 6$ | $20 - 12 = 8$ |
| ② Write a proportion. $\frac{\text{change}}{\text{original}} = \frac{\text{percent}}{100}$ | $\frac{6}{12} = \frac{n}{100}$ $6 \cdot 100 = 12n$ | $\frac{8}{20} = \frac{n}{100}$ $8 \cdot 100 = 20n$ |
| ③ Solve for $n$. | $n = 50$ | $n = 40$ |
|  | The percent of increase is 50%. | The percent of decrease is 40%. |

---

**State whether the change is an *increase* or *decrease*. Complete to find the percent of change.**

**1.** 40 to 60

$60 - 40 =$ _____

$\dfrac{\boxed{\phantom{xx}}}{40} = \dfrac{n}{100}$

_____ $\cdot 100 = 40n$

$n =$ _____

_____

**2.** 15 to 9

$15 - 9 =$ _____

$\dfrac{\boxed{\phantom{xx}}}{15} = \dfrac{n}{100}$

_____ $\cdot 100 = 15n$

$n =$ _____

_____

**3.** 0.4 to 0.9

$0.9 - 0.4 =$ _____

$\dfrac{\boxed{\phantom{xx}}}{0.4} = \dfrac{n}{\boxed{\phantom{xx}}}$

_____ $= 0.4n$

$n =$ _____

_____

**Find the percent of *increase*.**

**4.** 16 to 40      **5.** 22 to 66      **6.** 4 to 8      **7.** 20 to 22

_____      _____      _____      _____

**8.** 9 to 18      **9.** 28 to 35      **10.** 80 to 112      **11.** 150 to 165

_____      _____      _____      _____

**Find the percent of *decrease*.**

**12.** 20 to 15      **13.** 100 to 57      **14.** 52 to 26      **15.** 90 to 45

_____      _____      _____      _____

**16.** 140 to 126      **17.** 75 to 72      **18.** 1000 to 990      **19.** 420 to 357

_____      _____      _____      _____

# Practice 6-8

**Find each percent of change. State whether the change is an increase or a decrease.**

1. A $50 coat is put on sale for $35.

   _____

2. Mayelle earns $18,000 a year. After a raise, she earns $19,500.

   _____

3. Last year Anthony earned $24,000. After a brief lay-off this year, Anthony's income is $18,500.

   _____

4. In 1981, about $1.1 million was lost due to fires. In 1988, the loss was about $9.6 million.

   _____

5. In a recent year, certain colleges and universities received about $268 million in aid. Ten years later, they received about $94 million.

   _____

6. A coat regularly costing $125 is put on sale for $75.

   _____

7. Suppose that at a job interview, you are told that you would receive a 10% increase in your salary at the end of each of the first three years. How much would your starting salary have changed at the end of the third year?

   _____

8. Four years ago there were 35 students in the school band. Since then 12 students have joined the band.

   _____

9. Complete the table.

**Enrollment in Center City Schools From 1995 to 2000**

| Year | Enrollment | Change from Last Year (Number of Students) | Change from Last Year (%) | Increase or Decrease |
|------|-----------|-------------------------------------------|---------------------------|----------------------|
| 1995 | 18,500 | — | — | — |
| 1996 | 19,300 | | | |
| 1997 | 19,700 | | | |
| 1998 | 19,500 | | | |
| 1999 | 19,870 | | | |
| 2000 | 19,200 | | | |

# Reteaching 6-9
**Problem Solving: Write an Equation**

The cost for a car and driver on a car ferry is $15. Each additional
passenger is $2. If Brett pays a toll of $21, how many additional
passengers does he have?

**Read and Understand**  What information are you given? *You know the cost for the car and driver, and the cost for each passenger.* What are you asked to find? *You want to find the number of additional passengers.*

**Plan and Solve**  You are given a relationship between numbers. So, an equation may help solve the problem. The toll is $15 for the car and driver plus $2 for each passenger ($p$).

$$15 + 2p = \text{toll}$$
$$15 + 2p = 21$$

Solve the equation for $p$.

$$15 + 2p = 21$$
$$15 - 15 + 2p = 21 - 15 \quad \leftarrow \textbf{Subtract 15.}$$
$$2p = 6 \quad \leftarrow \textbf{Simplify.}$$
$$\frac{2p}{2} = \frac{6}{2} \quad \leftarrow \textbf{Divide by 2.}$$
$$p = 3 \quad \leftarrow \textbf{Simplify.}$$

There are 3 passengers.

**Look Back and Check**  $15 for car + $2 × 3 additional passengers = $21.

---

**Write and solve an equation for each problem.**

1. Mia is 8 years older than Kenji. Mia is 26 years old. How old is Kenji?

2. The perimeter of a rectangle is 100 in. The width is 18 in. Find the length.

3. A jacket costs $28 more than twice the cost of a pair of slacks. If the jacket costs $152, how much do the slacks cost?

4. Jennifer has $22.75 in her bank. She saves quarters and half dollars. She has $10.50 in half dollars. How many quarters does she have?

5. One number is 6 less than another number. Their sum is 20. Find the greater number.

6. Sari has 11 more markers than Sam. Together they have 61 markers. How many markers does Sam have?

*Course 2* Chapter 6

Lesson 6-9 Reteaching  **109**

# Practice 6-9

**Solve each problem by writing an equation. Check each answer in the original problem.**

1. In a pet store the number of dogs is 12 more than three times the number of cats. If the pet store has 21 dogs, how many cats does it have?

   _____

2. In the pet store the number of birds is 10 less than twice the number of rabbits. If the pet store has 56 birds, how many rabbits does it have?

   _____

3. A sweater cost $12 more than a shirt. Together they cost $46. What was the price of the shirt?

   _____

4. The perimeter of a rectangle is 84 cm. The length is twice the width. Find the length and width.

   _____

5. Mark and Melinda collect baseball caps. Mark has 7 more than Melinda. Together, they have 115 caps. How many baseball caps does each of them have?

   _____

**Use any strategy to solve each problem. Show your work.**

6. Lydia sold $\frac{4}{5}$ of her candles to raise money for the band. She has 8 candles left. How many candles did Lydia start with?

   _____

7. A coin purse contains quarters, dimes, and nickels. There are the same number of dimes as nickels and half as many quarters as dimes. The coins are worth $1.65. How many of each coin are in the coin purse?

   _____

8. The sum of two numbers is 20. The greater number is 4 more than the lesser number. What are the two numbers?

   _____

9. A garage charged Mr. Tilton $48 in parts and $36/h in labor. How many hours did the garage spend on Mr. Tilton's car if the total bill was $156?

   _____

# Reteaching 7-1

A plane is an infinite flat surface. A line is a series of points that extends in two opposite directions without end. Lines in a plane that never meet are called **parallel** lines. Lines that intersect to form a right angle (90°) are called **perpendicular** lines. Intersecting lines have exactly one common point.

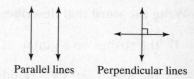

Parallel lines    Perpendicular lines

A line segment is formed by two endpoints and all the points between them.

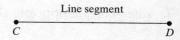

Line segment

- Use the figure to name a line segment, a point, two intersecting lines, and a pair of parallel lines.

Two endpoints are *S* and *U*, so they form a line segment, $\overline{SU}$.

There are 5 points, *R, S, M, U, T*.

Intersecting lines have exactly one point in common. So, $\overleftrightarrow{RU}$ and $\overleftrightarrow{SU}$ are intersecting lines.

Line $\overleftrightarrow{TU}$ never intersects line $\overleftrightarrow{RS}$, so $\overleftrightarrow{TU}$ and $\overleftrightarrow{RS}$ are parallel lines.

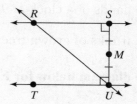

---

**Write *parallel* or *perpendicular* to describe the lines formed by this book.**

**1.** Top and bottom sides _____    **2.** Top and left sides _____

**Use the figure to name each of the following.**

**3.** a line segment _____

**4.** a point _____

**5.** two pairs of intersecting lines _____

**6.** a pair of parallel lines _____

**7.** Sketch a rectangle to represent a bulletin board.

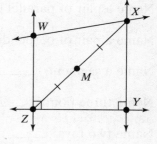

    **a.** Write *parallel* or *perpendicular* to describe the lines formed by the left and right sides of a bulletin board.

    **b.** Write *parallel* or *perpendicular* to describe the lines that meet at a corner of the bulletin board.

_____    _____

**Use a straightedge to draw each figure.**

**8.** $\overleftrightarrow{AB}$    **9.** $\overline{BC}$    **10.** $\overrightarrow{MN}$

Name _____ Class _____ Date _____

# Practice 7-1

**Write the word that describes the lines or line segments.**

1. the strings on a guitar _____

2. the marks left by a skidding car _____

3. sidewalks on opposite sides of a street _____

4. the segments that make up a + sign _____

5. the wires suspended between telephone poles _____

6. the hands of a clock at 9:00 P.M. _____

7. the trunks of grown trees in a forest _____

**Use the diagram below for Exercises 8–13.**

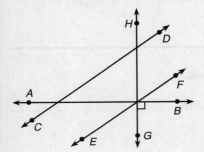

8. Name a pair of parallel lines. _____

9. Name a pair of perpendicular lines. _____

10. Name a segment. _____

11. Name three points. _____

12. Name two rays. _____

13. Name a pair of intersecting lines. _____

**Use a straightedge to draw each figure.**

14. Use a ruler to draw a line parallel to $\overline{UV}$.

15. Use a ruler and a protractor to draw a line perpendicular to $\overline{XY}$.

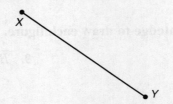

# Reteaching 7-2
**Measuring and Classifying Angles**

An **angle** is made up of two rays (the *sides* of the angle) with a common endpoint (the *vertex* of the angle).

You can name this angle ∠A, ∠BAC, or ∠CAB.

∠A is an **acute** angle because its measure is less than 90°. If an angle has a measure greater than 90° and less than 180°, it is an **obtuse** angle.

You can measure an angle using a protractor. Write the measure of ∠A as m∠A.

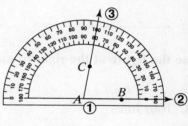

**acute** less than 90°

**obtuse** greater than 90° less than 180°

To measure an angle:

① Place the center point of your protractor on the vertex of the angle.

② Line up one side of the angle with zero on the protractor scale.

③ Read the scale at the second side of the angle. Since ∠A is an acute angle, read 80° and not 100°.

$m\angle A = 80°$

---

**Measure each angle. Then circle *acute* or *obtuse*.**

1.

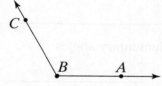

m∠B = —————

acute        obtuse

2.

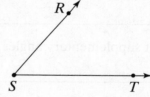

m∠S = —————

acute        obtuse

3.

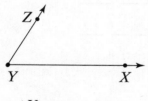

m∠Y = —————

acute        obtuse

4.

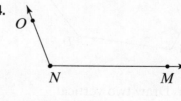

m∠N = —————

acute        obtuse

**Classify each angle with the given measure as *acute* or *obtuse*.**

5. 45° —————

6. 148° —————

7. 4° —————

8. 106° —————

9. 65° —————

10. 179° —————

11. 23° —————

12. 115° —————

# Practice 7-2

**Find the measure of each angle. Then classify the angle.**

1.

_____

2.

_____

3.

_____

**Classify each angle as _acute, right, obtuse,_ or _straight_.**

4. $m\angle A = 180°$     5. $m\angle B = 43°$     6. $m\angle C = 127°$     7. $m\angle D = 90°$

_____     _____     _____     _____

**Use the figure at the right to name the following.**

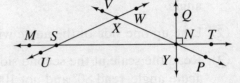

8. four lines          _____

9. three segments      _____

10. a pair of congruent angles _____

11. four right angles

_____

12. two pairs of obtuse vertical angles

_____

13. two pairs of adjacent supplementary angles

_____

14. two pairs of complementary angles

_____

15. Use a protractor to find $m\angle A, m\angle B, m\angle C, m\angle D$.

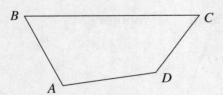

_____

_____

_____

_____

16. Use a protractor. Draw two vertical angles. One angle has a measure of 45°.

17. Use the dot grid to draw two supplementary angles, one of which is 45°. Do _not_ use a protractor.

# Reteaching 7-3

To bisect $\overline{AB}$:

① Open the compass more than half the length of $\overline{AB}$. With the compass tip on $A$, draw an arc.

② Without changing the opening, move the compass tip to $B$. Draw another arc.

③ Draw $\overleftrightarrow{CD}$ through the intersections of the arcs. $\overleftrightarrow{CD}$ is the bisector of $\overline{AB}$. Point $M$ is the midpoint of $\overline{AB}$.

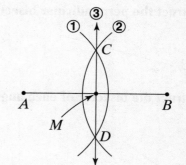

To bisect $\angle ABC$:

① Place the compass point on vertex $B$. Draw an arc intersecting the sides of the angle at points $P$ and $M$.

② Place the compass tip on point $M$. Draw an arc in the interior of the angle. Keep the opening the same and place the compass tip on point $P$. Draw a second arc intersecting the first at point $Q$.

③ Draw $\overrightarrow{BQ}$. $\overrightarrow{BQ}$ is the bisector of $\angle ABC$.

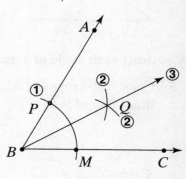

**Complete each construction to bisect the figure.**

1.

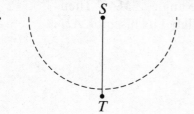

Bisect $\overline{ST}$.

2.

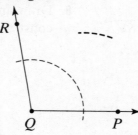

Bisect $\angle RQP$.

3.

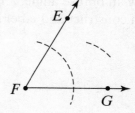

Bisect $\angle EFG$.

**Bisect each figure.**

4.

5.

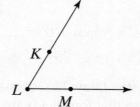

6.

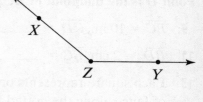

# Practice 7-3 ....................................................

**Construct the perpendicular bisector of each segment.**

**1.**

**2.**

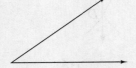

**Construct the bisector of each angle.**

**3.**

**4.**

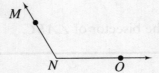

**Construct each angle or segment.**

**5.** Construct a segment with measure $\frac{3}{4}$ times that of $\overline{AB}$.

**6.** Construct an angle with measure $\frac{1}{4}$ times that of $\angle MNO$.

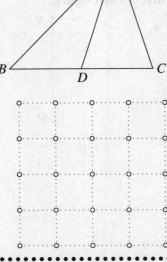

**7.** Draw an obtuse angle, $\angle RST$. Then construct and label its bisector $\overrightarrow{SV}$.

**8.** Draw an acute angle, $\angle MAT$. Then construct and label its bisector $\overrightarrow{AH}$.

**Point D is the midpoint of $\overline{BC}$. Complete.**

**9.** $\overline{BC} = 10$ in., $\overline{CD} =$ _____

**10.** $\overline{DC} = 9$ mm, $\overline{BD} =$ _____

**11.** $\overline{BD} = 2$ cm, $\overline{BC} =$ _____

**12.** $\overline{BC} = 12$ yd, $\overline{DC} =$ _____

**13.** Each square represents one acre of a farm. Draw 11 sections of fence along the dotted lines shown, so that four fields are formed, each containing four acres of land.

# Reteaching 7-4

| Classifying Triangles by Angles | Classifying Triangles by Sides |
|---|---|
| **Acute triangle:** three acute angles | **Equilateral triangle:** three congruent sides |
| **Right triangle:** one right angle | **Isosceles triangle:** at least two congruent sides |
| **Obtuse triangle:** one obtuse angle | **Scalene triangle:** no congruent sides |

The sum of the measures of the angles of a triangle is 180°.

Find the value of $x$ in the triangle at the right.

$$x = m\angle A$$
$$m\angle A + 40° + 78° = 180°$$
$$m\angle A + 118° = 180°$$
$$m\angle A = 180° - 118°$$
$$m\angle A = 62°$$
$$x = 62°$$

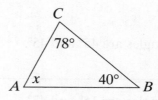

---

**Classify each triangle by its sides and then by its angles.**

1.
   _____

2.
   _____

3.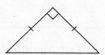
   _____

4.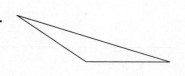
   _____

5.
   _____

6.
   _____

**Find the value of $x$ in each triangle.**

7.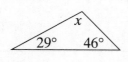
   _____

8.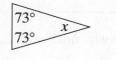
   _____

9.
   _____

# Practice 7-4

**Find the value of *x* in each triangle.**

1.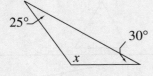

_____

2.

_____

3.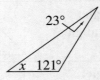

_____

4.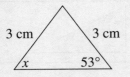

_____

5.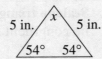

_____

6.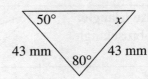

_____

**Classify each triangle.**

7. The measures of two angles are 45° and 45°.

_____

8. The measures of two angles are 15° and 47°.

_____

9. The measures of two angles are 53° and 76°.

_____

10. The measure of one angle is 18°.

_____

11. The measure of one angle is 90°.

_____

12. The measure of one angle is 115°.

_____

13. The measures of the angles of a triangle are 40°, 50°, and 90°.

   a. Classify the triangle by its angles. _____

   b. Can the triangle be equilateral? Why or why not? _____

   c. Can the triangle be isosceles? Why or why not? _____

   d. Can you classify the triangle by its sides? Why or why not? _____

# Reteaching 7-5

**Quadrilaterals and Other Polygons**

You name polygons by the number of sides. A **quadrilateral** is a polygon with four sides. The table shows the names and properties of some special quadrilaterals.

## Special Quadrilaterals

| Quadrilateral | Figure | Only 1 Pair of Parallel Sides | 2 Pairs of Parallel Sides | All Sides Must be Congruent | Opposite Sides Are Congruent | All Angles Must Be Right Angles |
|---|---|---|---|---|---|---|
| Square | | | ✔ | ✔ | ✔ | ✔ |
| Rectangle | | | ✔ | | ✔ | ✔ |
| Rhombus | | | ✔ | ✔ | ✔ | |
| Parallelogram | | | ✔ | | ✔ | |
| Trapezoid | | ✔ | | | | |

Look at the rhombus. It is also a parallelogram, but the name rhombus is best because it gives the most information about the figure.

---

**Write the best name for each quadrilateral.**

1.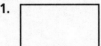

2.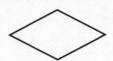

3.

4.

_____  _____  _____  _____

**Draw each of the following.**

5. a trapezoid with a right angle

6. a quadrilateral with opposite sides parallel and a right angle

7. a regular octagon

8. an irregular pentagon

# Practice 7-5

**Identify each polygon and classify it as *regular* or *irregular*.**

1.

_____

_____

2.

_____

_____

3.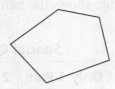

_____

_____

4.

_____

_____

**State all correct names for each quadrilateral. Then circle the best name.**

5.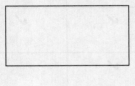

_____

_____

_____

6.

_____

_____

_____

7.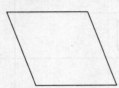

_____

_____

_____

8.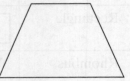

_____

_____

_____

**Use dot paper to draw each quadrilateral.**

9. a rectangle that is not a square

10. a rhombus with two right angles

11. a trapezoid with no right angles

12. Draw a pair of quadrilaterals where the angles of the first quadrilateral are congruent to the angles of the second quadrilateral. No side of one quadrilateral is to be congruent to any side of the other quadrilateral.

# Reteaching 7-6

**Problem Solving: Draw a Diagram and Look for a Pattern**

One acute angle of a right triangle is 35°. What is the measure of the other acute angle?

| | |
|---|---|
| **Read and Understand** | What kind of triangle is given? *A right triangle is given.* What do you know about a right triangle? *It has one 90° angle and two acute angles.* What are you given? *You are given one acute angle that measures 35°.* What do you want to find? *You want to find the measure of the other acute angle.* |

**Plan and Solve**   A good strategy for this problem is to draw a diagram. Show a right triangle with the acute angle labeled and the right angle marked.

Remember that the sum of the angle measures of a triangle is 180°. The diagram reminds you that the right angle measures 90°.

$$180° − (90° + 35°) = 180° − 125°$$
$$= 55°$$

The measure of the third angle is 55°.

**Look Back and Check**   Check by adding: $55° + 35° + 90° = 180°$

---

**Solve each problem by drawing a diagram.**

1. One acute angle of a right triangle is 42°. What is the measure of the other acute angle?

   _____

2. One of the two equal angles of an isosceles triangle is 48°. What are the measures of the other two angles?

   _____

3. A square garden is enclosed by a fence that has 9 posts on each side. How many posts are there in all?

   _____

4. A piece of string is cut in half. Then each piece is cut in half. Each of those pieces is cut in half. How many cuts were made?

   _____

5. You planned to bike 120 mi on your vacation. On the first day you biked $\frac{1}{2}$ of the distance. On the next day you biked $\frac{1}{4}$ of the remaining distance. How far did you have left to go?

   _____

6. Newtown is 522 km west of Jamesburg. Pottsville is 356 km east of Jamesburg and 928 km east of Mayfield. How far and in what direction is Newtown from Mayfield?

   _____

# Practice 7-6

**Problem Solving: Draw a Diagram and Look for a Pattern**

**Solve each problem by drawing a diagram.**

1. One angle of an isosceles triangle measures 56°. What are the measures of the other two angles?

   _____

2. The eight members of the Ping Pong Paddlers Club have a tournament in which every player plays a game against every other player. How many games are there in the tournament?

   _____

3. You took a train trip to visit your cousin. By 10:15 the train had traveled 20 mi. By 10:30 the train had traveled an additional 10 mi. You are now halfway to your cousin's town. At what time will you reach your cousin's town if the train's speed is constant?

   _____

4. A cat likes to play on stairs. Starting at the bottom landing, the cat jumped up 4 steps, then down 2. Then the cat jumped up 5 steps and fell down 3. In two more jumps of 4 steps and then 2 steps, the cat reached the top of the stairs. How many steps are in the staircase?

   _____

**Use any strategy to solve each problem. Show your work.**

5. Carla is five years older than her sister Julie. The product of their ages is 234. How old is Julie?

   _____

6. Your teacher bought pens for your class. The pens all cost the same price. She bought as many pens as the cost (in cents) of each pen. She spent a total of $56.25. How many pens did she buy?

   _____

7. If the pattern at the right continues, how many dots will there be in the fifth figure?

   1 dot      5 dots      12 dots

8. Frank, Bill, and Pam each ordered a salad at a restaurant. A spinach salad, a chef's salad, and a tuna salad were ordered. Bill did not order the spinach salad. Pam sat to the right of the one who ordered the spinach salad and to the left of the one who ordered the chef's salad. Who ordered which salad?

   _____

# Reteaching 7-7

**Congruent polygons** have congruent sides and angles. These are called the *corresponding parts* of the congruent figures.

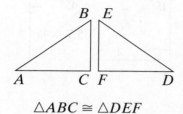

$$\triangle ABC \cong \triangle DEF$$

| Corresponding Angles | Corresponding Sides |
|---|---|
| $\angle A \cong \angle D$ | $BC \cong EF$ |
| $\angle B \cong \angle E$ | $CA \cong FD$ |
| $\angle C \cong \angle F$ | $AB \cong DE$ |

**Complete each congruence statement.**

1. $\triangle LMN \cong \triangle RPQ$

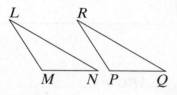

$\overline{MN} \cong \overline{PQ}$ $\qquad$ $\angle M \cong \angle P$

$\overline{NL} \cong$ _____ $\qquad$ $\angle L \cong$ _____

2. $\triangle FGJ \cong \triangle YWX$

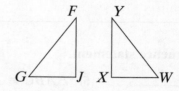

$\overline{JF} \cong \overline{XY}$ $\qquad$ $\angle G \cong \angle W$

$\overline{FG} \cong$ _____ $\qquad$ $\angle J \cong$ _____

3. $\triangle ABC \cong \triangle DEF$ $\qquad$ **a.** $\angle A \cong$ _____ $\qquad$ **b.** $\angle B \cong$ _____ $\qquad$ **c.** $\angle C \cong$ _____

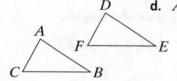

**d.** $\overline{AC} \cong$ _____ $\qquad$ **e.** $\overline{BC} \cong$ _____ $\qquad$ **f.** $\overline{AB} \cong$ _____

**Are the figures below *congruent* or *not congruent*? Explain.**

4.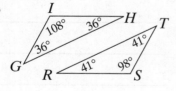

_____

_____

_____

5.

_____

_____

_____

# Practice 7-7

**Congruent Figures**

**Are the figures congruent or not congruent? Explain.**

**1.**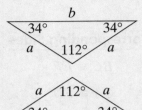

**2.**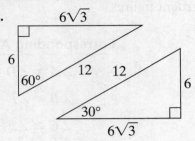

**3.**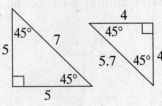

_____    _____    _____

_____    _____    _____

_____    _____    _____

_____    _____    _____

**Complete each congruence statement.**

**4.** $\triangle ABC \cong$ _____

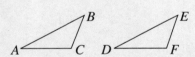

**5.** $\triangle ABC \cong$ _____

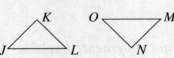

**6.** $\triangle ABC \cong$ _____

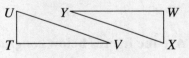

**Write six congruences involving corresponding sides and angles for each pair of triangles.**

**7.** $\triangle ABC \cong \triangle DEF$

**8.** $\triangle JKL \cong \triangle MNO$

**9.** $\triangle TUV \cong \triangle WXY$

_____    _____    _____

_____    _____    _____

_____    _____    _____

**Use the diagram at the right to complete each of the following.**

**10. a.** $\angle ABC \cong$ _____

**b.** $\overline{AB} \cong$ _____

**c.** $\angle F \cong$ _____

**11. a.** $\triangle ABC \cong$ _____

**b.** $\triangle BAC \cong$ _____

**c.** $\triangle CAB \cong$ _____

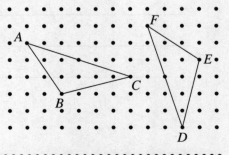

# Reteaching 7-8

A **circle** is the set of points in a plane that are all the same distance from a point, called the *center*. This circle is called circle *A*.

$\overline{AB}$ is a **radius** of circle *A*. It is a segment that has one endpoint on the circle and the other at the center. $\overline{AC}$ and $\overline{AD}$ are also *radii* of circle *A*.

$\overline{DC}$ is a **diameter** of circle *A*. It is a segment that passes through the center of the circle and has both endpoints on the circle.

$\overline{DE}$ is a chord of circle *A*. A **chord** is a segment that has both endpoints on the circle.

$\overset{\frown}{DB}$ is an arc of circle *A*. An **arc** is part of a circle.

$\angle DAB$ is a **central angle** of circle *A*. It is an angle with its vertex at the center of the circle.

$\overset{\frown}{DEC}$ is a **semicircle**. A semicircle is an arc that is half a circle.

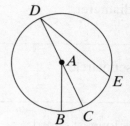

---

**Name each of the following for circle *P*.**

1. all radii _____

2. all chords _____

3. 3 arcs _____

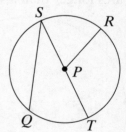

**Name each of the following shown for circle *M*.**

4. all diameters

_____

5. 3 central angles

_____

6. all chords

_____

7. 2 semicircles

_____

8. two radii

_____

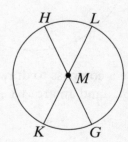

# Practice 7-8

**Name each of the following for circle *O*.**

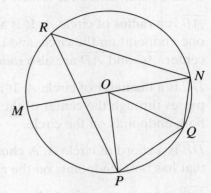

**1.** two chords

_____

**2.** three radii

_____

**3.** a diameter

_____

**4.** a central angle

_____

**5.** a semicircle

_____

**6.** two arcs

_____

**7.** the longest chord

_____

**8.** the shortest chord

_____

**Name all of the indicated arcs for circle *Q*.**

**9.** all arcs shorter than a semicircle _____

**10.** all arcs longer than a semicircle _____

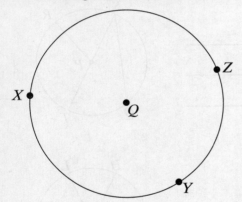

**11.** Use a compass to draw and label a circle *Q*. Label a semicircle $\overarc{ABC}$ and an arc $\overarc{AX}$.

# Reteaching 7-9

**Use the information in the table to create a circle graph.**

The class took a survey of what time students usually go to sleep.
To make a circle graph:

①  Find the total number of students.

②  Use a proportion to find the measure
of each central angle. Round to the
nearest degree.

③  Use a compass. Draw a circle. Use a
protractor. Draw the central angles.
Label each sector.

**Time Students Go to Sleep**

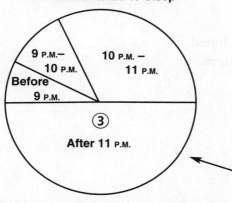

| Time Students Go to Sleep | Number of Students | ② Central Angle Measure |
|---|---|---|
| Before 9 P.M. | 2 | $\frac{2}{28} = \frac{a}{360°}$ $a \approx 26°$ |
| 9 P.M.–10 P.M. | 3 | $\frac{3}{28} = \frac{b}{360°}$ $b \approx 39°$ |
| 10 P.M.–11 P.M. | 9 | $\frac{9}{28} = \frac{c}{360°}$ $c \approx 116°$ |
| After 11 P.M. | 14 | $\frac{14}{28} = \frac{d}{360°}$ $d \approx 180°$ |
| ① Total | 28 | |

The central angle measures add to 361° because of
rounding, but the difference does not show in the graph.

---

**Complete the table. Draw a circle graph of the data.**

**Tuesday's Music CD Sales**

| Type of Music | Number of CDs Sold | Central Angle Measure |
|---|---|---|
| Country | 10 | |
| Rock | 8 | |
| Jazz | 16 | |
| Rap | 14 | |
| **Total** | | |

**Tuesday's Music CD Sales**

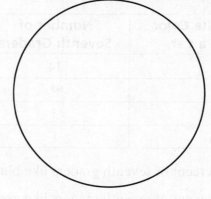

# Practice 7-9

**Use the information in each table to create a circle graph.**

1. The data show the total number of space vehicles that either successfully reached or exceeded orbit around Earth.

| Years | Number of Successful United States Space Launches |
|-------|:---:|
| 1957–1959 | 15 |
| 1960–1969 | 470 |
| 1970–1979 | 258 |
| 1980–1989 | 153 |
| 1990–1995 | 146 |

2. The data represent the percent of private schools in the United States that have an annual tuition in each of the given ranges.

| Annual Tuition | % of Private Schools |
|----------------|:---:|
| Less than $500 | 13 |
| $500–$1,000 | 28 |
| $1,001–$1,500 | 26 |
| $1,501–$2,500 | 15 |
| More than $2,500 | 18 |

3. The data represent a poll taken in a seventh-grade class.

| Favorite Color for a Car | Number of Seventh Graders |
|--------------------------|:---:|
| Red | 14 |
| Blue | 9 |
| White | 3 |
| Green | 1 |

a. What percent of seventh graders like blue cars? _____

b. What percent of seventh graders like green cars? _____

c. What percent of seventh graders like either red *or* blue cars?

_____

d. What percent of seventh graders like a car color *other than* white?

_____

# Reteaching 8-1

To choose a reasonable estimate, determine if the measurement is small like inches or centimeters or big like feet, yards, or meters.

**Choose a reasonable estimate. Explain your choice.**

- Which is a better estimate for the height of an office building, 20 in. or 20 yd?

The height of an office building is tall, so 20 yd is the better estimate.

- To estimate the area of a figure, estimate the number of square units contained in the figure.

Each square unit represents 1 ft$^2$.
Estimate the area.

12 whole squares
partial squares $\approx$ 2 whole squares

$12 + 2 = 14$

The area is about 14 ft$^2$.

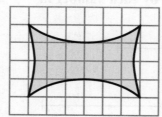

---

**Estimate the length of the line segment by each number in inches.**

1. |⊢——————————————————⊣|          2. |⊢————⊣|

_____                              _____

**Estimate the length of the line segment by each number in centimeters.**

3. |⊢——————————⊣|                        4. |⊢————⊣|

_____                              _____

**Choose a reasonable estimate. Explain your choice.**

5. height of a refrigerator: 6 in. or 6 ft

_____

_____

6. height of a stop sign: 8 ft or 8 yd

_____

_____

**Each square on the grids below represents 10 mi$^2$. Estimate the area of each region.**

7.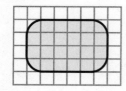

_____

8.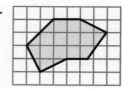

_____

# Practice 8-1

**Estimate the length of the line segment by each number in inches.**

1. |————————————————————|

_____

2. |————————————————————————————|

_____

**Estimate the length of the line segment by each number in centimeters.**

3. |————————————————————|

_____

4. |————————————————————————|

_____

**Choose a reasonable estimate. Explain your choice.**

5. height of a truck cab: 12 in. or 12 ft    _____

6. width of a book: 8 in. or 8 ft    _____

7. diameter of a pizza: 8 in. or 8 ft    _____

8. depth of a bathtub: 2 ft. or 2 yd    _____

**Suppose each square on the grids below is 1 cm by 1 cm. Estimate the area of each figure.**

9.     10. 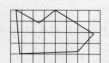    11. 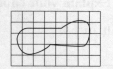    12.

_____    _____    _____    _____

**Choose the metric unit of measure listed that you would use to estimate the given length or area.**

13. the height of a tree:
    mm, cm, m, km    _____

14. the perimeter of the cover of a book:
    in., ft, yd, mi    _____

15. the area of an ocean:
    $ft^2$, $yd^2$, $in.^2$, $mi^2$    _____

# Reteaching 8-2

**Areas of Parallelograms and Triangles**

You can use the area of a rectangle to find the area of a parallelogram.

① Draw a perpendicular segment from one vertex to the opposite side to form a triangle.

② Move the triangle to the right side of the parallelogram to form a rectangle.

③ Find the area of the rectangle.
$A$ = length × width = base × height = $bh$

The parallelogram has the same base, height, and area as the rectangle.

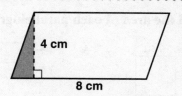

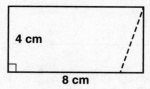

$A = bh$
$\phantom{A} = 8 \cdot 4$
$\phantom{A} = 32 \text{ cm}^2$

You can use the area of a parallelogram to find the area of a triangle. Two identical triangles, together as shown, form a parallelogram. Each triangle has half the area of the parallelogram.

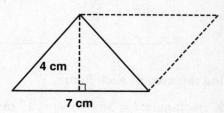

Area of parallelogram: $A = bh$

Area of triangle: $\qquad = \frac{1}{2}bh = \frac{1}{2} \cdot 7 \cdot 4 = 14 \text{ cm}^2$

**Find the area of each figure.**

1.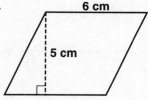
_____

2.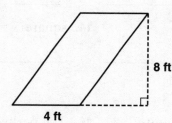
_____

3.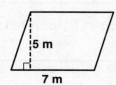
_____

4.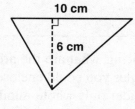
_____

5.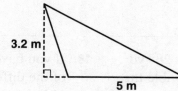
_____

6.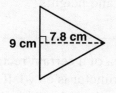
_____

**Find the area of a parallelogram with base length $b$ and height $h$.**

7. $b = 7$ in., $h = 4$ in.

8. $b = 9$ m, $h = 1.5$ m

9. $b = 1.25$ cm, $h = 2$ cm

_____ _____ _____

# Practice 8-2

**Areas of Parallelograms and Triangles**

**Find the area of each parallelogram and triangle.**

1.
4 m
4 m

_____

2.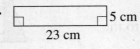
5 cm
23 cm

_____

3.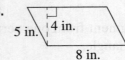
5 in.  4 in.
8 in.

_____

4.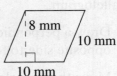
8 mm
10 mm
10 mm

_____

5.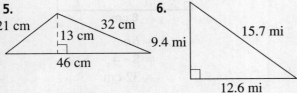
21 cm    32 cm
13 cm
46 cm

_____

6.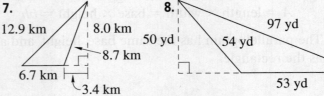
15.7 mi
9.4 mi
12.6 mi

7.
12.9 km    8.0 km
8.7 km
6.7 km    3.4 km

_____

8.
97 yd
50 yd    54 yd
53 yd

_____

**Find the area of each figure.**

9.  rectangle: $l = 16$ mm, $w = 12$ mm

_____

10. triangle: $b = 23$ km, $h = 14$ km

_____

11. square: $s = 27$ ft

_____

12. rectangle: $l = 65$ mi, $w = 48$ mi

_____

13. triangle: $b = 19$ in., $h = 15$ in.

_____

14. square: $s = 42$ m

_____

**Solve.**

15. The area of a triangle is 6 square units. Both the height and the length of the base are whole numbers. What are the possible lengths and heights?

_____

16. The perimeter of a rectangle is 72 m. The width of the rectangle is 16 m. What is the area of the rectangle?

_____

17. The area of a certain rectangle is 288 yd². The perimeter is 68 yd. If you double the length and width, what will be the area and perimeter of the new rectangle?

_____

18. If you have 36 ft of fencing, what are the areas of the different rectangles you could enclose with the fencing? Consider only whole-number dimensions.

_____

# Reteaching 8-3

**Trapezoid**

Two identical trapezoids, together as shown, form a parallelogram. The trapezoid has half the area of the parallelogram.

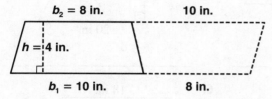

Area of parallelogram:  $A = (b_1 + b_2)h$

Area of trapezoid:  $A = \frac{1}{2}h(b_1 + b_2)$
$= \frac{1}{2}(4)(10 + 8)$
$= 2(18) = 36$ in.$^2$

**Irregular Figures**

Not all geometric figures are shapes with which you are familiar. Some of them, however, can be divided into familiar shapes.

Find the area of the figure.

Use the area formulas to find the areas of the triangle and the rectangle.

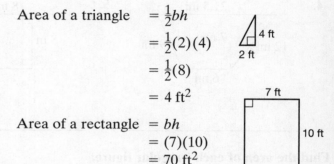

Area of a triangle $= \frac{1}{2}bh$
$= \frac{1}{2}(2)(4)$
$= \frac{1}{2}(8)$
$= 4$ ft$^2$

Area of a rectangle $= bh$
$= (7)(10)$
$= 70$ ft$^2$

Find the total area by adding the area of each figure.

Total area = area of triangle + area of rectangle
$= 4 + 70$
$= 74$

The total area is 74 ft$^2$.

**Find the area of each figure.**

**1.**

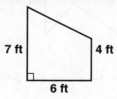

_____

**2.**

_____

**3.**

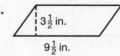

_____

**4.**

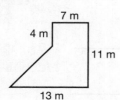

**5.**

**6.**

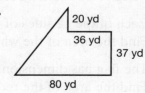

Name _____  Class _____  Date _____

# Practice 8-3

**Areas of Other Figures**

**Find the area of each trapezoid.**

**1.**
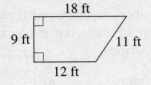
18 ft
9 ft
11 ft
12 ft

_____

**2.**
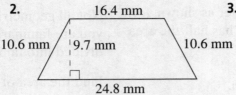
16.4 mm
10.6 mm  9.7 mm  10.6 mm
24.8 mm

_____

**3.**
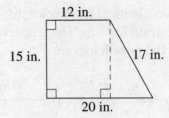
12 in.
15 in.  17 in.
20 in.

_____

**4.**
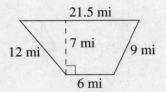
21.5 mi
12 mi  7 mi  9 mi
6 mi

_____

**5.**
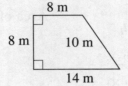
8 m
8 m  10 m
14 m

_____

**6.**
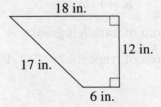
18 in.
12 in.
17 in.
6 in.

_____

**Find the area of each irregular figure.**

**7.**
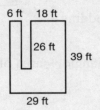
6 ft  18 ft
26 ft  39 ft
29 ft

_____

**8.**
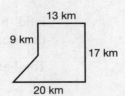
13 km
9 km  17 km
20 km

_____

**9.**
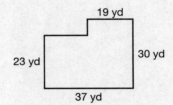
19 yd
23 yd  30 yd
37 yd

_____

**10.**
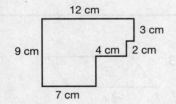
12 cm
3 cm
9 cm  4 cm  2 cm
7 cm

_____

**11.**
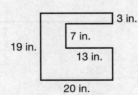
3 in.
7 in.
19 in.  13 in.
20 in.

_____

**12.**
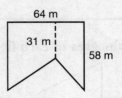
64 m
31 m  58 m

_____

**Solve.**

**13.** The flag of Switzerland features a white cross on a red background.

  **a.** Each of the 12 sides of the cross has a length of 15 cm.
  Find the area of the white cross. _____

  **b.** The flag has dimensions 60 cm by 60 cm.
  Find the area of the red region. _____

**14.** A trapezoid has an area of 4 square units, and a height of 1 unit.
What are the possible whole number lengths for the bases? _____

**134**  Lesson 8-3 Practice                    *Course 2* Chapter 8

# Reteaching 8-4

**Circumferences and Areas of Circles**

The **circumference** of a circle is the distance around it. To find the circumference of a circle with radius $r$ and diameter $d$, use either the formula $C = 2\pi r$ or $C = \pi d$. Use 3.14 for $\pi$.

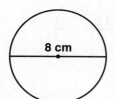

$d = 8$ cm
$C = \pi d$
$\quad = 3.14 \cdot 8$
$\quad = 25.12$ cm

$r = 6$ ft
$C = 2\pi r$
$\quad = 2 \cdot 3.14 \cdot 6$
$\quad = 37.68$ ft

To the nearest centimeter, the circumference is 25 cm.

To the nearest foot, the circumference is 38 ft.

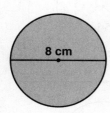

To find the area of a circle, use $A = \pi r^2$.
The diameter of the circle is 8 cm, so the radius is 4 cm.

$A = \pi r^2$
$\quad = 3.14 \cdot 4 \cdot 4$
$\quad = 50.24$ cm$^2$

To the nearest square centimeter, the area is 50 cm$^2$.

---

**Find the circumference and area of each circle. Round your answer to the nearest whole unit.**

**1.**

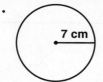

7 cm

_____

**2.**

2 in.

_____

**3.**

10 m

_____

**4.**

2 cm

_____

**5.**

3 ft

_____

**6.**

8 yd

_____

# Practice 8-4

**Circumferences and Areas of Circles**

**Find the circumference and area of each circle. Round your answer to the nearest tenth.**

**1.**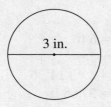

3 in.

_____

**2.**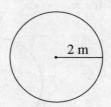

2 m

_____

**3.**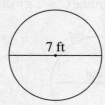

7 ft

_____

**4.**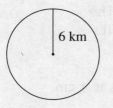

6 km

_____

**5.**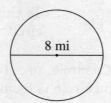

8 mi

_____

**6.**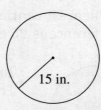

15 in.

_____

**7.**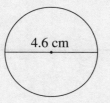

4.6 cm

_____

**8.**

9.3 mm

_____

**9.**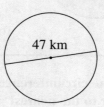

47 km

_____

**10.**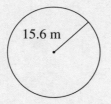

15.6 m

_____

**11.**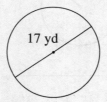

17 yd

_____

**12.**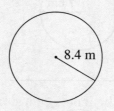

8.4 m

_____

**Estimate the radius of each circle with the given circumference. Round your answer to the nearest tenth.**

**13.** 80 km

_____

**14.** 92 ft

_____

**15.** 420 in.

_____

**16.** 700 km

_____

**17.** The radius of the large circle is 8 in. The radius of each of the smaller circles is 1 in. Find the area of the shaded region to the nearest unit.

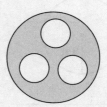

_____

# Reteaching 8-5

**Square Roots and Irrational Numbers**

The number 25 is a **perfect square.**

It is the square of the whole number 5.     $5^2 = 25$
5 is the **square root** of 25.                $5 = \sqrt{25}$

You can find the length of a side of a square
by finding the square root of the area.
$$s^2 = A = 225$$
$$s = \sqrt{A} = \sqrt{225} = 15$$
The length of each side is 15 in.

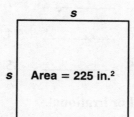

You can use patterns to find the square roots
of some larger numbers.
$$9^2 = 81 \rightarrow 90^2 = 8{,}100$$
$$9 = \sqrt{81} \rightarrow 90 = \sqrt{8{,}100}$$

A **rational number** is a ratio of two integers, $\frac{a}{b}$, where $b \neq 0$. Since terminating decimals and repeating decimals can be written as ratios, they are rational. Irrational numbers are numbers that cannot be written as ratios. Decimals that do not end or repeat are irrational numbers.

---

**Find each of the following.**

**1.** $\sqrt{144}$

_____

**2.** $\sqrt{36}$

_____

**3.** $\sqrt{100}$

_____

**4.** $\sqrt{2{,}500}$

_____

**5.** $\sqrt{324}$

_____

**6.** $\sqrt{400}$

_____

**Find the length of a side of a square with the given area.**

**7.** $A = 49$ cm$^2$
side $= \sqrt{49} =$ _____

**8.** $A = 81$ in.$^2$
side $= \sqrt{81} =$ _____

**9.** $A = 144$ cm$^2$
side $= \sqrt{144} =$ _____

**10.** $A = 625$ in.$^2$

_____

**11.** $A = 676$ ft$^2$

_____

**12.** $A = 3{,}600$ yd$^2$

**Identify each number as rational or irrational.**

**13.** $1\frac{1}{3}$

_____

**14.** $\sqrt{15}$

_____

**15.** 7

_____

**16.** $\sqrt{144}$

_____

# Practice 8-5

**Simplify each square root.**

1. $\sqrt{64}$ _____
2. $\sqrt{81}$ _____
3. $\sqrt{100}$ _____
4. $\sqrt{144}$ _____

5. $\sqrt{121}$ _____
6. $\sqrt{1}$ _____
7. $\sqrt{36}$ _____
8. $\sqrt{169}$ _____

9. $\sqrt{25}$ _____
10. $\sqrt{16}$ _____
11. $\sqrt{256}$ _____
12. $\sqrt{9}$ _____

13. $\sqrt{196}$ _____
14. $\sqrt{49}$ _____
15. $\sqrt{225}$ _____
16. $\sqrt{4}$ _____

**Identify each number as rational or irrational.**

17. $0.363636\ldots$
18. $\sqrt{10}$
19. $-\frac{1}{9}$
20. $-3.25$

_____     _____     _____     _____

**For each number, write all the sets to which it belongs. Choose from rational number, irrational number, whole number, and integer.**

21. $\frac{3}{8}$
22. $\sqrt{49}$
23. $\sqrt{98}$
24. $0$

_____     _____     _____     _____

**Find the length of the side of a square with the given area.**

25. $64 \text{ km}^2$
26. $81 \text{ m}^2$
27. $121 \text{ ft}^2$
28. $4 \text{ mi}^2$

_____     _____     _____     _____

29. $225 \text{ in.}^2$
30. $196 \text{ yd}^2$
31. $169 \text{ cm}^2$
32. $144 \text{ mm}^2$

_____     _____     _____     _____

**Solve.**

33. The square of a certain number is the same as three times the number. What is the number?

_____

34. The area of a square lawn is $196 \text{ yd}^2$. What is the perimeter of the lawn?

_____

**Find two consecutive whole numbers that each number is between.**

35. $\sqrt{80}$
36. $\sqrt{56}$
37. $\sqrt{130}$
38. $\sqrt{150}$

_____     _____     _____     _____

39. $\sqrt{70}$
40. $\sqrt{190}$
41. $\sqrt{204}$
42. $\sqrt{159}$

_____     _____     _____     _____

# Reteaching 8-6

**The Pythagorean Theorem**

**Pythagorean Theorem**

$$a^2 + b^2 = c^2$$

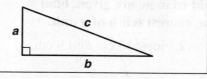

If you know the lengths of two sides of a right triangle, you can find the length of the third side.

Find the length of $a$.

$$a^2 + b^2 = c^2$$
$$a^2 + 12^2 = 13^2$$
$$a^2 + 144 = 169$$
$$a^2 = 169 - 144$$
$$a^2 = 25$$
$$a = 5$$

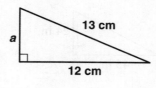

If $a^2 + b^2 = c^2$, then the triangle is a right triangle.

Is this triangle a right triangle?

$$\underline{3^2 + 4^2} = 9 + 16 = 25 = \underline{5^2}$$

Yes, the triangle is a right triangle.

---

**Find each missing length. Round your answer to the nearest tenth of a unit.**

1.

    _____

2.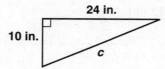

    _____

3.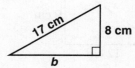

    _____

4.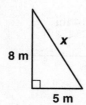

    _____

5.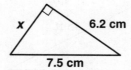

    _____

6.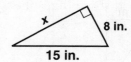

    _____

7.  A ladder leans against a wall 6 ft above the ground. The base of the ladder is 3 ft from the wall. How long is the ladder?

    _____

8.  A small rectangular tray measures 16 cm by 18 cm. How long is the diagonal?

    _____

# Practice 8-6

**The lengths of two sides of a right triangle are given. Find the length of the third side to the nearest tenth of a unit.**

**1.** legs: 5 ft and 12 ft

**2.** legs: 13 cm and 9 cm

**3.** leg: 7 m; hypotenuse: 14 m

_____

**4.** legs: 17 ft and 6 ft

**5.** legs: 11 cm and 21 cm

**6.** leg: 15 m; hypotenuse: 20 m

_____

**Find each missing length. Round to the nearest tenth of a unit, if necessary.**

**7.**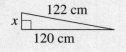
122 cm
$x$
120 cm

_____

**8.**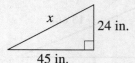
$x$
24 in.
45 in.

_____

**9.**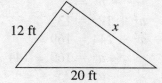
12 ft
$x$
20 ft

_____

**10.**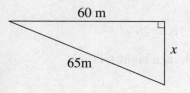
60 m
65m
$x$

_____

**11.**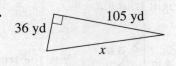
36 yd
105 yd
$x$

_____

**12.**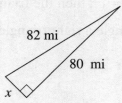
82 mi
80 mi
$x$

_____

**13.**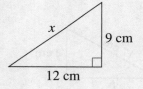
$x$
9 cm
12 cm

_____

**14.**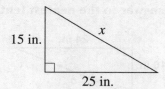
$x$
15 in.
25 in.

_____

**15.**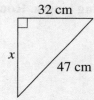
32 cm
$x$
47 cm

_____

**16.**
16 m
28 m
$x$

_____

**17.**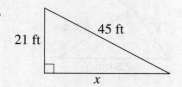
45 ft
21 ft
$x$

_____

**18.**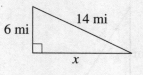
14 mi
6 mi
$x$

_____

**Solve.**

**19.** A playground is 50 yd by 50 yd. Amy walked across the playground from one corner to the opposite corner. How far did she walk?

_____

**20.** A 70-ft ladder is mounted 10 ft above the ground on a fire truck. The bottom of the ladder is 40 ft from the wall of a building. The top of the ladder is touching the building. How high off the ground is the top of the ladder?

_____

# Reteaching 8-7

**Three-Dimensional Figures**

A **prism** is a three-dimensional figure with two parallel and congruent polygonal **bases**. It is named by the shape of a base.

**Rectangular prism**
The bases are rectangles.

rectangular
prism

**Triangular prism**
The bases are triangles.

triangular
prism

**Hexagonal prism**
The bases are hexagons.

hexagonal
prism

A **pyramid** is a three-dimensional figure with only one base.

**Triangular pyramid**
The base is a triangle.

triangular
pyramid

**Square pyramid**
The base is a square.

square
pyramid

The **cylinder, cone,** and **sphere** are also three-dimensional figures.

cylinder    cone    sphere

---

**Give the best name for each figure.**

1.

_____

2.

_____

3.

_____

4.

_____

5.
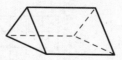

_____

6.

_____

7.

_____

8.
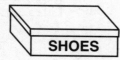

_____

9.

_____

# Practice 8-7

**Describe the base and name the figure.**

1.

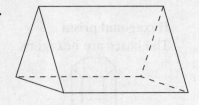

_____
_____

2.

_____
_____

3.

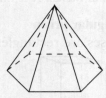

_____
_____

4.

_____
_____

5.

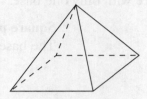

_____
_____

6.

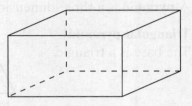

_____
_____

**Draw each figure named.**

7. a triangular pyramid

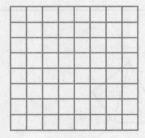

8. a square prism

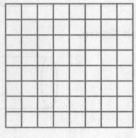

9. a cone

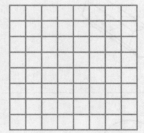

10. a pentagonal pyramid

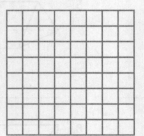

Name _____ Class _____ Date _____

# Reteaching 8-8

**Surface Areas of Prisms and Cylinders**

The **surface area** of a prism is the sum of the areas of its faces. You can use a **net,** or pattern, for the prism to help you find its surface area.

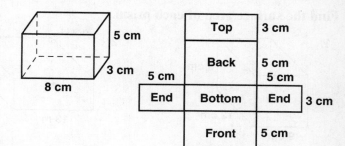

• Add the areas of all the surfaces.

Surface Area
= front + back + top + bottom + end + end
= $(8 \cdot 5) + (8 \cdot 5) + (8 \cdot 3) + (8 \cdot 3) + (5 \cdot 3) + (5 \cdot 3)$
= $40 + 40 + 24 + 24 + 15 + 15$
= $158 \text{ cm}^2$

• To find the surface area of a cylinder, add the area of the rectangle and the areas of the bases. Use 3.14 for $\pi$.

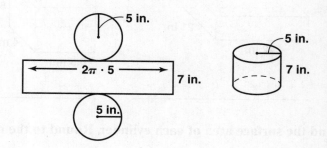

Surface area
= top + bottom + side (rectangle)
= $(\pi \cdot 5 \cdot 5) + (\pi \cdot 5 \cdot 5) + (2\pi \cdot 5 \cdot 7)$
= $(25\pi) + (25\pi) + (70\pi)$
≈ $120 \cdot 3.14 = 376.8 \text{ in.}^2$

---

**Use the net to find the surface area. Round your answers to the nearest whole unit.**

1.

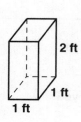

2.

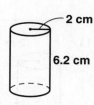

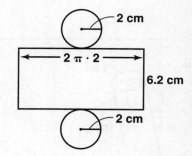

_____          _____

**Draw a net for each figure. Then find the surface area to the nearest tenth of a unit.**

3.

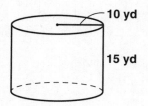

4.

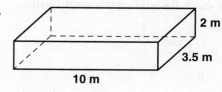

_____          _____

# Practice 8-8

**Surface Areas of Prisms and Cylinders**

**Find the surface area of each prism.**

**1.**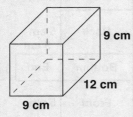

9 cm
12 cm
9 cm

_____

**2.**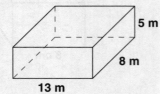

5 m
8 m
13 m

_____

**3.**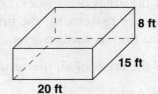

8 ft
15 ft
20 ft

_____

**4.**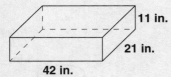

11 in.
21 in.
42 in.

_____

**5.**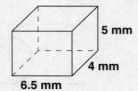

5 mm
4 mm
6.5 mm

_____

**6.**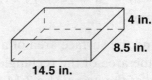

4 in.
8.5 in.
14.5 in.

_____

**Find the surface area of each cylinder. Round to the nearest unit.**

**7.**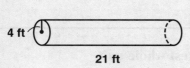

4 ft
21 ft

_____

**8.**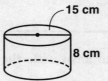

15 cm
8 cm

_____

**9.**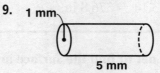

1 mm
5 mm

_____

**10.**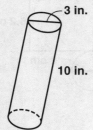

3 in.
10 in.

_____

**11.**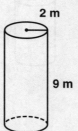

2 m
9 m

_____

**12.**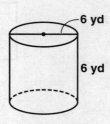

6 yd
6 yd

_____

**Draw a net for each three-dimensional figure.**

**13.**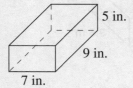

5 in.
9 in.
7 in.

**14.**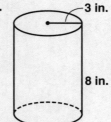

3 in.
8 in.

# Reteaching 8-9

**Volumes of Rectangular Prisms and Cylinders**

The **volume** of a three-dimensional figure is the number of cubic units needed to fill the space inside the figure. A **cubic unit** is a cube whose edges are 1 unit long. You can find the volume of a prism or a cylinder by finding the *area of the base* (B) and multiplying by the *height* (h). Use 3.14 for $\pi$.

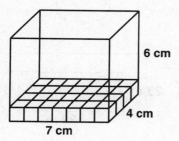

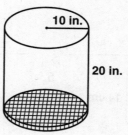

$B = lw$
$B = 7 \cdot 4 = 28$ cm$^2$
$V = Bh$
$V = 28 \cdot 6 = 168$ cm$^3$
The volume is 168 cubic centimeters.

$B = \pi r^2$
$B \approx 3.14 \cdot 10 \cdot 10 = 314$ in.$^2$
$V = Bh$
$V \approx 314 \cdot 20 = 6,280$ in.$^3$
The volume is 6,280 cubic inches.

---

**Complete to find the volume to the nearest tenth of a unit.**

**1.**

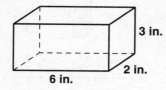

$V = Bh = lwh$

$= \underline{\hspace{1cm}} \cdot \underline{\hspace{1cm}} \cdot \underline{\hspace{1cm}}$

$= \underline{\hspace{2cm}}$

**2.**

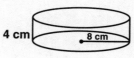

$V = Bh = \pi r^2 h$

$\approx 3.14 \cdot \underline{\hspace{1cm}} \cdot \underline{\hspace{1cm}} \cdot \underline{\hspace{1cm}}$

$= \underline{\hspace{2cm}}$

**Find the volume. Round to the nearest cubic unit.**

**3.**

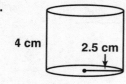

_____

**4.**

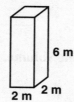

_____

**5.**

_____

# Practice 8-9
**Volumes of Rectanglar Prisms and Cylinders**

**Find each volume. Round to the nearest cubic unit.**

1.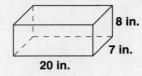
8 in.
7 in.
20 in.

2.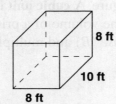
8 ft
10 ft
8 ft

3.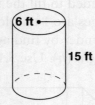
6 ft
15 ft

_____

_____

_____

4.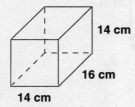
14 cm
16 cm
14 cm

5.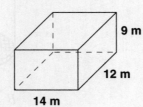
9 m
12 m
14 m

6.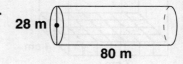
28 m
80 m

_____

_____

_____

7.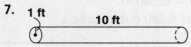
1 ft
10 ft

8.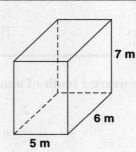
7 m
6 m
5 m

9.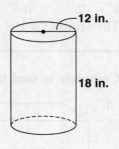
12 in.
18 in.

_____

_____

_____

**Find the volume of each rectangular prism.**

10.
$x$
$4x$
$2x$

11.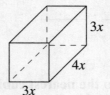
$3x$
$4x$
$3x$

_____

_____

**Find the height of each rectangular prism given the volume, length, and width.**

12. $V = 122{,}500 \text{ cm}^3$
$l = 50 \text{ cm}$
$w = 35 \text{ cm}$

13. $V = 22.05 \text{ ft}^3$
$l = 3.5 \text{ ft}$
$w = 4.2 \text{ ft}$

14. $V = 3{,}375 \text{ m}^3$
$l = 15 \text{ m}$
$w = 15 \text{ m}$

_____

_____

_____

# Reteaching 8-10

**Problem Solving: Try, Check, and Revise and Written Equation**

The length and width of a rectangular prism are equal and the height is 2 times that amount. If the volume of the prism is 3,456 m³, what are the dimensions of the rectangle?

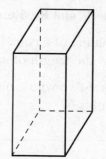

**Read and Understand**  What is the volume of the prism? What do you know about the dimensions? *The volume is 3,456 m³. The length and width are the same. The height is 2 times that dimension.*

**Plan and Solve**  You can use a Try, Check, and Revise strategy and the prism volume formula. Try the length, then find the width and height. Multiply to find volume, then check.

① Start with 10 for the length. The width would be 10 and the height 20. Volume of 2,000 is not enough.

② Try 15 for the length. The width would be 15 and the height 30. Volume of 6,750 is too much.

③ Try 12 m. A length of 12 m gives the correct volume.

| Length | Width | Height | Volume |
|--------|-------|--------|--------|
| ① 10 | 10 | 20 | 2,000 |
| ② 15 | 15 | 30 | 6,750 |
| ③ 12 | 12 | 24 | 3,456 |

**Look Back and Check**  The guesses of 10 and 15 helped you make the next guess of 12.

---

## Use Try, Check, and Revise, or write an equation to solve each problem.

1. The product of two numbers is 2,250. Their difference is 5. What are the two numbers?

2. The length of a rectangle is twice the width. The area of the rectangle is 648 ft². How long is the rectangle?

3. Kevin opened a book. The product of the 2 page numbers was 7,832. What are the page numbers?

4. The base of a triangle is 8 cm and the area is 36 cm². What is the height?

5. One leg of a right triangle measures 8 m. The other leg measures 6 m. Find the length of the hypotenuse.

6. Jason purchased three pennants for $5.60, two sweatshirts, and 1 ball hat for $15.50. He paid the cashier $100 and received $49.90 in change. If the sweatshirts were the same price, how much was one sweatshirt?

# Practice 8-10

**Problem Solving: Try, Check, and Revise and Write an Equation**

**Use Try, Check, and Revise, or write an equation to solve each problem.**

1. The volume of a cube is 79,507 in.$^3$.
   What is the length of each edge of the cube? _____

2. What are two whole numbers whose product is 294 and whose
   quotient is 6?

   _____

3. Tickets for a concert sold for $8 for floor seats and $6 for balcony
   seats. For one performance, 400 tickets were sold, bringing in
   $2,888. How many of each ticket were sold?

   _____

4. Aaron bought 6 books and 2 notebooks for $46.86. Erin bought
   2 books and 6 notebooks for $27.78. How much does one book cost?

   _____

**Solve if possible. If not, tell what information is needed.**

5. Find the volume of a rectangular prism. The width is half the
   length. The height is twice the length.

   _____

   _____

6. Sal raises pigs and chickens. She has 420 creatures, with a total of
   1,240 legs. How many pigs does Sal raise?

   _____

7. The width of a rectangle is 6 in. less than the length. The area of
   the rectangle is 135 in.$^2$. Find the length and width.

   _____

8. A cube has a volume of 4,096 cm$^3$. What is the length of each
   edge of the cube?

   _____

9. Tom is 26 years older than Paul. The product of their ages is 560.
   How old is Paul?

   _____

*Course 2* Chapter 8

# Reteaching 9-1

Graphs can help you visualize the relationship between data. A graph includes two scales, the horizontal axis and the vertical axis. An interval is the distance between the values on a scale.

**Graph the data in the table.**

**Step 1** Choose the scales and intervals.

Graph the data in the first column on the horizontal axis. Graph the data in the second column on the vertical axis.

Choose the interval for the scale on the horizontal axis. The greatest number of hours worked is 9. If each interval is 1 hour, then the number of intervals is $9 \div 1 = 9$.

Choose the interval for the scale on the vertical axis. The greatest amount of money earned is $74.25. If each interval is $5, then the number of intervals is $74.25 \div 5 = 14.85$, or 15 intervals.

**Step 2** Draw the graph and plot the data. Estimate the position of data points that fall between intervals.

| Hours Worked | Money Earned |
|---|---|
| 5 | $41.25 |
| 6 | $49.50 |
| 7 | $57.75 |
| 8 | $66.00 |
| 9 | $74.25 |

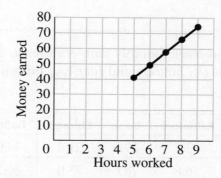

---

**Graph the data in each table.**

**1.**

| Hours | Miles Run |
|---|---|
| 2 | 10 |
| 2.8 | 14 |
| 3.2 | 16 |
| 3.6 | 18 |

**2.**

| Gallons of Gas | Miles Driven |
|---|---|
| 0.5 | 13 |
| 1.5 | 39 |
| 2.5 | 65 |
| 3 | 78 |

# Practice 9-1

**1.** The table shows prices of packages containing 100-megabyte computer disks. Graph the data in the table.

| Number of disks | 1 | 2 | 3 | 6 | 10 |
|---|---|---|---|---|---|
| Price ($) | 20 | 37 | 50 | 100 | 150 |

**100 MB Computer Disks**

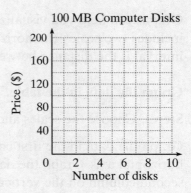

The graph shows the 1989 median income of some year-round workers and the number of years of school. The trend line is shown. Use this graph for Exercises 2–3.

**2.** Predict the median income for the workers who have spent 20 years in school.

_____

**3.** Do you think you can use this graph to predict the median salary for workers who have spent less than 8 years in school? Explain.

_____

**Median Income**

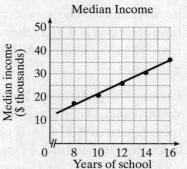

The table shows average monthly temperatures in degrees Fahrenheit for American cities in January and July. Use this information for Exercises 4–6.

| City | Seattle | Baltimore | Boise | Chicago | Dallas | Miami | LA |
|---|---|---|---|---|---|---|---|
| Jan. | 39.1 | 32.7 | 29.9 | 21.4 | 44.0 | 67.1 | 56.0 |
| Jul. | 64.8 | 76.8 | 74.6 | 73.0 | 86.3 | 82.5 | 69.0 |

| City | Anchorage | Honolulu | New York | Portland | New Orleans |
|---|---|---|---|---|---|
| Jan. | 13.0 | 72.6 | 31.8 | 21.5 | 52.4 |
| Jul. | 58.1 | 80.1 | 76.4 | 68.1 | 82.1 |

**4.** Graph the data in the table.

**5.** Use your graph to estimate the July temperature of a city whose average January temperature is 10°F.

_____

**6.** Use your graph to estimate the January temperature of a city whose average July temperature is 75°F.

_____

**Average Monthly Temperatures**

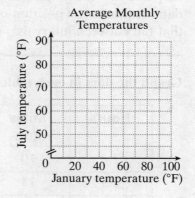

# Reteaching 9-2

A set of numbers that follows a pattern forms a **sequence**. The numbers 2, 4, 6, 8, . . . form a sequence. The three dots ". . ." tell you that the pattern continues. The numbers 2, 4, 6, 8, and so on are the **terms** of the sequence.

**Arithmetic Sequence**

Add the same number to each term to get the next term. In the sequence 2, 4, 6, 8, . . . , you add 2 to each term to get the next term.

Write a rule to describe this sequence, and find the next three terms.
5, 10, 15, 20, . . .

$$5 \underset{+5}{\nearrow} 10 \underset{+5}{\nearrow} 15 \underset{+5}{\nearrow} 20$$

*Start with 5 and add 5 repeatedly.*

To find the next three terms, add 5.

$$20 + 5 = 25$$
$$25 + 5 = 30$$
$$30 + 5 = 35$$

The next three terms are 25, 30, and 35.

**Geometric Sequence**

Multiply each term by the same number to get the next term. In the sequence 1, 4, 16, 64, . . . , you multiply each term by 4 to get the next term.

Write a rule to describe this sequence, and find the next three terms.
2 , 4, 8, 16, . . .

$$2 \underset{\times 2}{\nearrow} 4 \underset{\times 2}{\nearrow} 8 \underset{\times 2}{\nearrow} 16$$

*Start with 2 and multiply by 2 repeatedly.*

To find the next three terms, multiply by 2.

$$16 \times 2 = 32$$
$$32 \times 2 = 64$$
$$64 \times 2 = 128$$

The next three terms are 32, 64, and 128.

**Write a rule for each arithmetic sequence. Then find the next three terms.**

**1.** 4, 7, 10, 13, . . .

_____

_____

_____

**2.** 2, 4, 6, 8, . . .

_____

_____

_____

**3.** 20, 35, 50, . . .

_____

_____

_____

**Write a rule for each geometric sequence. Then find the next three terms.**

**4.** 5, 25, 125, 625, . . .

_____

_____

_____

**5.** 7, 49, 343, 2,401, . . .

_____

_____

_____

**6.** 0.3, 0.9, 2.7, 8.1, . . .

_____

_____

_____

# Practice 9-2

**Identify each sequence as arithmetic, geometric, or neither.**
**Write a rule for each sequence.**

**1.** 2, 6, 18, 54, . . .

_____

_____

**2.** 5, −10, 20, −40, . . .

_____

_____

**3.** 3, 5, 7, 9, . . .

_____

_____

**4.** 5, 6, 8, 11, 15, . . .

_____

_____

**5.** 1, 2, 6, 24, . . .

_____

_____

**6.** 17, 16, 15, 14, . . .

_____

_____

**7.** 50, −50, 50, −50, . . .

_____

_____

**8.** 1, 2, 4, 5, 10, 11, 22, . . .

_____

_____

**Find the next three numbers in each sequence.**

**9.** 15, −14, 13, −12, . . .

_____

**10.** 243, 81, 27, . . .

_____

**11.** 5, 12, 26, . . .

_____

**12.** 2, 5, 9, 14, . . .

_____

**Write the first five terms in the sequence described by the rule.**
**Identify the sequence as arithmetic, geometric, or neither.**

**13.** Start with 2 and multiply by −3 repeatedly.

_____

**14.** Start with 27 and add −9 repeatedly.

_____

**15.** Start with 18 and multiply by 0.1, then by 0.2, then by 0.3, and so on.

_____

# Reteaching 9-3

**A table can help you write a variable expression that describes a sequence.**

Give the next two terms in this sequence: 6, 12, 18, 24, 30 . . .

| Term number | 1 | 2 | 3 | 4 | 5 |
|---|---|---|---|---|---|
| Term | 6 | 12 | 18 | 24 | 30 |

The rule is *"multiply the term number by 6."*

So, the next two terms will be 36 and 42.

---

**Give the next two terms in this sequence: 4, 8, 12, 16, 20, . . .**

1. What will you multiply the term number by to find the corresponding term? _____

2. Let $n$ = term number. Write an expression that shows this relationship. _____

3. How will you find the sixth term in the sequence? the seventh term? _____

4. What are the sixth and seventh terms?

   _____

**Give the next two terms in this sequence: 5, 7, 9, 11, 13, . . .**

5. If $n$ equals the term number, circle the expression that gives the rule for this sequence.

   $2n + 1$ $\qquad$ $n - 3$ $\qquad$ $2n + 3$ $\qquad$ $n + 3$

6. How will you find the sixth term in the sequence? the seventh term?

   _____

7. What are the sixth and seventh terms?

   _____

**Let $n$ equal the term number. Circle the expression that gives the rule for each sequence.**

8. 2, 5, 8, 11, 14 . . . $\qquad$ $2n - 1$ $\qquad$ $3n - 1$ $\qquad$ $3n + 1$

9. 1, 4, 9, 25, 36, . . . $\qquad$ $n + 5$ $\qquad$ $n^2$ $\qquad$ $n^2 - 1$

10. 5, 10, 15, 20, 25 . . . $\qquad$ $5n$ $\qquad$ $n^5$ $\qquad$ $n + 5$

# Practice 9-3

**Complete each table.**

**1.**

| Time (h) | 1 | 2 | 3 | 4 | 7 |
|---|---|---|---|---|---|
| Distance cycled (mi) | 8 | 16 | 24 | 32 | |

**2.**

| Time (min) | 1 | 2 | 3 | 4 | 7 |
|---|---|---|---|---|---|
| Distance from surface of water (yd) | −3 | −2 | −1 | 0 | |

**Write a variable expression to describe the rule for each sequence. Then find the 100th term.**

**3.** 35, 36, 37, . . .

Expression: _____

100th term: _____

**4.** 8, 10, 12, 14, . . .

Expression: _____

100th term: _____

**5.** 1.5, 3, 4.5, 6, . . .

Expression: _____

100th term: _____

**Find the values of the missing entries in each table.**

**6.**

| m | 4 | 6 | | 10 |
|---|---|---|---|---|
| n | 24 | 26 | 28 | |

**7.**

| p | 2 | | 10 | 14 |
|---|---|---|---|---|
| q | 1 | 13 | 25 | |

**8.** A pattern of squares is shown.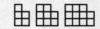

   **a.** Sketch the 4th and 5th figure in this pattern. _____

   **b.** Make a table comparing the figure number to the number of squares.
       Write an expression for the number of squares in the $n$th figure.

   **c.** How many squares would there be in the 80th figure? _____

**Write a variable expression to describe the rule for each sequence. Then find the 20th term.**

**9.** 6, 12, 18, 24, . . .

Expression: _____

20th term: _____

**10.** 3, 6, 9, 12, . . .

Expression: _____

20th term: _____

**11.** 1, 5, 9, 13, . . .

Expression: _____

20th term: _____

**12.** One month's average price for ground beef is $2.39 per pound.
    Using this relationship, make a table that shows the price for 1, 2,
    3, and 4 pounds of ground beef.

# Reteaching 9-4

The function table shows the relationship between inputs and outputs.
A function rule for this table is:

output = 4 · input

| Input | Output |
|-------|--------|
| 1 | 4 |
| 2 | 8 |
| 3 | 12 |

You can use the function rule $y = 2x + 3$ to find $y$ when $x = 0, 1, 2,$ and 3.
Replace $x$ with 0, 1, 2, and 3.

| $x$ | $y = 2x + 3$ |
|-----|--------------|
| 0 | $2(0) + 3 = 3$ |
| 1 | $2(1) + 3 = 5$ |
| 2 | $2(2) + 3 = 7$ |
| 3 | $2(3) + 3 = 9$ |

**Write input-output function rules for each table of values.**

**1.**

| Input | Output |
|-------|--------|
| 3 | 6 |
| 4 | 8 |
| 5 | 10 |
| 6 | 12 |

_____

**2.**

| Input | Output |
|-------|--------|
| 1 | 3 |
| 2 | 4 |
| 3 | 5 |
| 4 | 6 |

_____

**3.**

| Input | Output |
|-------|--------|
| 1 | 45 |
| 2 | 90 |
| 3 | 135 |
| 4 | 180 |

_____

**Make a table for the function represented by each rule. Find $y$ when $x = 0, 1, 2,$ and 3.**

**4.** $y = 10x$

| $x$ | $y$ |
|-----|-----|
| 0 | |
| 1 | |
| 2 | |
| 3 | |

**5.** $y = x - 4$

| $x$ | $y$ |
|-----|-----|
| 0 | |
| 1 | |
| 2 | |
| 3 | |

**6.** $y = 2x + 4$

| $x$ | $y$ |
|-----|-----|
| 0 | |
| 1 | |
| 2 | |
| 3 | |

**7.** $y = 3x - 1$

| $x$ | $y$ |
|-----|-----|
| 0 | |
| 1 | |
| 2 | |
| 3 | |

**8.** A printer can print 9 black and white pages per minute.

    **a.** Write a function rule to represent the relationship between the number of black and white printed pages and the time it takes to print them. _____

    **b.** How many black and white pages can be printed in 15 minutes? _____

    **c.** How long would it take to print a 75 page black and white report? _____

# Practice 9-4

**Use each function rule. Find *y* for *x* = 1, 2, 3, and 4.**

**1.** $y = 2x$

**2.** $y = x + 4$

**3.** $y = x^2 - 1$

_____

_____

_____

**4.** $y = -2x$

**5.** $y = 3x + 1$

**6.** $y = 8 - 3x$

_____

_____

_____

**7.** $y = 6 + 4x$

**8.** $y = x - 5$

**9.** $y = 2x + 7$

_____

_____

_____

**10.** $y = -5x + 6$

**11.** $y = 3x + 9$

**12.** $y = \frac{x}{2}$

_____

_____

_____

**Write a rule for the function represented by each table.**

**13.**

| $x$ | $y$ |
|-----|-----|
| 1 | 6 |
| 2 | 7 |
| 3 | 8 |
| 4 | 9 |

**14.**

| $x$ | $y$ |
|-----|-----|
| 1 | 4 |
| 2 | 8 |
| 3 | 12 |
| 4 | 16 |

**15.**

| $x$ | $y$ |
|-----|-----|
| 1 | −6 |
| 2 | −9 |
| 3 | −12 |
| 4 | −15 |

_____

_____

_____

**16.**

| $x$ | $y$ |
|-----|-----|
| 1 | 5 |
| 2 | 7 |
| 3 | 9 |
| 4 | 11 |

**17.**

| $x$ | $y$ |
|-----|-----|
| 1 | 4 |
| 2 | 7 |
| 3 | 10 |
| 4 | 13 |

**18.**

| $x$ | $y$ |
|-----|-----|
| 1 | −1 |
| 2 | −3 |
| 3 | −5 |
| 4 | −7 |

_____

_____

_____

**19.** A typist types 45 words per minute.

   **a.** Write a function rule to represent the relationship between the number of typed words and the time in which they are typed.

_____

   **b.** How many words can the typist type in 25 minutes?

_____

   **c.** How long would it take the typist to type 20,025 words?

_____

# Reteaching 9-5

If you ride a bicycle at 12 mi/h, the distance you ride is a **function** of time. For each input value (time), there is exactly one output value (distance).

- You can represent the relationship between time and distance with a table.

| Input (hours) | 1 | 2 | 3 | 4 |
|---|---|---|---|---|
| Output (miles) | 12 | 24 | 36 | 48 |

- You can represent the relationship, or function, with a rule.

  output $= 12 \cdot$ input

  distance $= 12 \cdot$ time

- You can represent the relationship, or function, with a graph.

① Graph the points from the table. $(1, 12), (2, 24), (3, 36), (4, 48)$

② Draw a line through the points.

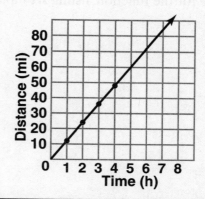

---

**Graph the equation $y = -2x$.**

1. Complete the table of values for the equation $y = -2x$.
   Then write each pair of values as ordered pairs.

   Table of values        Ordered pairs

   | x | y |
   |---|---|
   | −2 |  |
   | 0 |  |
   | 1 |  |
   | 3 |  |
   | 4 |  |

   → _____

   → _____

   → _____

   → _____

   → _____

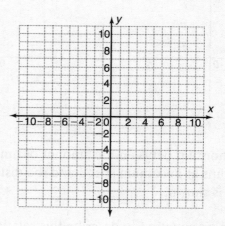

2. Plot the points on the coordinate grid.
   Then connect the points.

Name _____ Class _____ Date _____

# Practice 9-5

**The graph at the right shows the relationship between distance and time for a car driven at a constant speed.**

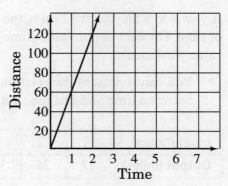

1. What is the speed? _____

2. Is this a function relationship? _____

3. If this is a function, write a rule to represent it.

   _____

4. Make a table for the function, listing six input/output pairs.

**Graph each function. Use input values of 1, 2, 3, 4, and 5.**

5. $y = -4x$

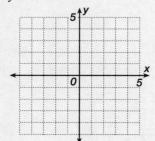

6. $y = x - 3$

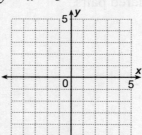

7. $y = -2x + 4$

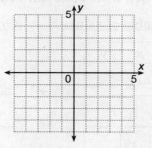

8. The relationship between the amount of time a zebra runs at maximum speed and the distance it covers is shown.

| Time (min) | 3 | 6 | 9 | 12 | 15 |
|---|---|---|---|---|---|
| Distance (mi) | 2 | 4 | 6 | 8 | 10 |

   a. Write an equation to describe this relationship.

   _____

   b. Use the equation to find the distance the zebra would travel in 48 minutes.

   _____

# Reteaching 9-6

You can describe a situation shown by a graph.

- An airplane ascends to its cruising altitude of 20,000 ft in 20 min. After 50 min it begins its descent into Atlanta. The descent takes 15 min.

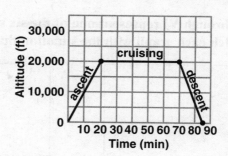

The graph at the right shows time and altitude for the airplane trip. Each part of the trip is labeled.

You can sketch a graph to describe a situation.

- When Ahmad goes out for a run, he walks for a few minutes to warm up, runs for a while, jogs in place while he waits for a light to change, and then walks the rest of the way to cool down.

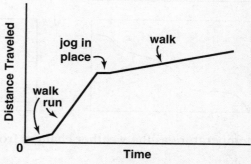

The graph at the right shows the distance Ahmad travels and each type of movement.

**Match each graph with its situation.**

A.

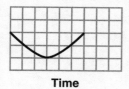

B.

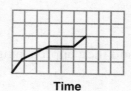

C.

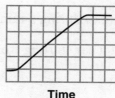

1. A car travels 10 mph for 5 min, 50 mph for 27 min, and then is stopped for 10 min.

_____

2. Total rainfall over a 24-hour period

_____

3. Water level in a bay

_____

**Sketch a graph for the situation. Include labels.**

4. You walk to a park, visit with a friend for few minutes, and then jog home.

5. You climb up a ladder, then climb down the ladder.

# Practice 9-6

**Graphs I through VI represent one of the six situations described below. Match each graph with the situation that describes it.**

I.
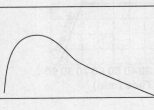

II.
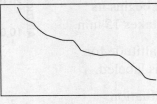

III.
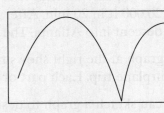

IV.

V.
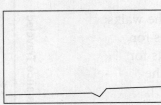

VI.
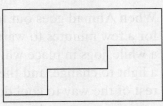

1. temperature as the weather changes from rainy to snowy

   _____

2. number of fish caught per hour on a bad fishing day _____

3. total rainfall during a rainy day _____

4. speed of a car starting from a stop sign and then approaching a

   stoplight _____

5. height of a cricket as it jumps _____

6. total amount of money spent over time during a trip to the mall

   _____

**Sketch a graph for each situation.**

7. The speed of a runner in a 1-mi race.

8. The height above ground of the air valve on a tire of a bicycle ridden on flat ground. (You can model this using a coin.)

# Reteaching 9-7

**Simple and Compound Interest**

When you deposit money in a bank, the bank pays interest.
**Simple interest** is interest paid only on the amount you deposited,
called the **principal. Compound interest** is paid on the original
principal and on any interest that has been left in the account.

| **Simple Interest** | **Compound Interest** |
|---|---|
| To find simple interest, use this formula. | To find compound interest, use this formula. |
| Interest = principal · rate · time in years | Balance = principal · (1 + rate)$^{\text{time in years}}$ |
| $I = p \cdot r \cdot t$ | $B = p(1 + r)^t$ |
| Find the simple interest on $1,800 invested at 5% annual interest for 3 years. | You put $1,800 in the bank. The interest rate is 5% compounded annually. How much will be in the account after 3 years? |
| $I = p \cdot r \cdot t$ | $B = p(1 + r)^t$ |
| $= 1,800 \cdot 0.05 \cdot 3$ ← **Use 0.05 for 5%.** | $= 1,800(1 + 0.05)^3$ ← **Use 0.05 for 5%.** |
| $= 270$ | $= 1,800 \cdot (1.05)^3$ |
| | $\approx 2,083.73$ |
| The interest is $270. (The balance will be $1,800 + $270, or $2,070.) | The balance is $2,083.73. |

**Find the simple interest earned by each account.**

**1.** $800 principal
4% interest rate
5 years
$I = p \cdot r \cdot t$

= _____ · _____ · _____

= _____

**2.** $1,200 principal
5.5% interest rate
25 years
$I = p \cdot r \cdot t$

= _____ · _____ · _____

= _____

**3.** $800 principal
3% interest
4 years

_____

**4.** $1,900 principal
4.5% interest
20 years

_____

**5.** $20,000 principal
3.5% interest
15 years

_____

**Find the balance of each account earning compound interest.**

**6.** $600 principal, 6% interest rate,
3 years
$B = p(1 + r)^t$

= _____ (1+ _____ )$^3$

= _____

**7.** $9,000 principal, 5% interest rate,
4 years
$B = p(1 + r)^t$

= _____ (1+ _____ )—

= _____

# Practice 9-7

**Simple and Compound Interest**

## Find the *simple* interest earned in each account.

**1.** $700 principal
3% interest rate
2 years

_____

**2.** $950 principal
8% interest rate
5 years

_____

**3.** $5,000 principal
6.5% interest rate
3 years

_____

## Find the balance in each *compound* interest account.

**4.** $800 principal
6% interest rate
9 years

_____

**5.** $5,200 principal
5% interest rate
4 years

_____

**6.** $3,500 principal
4.5% interest rate
10 years

_____

## Solve.

**7.** You borrow $600. You pay 5% interest compounded annually.
How much do you owe at the end of 4 years?

_____

**8.** You deposit $2,000 in an account that pays 6% interest
compounded annually. How much money is in the account
at the end of 12 years?

_____

**9.** You invest $5,000 in an account earning simple interest. The
balance after 6 years is $6,200. What is the interest rate?

_____

## Find the simple interest earned in each account.

**10.** $2,000 at 4% for 6 months

_____

**11.** $10,000 at 10% for 2 years

_____

**12.** $500 at 3% for 3 months

_____

**13.** $25,000 at 4.25% for 5 years

_____

**14.** $1,400 at 8% for 10 months

_____

**15.** $40 at 12% for 8 months

_____

# Reteaching 9-8

You can use your equation-solving abilities to help you solve real-world problems.

Cory wants to buy new track shoes that cost $75. So far, she has saved $25. She usually earns $10 each week cutting lawns. How many weeks will it take her to earn the rest of the money needed to buy the shoes?

You can often use these three steps to help you solve problems.

**Read and Understand:** Choose a variable to represent what you want to find.

Let $w$ = the number of weeks.

**Plan and Solve:** Write an equation to show the information in the problem.

**Cost of shoes = Money saved + Money earned**

$$\downarrow \qquad\qquad \downarrow \qquad\qquad \downarrow$$

$$75 \quad = \quad 25 \quad + \quad 10w$$

Solve your equation.

$$75 = 25 + 10w$$
$$75 - 25 = 25 - 25 + 10w$$
$$\frac{50}{10} = \frac{10w}{10}$$
$$5 = w$$

**Look Back and Check:** Answer the question in the problem.

It will take Cory 5 weeks to earn the money.

---

**Solve.**

1. The area of Jared's computer room floor is 168 ft². The formula for area of a rectangle is $A = l \times w$. If the length of the room is 14 feet, what is the width? Let $w$ = width.

   Write an equation. Use the formula to help you. _____

   Solve the equation. $w =$ _____

   Answer the question. _____

2. A skirt costs $15 more than a blouse. The skirt costs $48. What is the price of the blouse? Write an equation. Then solve the problem.

   _____

3. Mary ate one of the muffins she baked and had 12 left. How many muffins did Mary bake? Write an equation. Then solve the problem.

   _____

# Practice 9-8

**Use any strategy or a combination of strategies to solve each problem.**

1. Suppose the temperature increases 8° to −7°F. What was the starting temperature?

   _____

2. A typical giant squid is about 240 in. long, which is 16 times the diameter of one of its eyes. What is the diameter of the eye?

   _____

3. James went to the store to return a defective $45 tape recorder for a refund. At the same time, he bought some batteries for $3 per package. If he received $33 of his refund, how many packages of batteries did he buy?

   _____

4. The Rugyong Hotel in Pyongyang, North Korea, has 105 stories. This is 9 more than twice the number of stories of the Transamerica Pyramid in San Francisco, California. How many stories does the Transamerica Pyramid have?

   _____

5. Rome, Italy, gets an average of 2 in. of rain in April. This is about $\frac{1}{4}$ the average April rainfall in Nairobi, Kenya. How much rain falls in Nairobi in April?

   _____

6. Neptune has 8 known moons. This is 2 more than $\frac{1}{3}$ of the number of known moons of Saturn. How many moons is Saturn known to have?

   _____

7. Ohm's Law states that the electrical current, $I$ in amperes, through a resistor is given by the formula $I = \frac{V}{R}$, where $V$ is the voltage in volts and $R$ is the resistance in ohms. If the current is 6 amperes and the resistance is 18 ohms, what is the voltage?

   _____

8. Fahrenheit and Celsius temperatures are related by the formula $F = \frac{9}{5}C + 32$. What is the Celsius temperature if

   a. the temperature is 77°F?

   _____

   b. the temperature is −22°F?

   _____

# Reteaching 9-9
**Transforming Formulas**

A **formula** such as $I = prt$ states the relationship among unknown quantities represented by the variables $I$, $p$, $r$, and $t$. It means that *interest* equals the *principal* times the *rate* times the *time*.

You can use a formula by **substituting** values for the variables. Some formulas have numbers that do not vary, such as this formula for finding the perimeter of a square: $P = 4s$. The number 4 is a **constant.**

A Boeing 747 airplane traveled at 600 mi/hr. At this speed how many hours did it take to travel 2,100 miles?

| | |
|---|---|
| $d = r \cdot t$ | Use the formula $d = rt$. |
| $2,100 = 600 \cdot t$ | Substitute the known values. |
| $3.5 = t$ | Divide to find the unknown value. |

The Boeing 747 airplane traveled 2,100 miles in 3.5 hours.

---

1. Lisa rides her bike for 2 hours and travels 12 miles. Find her rate of speed.

   **a.** Which formula should you use to find the rate? _____

   **b.** What is the rate of speed? _____

**Solve each formula for the values given.**

2. $A = lw$ for $A$, given $l = 35$ m and $w = 22$ m

3. $P = 2l + 2w$ for $l$ given $P = 30$ in. and $w = 7$ in.

4. $r = \frac{d}{t}$ for $t$, given $d = 366$ mi and $r = 30.5$ mi/hr

5. $C = 2\pi r$ for $r = 10$ cm. Use 3.14 for $\pi$.

6. $V = lwh$ for $l$ given $V = 60$ ft$^3$, $w = 3$ ft, and $h = 5$ ft

7. $I = prt$ for $p = \$100$, $r = 0.05$, and $t = 2$ years

# Practice 9-9

**Solve each formula for the indicated variable.**

1. $d = rt$, for $r$ _____

2. $P = 4s$, for $s$ _____

3. $K = C + 273$, for $C$ _____

4. $S = 180(n - 2)$, for $n$ _____

5. $m = \dfrac{a + b + c}{3}$, for $a$ _____

6. $A = \pi r^2$, for $\pi$ _____

7. $P = 2b + 2h$, for $b$ _____

8. $V = \dfrac{1}{3} Bh$, for $B$ _____

9. $A = 2(\ell w + wh + \ell h)$, for $\ell$ given, $w = 5$, $h = 3$, and $A = 158$

   _____

10. $C = \dfrac{5}{9}(F - 32)$, for $F$, given $C = 25$

    _____

11. $T = 0.0825p$, for $p$, given $T = 13.2$

    _____

12. $F = ma$, for $m$, given $a = 9.8$ and $F = 117.6$

    _____

**Solve.**

13. In 1989, Dutch ice skater Dries van Wijhe skated 200 km at an average speed of 35.27 km/hr. How long was he skating?

    _____

14. A roofer calculates his bid price using the formula $P = 1.85s + 4.2f$, where $s$ is the area of the roof in square feet and $f$ is the length of the fascia in feet. Find the area of the roof with 190 feet of fascia and a price of $4,148.

    _____

# Reteaching 10-1

**Graphing Points in Four Quadrants**

The intersection of a horizontal number line and a vertical number line forms the **coordinate plane.** The coordinate plane below shows point $A$ for the **ordered pair** $(3, -4)$.

To graph point $A$ with **coordinates** $(3, -4)$:

① Start at the origin, $O$. Move 3 units to the right.

② Move 4 units down for $-4$. Draw point $A$.

The axes form four **quadrants** in the coordinate plane.

*   The point $(3, -4)$ is located in quadrant IV.

*   Point $B$ is located in quadrant II.

The line containing two points with the same $x$-coordinate is a vertical line. The line containing two points with the same $y$-coordinate is a horizontal line.

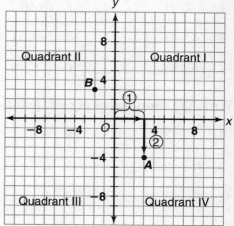

**Name the point with the given coordinates.**

1. $(8, 0)$ _____

2. $(8, -8)$ _____

3. $(1, 4)$ _____

4. $(-7, -4)$ _____

5. $(-5, 6)$ _____

6. $(-2, 0)$ _____

7. $(6, -5)$ _____

8. $(-5, -3)$ _____

**Write the coordinates of each point.**

9. $D$ _____

10. $G$ _____

11. $I$ _____

12. $J$ _____

13. $K$ _____

14. $L$ _____

15. $M$ _____

16. $S$ _____

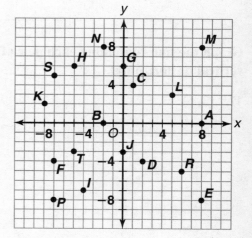

**Identify the quadrant in which each point lies.**

17. $F$ _____

18. $C$ _____

19. $D$ _____

20. $H$ _____

21. $N$ _____

22. $P$ _____

23. $S$ _____

24. $R$ _____

**Without graphing, tell whether the line containing each pair of points is vertical or horizontal.**

25. $F$ and $P$

26. $H$ and $G$

27. $A$ and $M$

_____    _____    _____

Name _____ Class _____ Date _____

# Practice 10-1

**Graphing Points in Four Quadrants**

• • • • • • • • • • • • • • • • • • • • • • • • • • • • • • • • • • • • • • • • • • • • • • • • • • • • •

**Name the point with the given coordinates.**

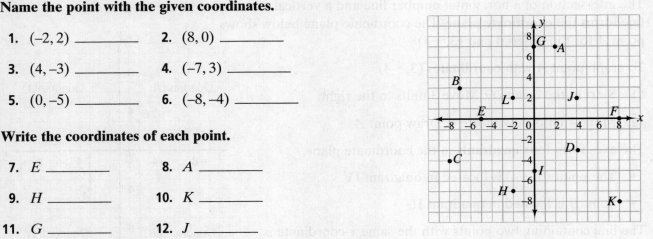

**1.** $(-2, 2)$ _____

**2.** $(8, 0)$ _____

**3.** $(4, -3)$ _____

**4.** $(-7, 3)$ _____

**5.** $(0, -5)$ _____

**6.** $(-8, -4)$ _____

**Write the coordinates of each point.**

**7.** $E$ _____

**8.** $A$ _____

**9.** $H$ _____

**10.** $K$ _____

**11.** $G$ _____

**12.** $J$ _____

**Identify the quadrant in which each point lies.**

**13.** $(-4, 3)$

**14.** $(7, 21)$

**15.** $(5, -8)$

**16.** $(-2, -7)$

_____    _____    _____    _____

**Graph the line containing each pair of points. Identify the line as vertical or horizontal.**

**17.** $(3, 6), (3, -2)$

**18.** $(-1, 5), (3, 5)$

_____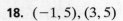

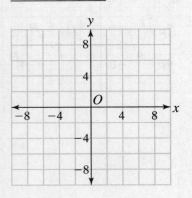    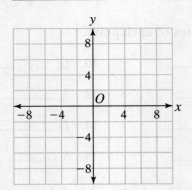

**Without graphing, tell whether the line containing each pair of points is vertical or horizontal.**

**19.** $(10, -1), (10, 5)$

**20.** $(3, -2), (8, -2)$

**21.** $(0, 6), (0, -7)$

_____    _____    _____

Name _____ Class _____ Date _____

# Reteaching 10-2

The **solutions** of $y = x + 3$ are the $(x, y)$ pairs that make the equation true.

The solutions can be listed in a table.

| x | x + 3 | y | (x, y) |
|---|-------|---|--------|
| 0 | 0 + 3 | 3 | (0, 3) |
| 1 | 1 + 3 | 4 | (1, 4) |
| −2 | −2 + 3 | 1 | (−2, 1) |

If all the solutions lie on a line, the equation is a **linear equation** and the line is its **graph.**

$y = x + 3$ is a linear equation.

The solutions can be graphed in the coordinate plane, as shown.

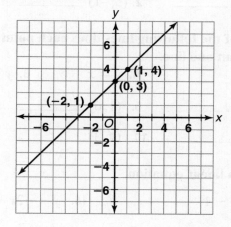

**Complete each table.**

**1.** $y = x - 4$

| x | x − 4 | y | (x, y) |
|---|-------|---|--------|
| 2 | | | |
| 4 | | | |
| 6 | | | |

**2.** $y = 3x$

| x | 3x | y | (x, y) |
|---|----|---|--------|
| −1 | | | |
| 0 | | | |
| 3 | | | |

**3.** $y = -x + 1$

| x | −x + 1 | y | (x, y) |
|---|--------|---|--------|
| 0 | | | |
| 2 | | | |
| −3 | | | |

**Graph each linear equation.**

**4.** $y = x - 5$

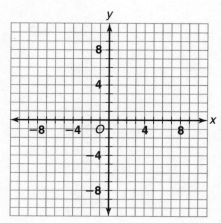

**5.** $y = 3x - 4$

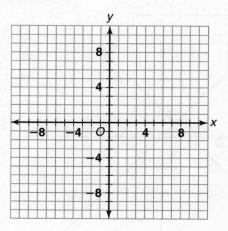

# Practice 10-2

**Graphing Linear Equations**

**Determine whether each ordered pair is a solution of $y = x - 4$.**

**1.** $(0, -4)$ _____

**2.** $(5, -1)$ _____

**3.** $(-3, -7)$ _____

**4.** $(-7, -3)$ _____

**On which of the following lines does each point lie? A point may lie on more than one line.**

**A.** $y = x + 5$     **B.** $y = -x + 7$     **C.** $y = 2x - 1$

**5.** $(0, 5)$ _____

**6.** $(1, 6)$ _____

**7.** $\frac{8}{3}, \frac{13}{3}$ _____

**8.** $(0, -1)$ _____

**9.** $(4, 9)$ _____

**10.** $(4, 3)$ _____

**11.** $(-2, -5)$ _____

**12.** $(-8, 15)$ _____

**Graph each linear equation.**

**13.** $y = 3x - 1$

**14.** $y = -2x + 1$

**15.** $y = 2x - 4$

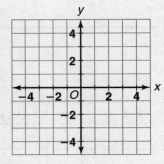
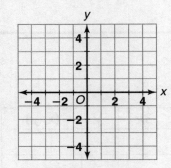
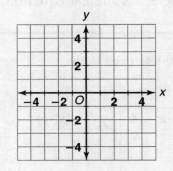

**16.** The graph of $y = -x$ passes through which quadrants?

_____

**17.** Use the graph below to determine the coordinates of the point that is a solution of the equations of lines $p$ and $q$.

_____

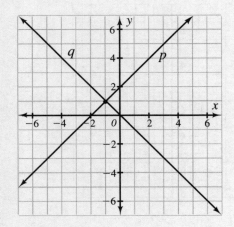

# Reteaching 10-3

**Finding the Slope of a Line**

The steepness of a line is measured by its **slope.** To find the slope of a line, follow these steps.

① Pick any two points on the line. Find the *rise,* or vertical change. Here, the rise is −4.

② Find the *run,* or horizontal change. Here, the run is 2.

③ Find the ratio of rise to run.

$$\text{slope} = \frac{\text{rise}}{\text{run}} = \frac{-4}{2} = -2$$

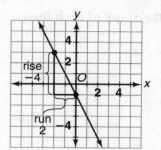

Sometimes the two points are given, such as (2, 3) and (4, 6). Graph both points. Draw their line. Then determine the slope.

$$\text{slope} = \frac{\text{rise}}{\text{run}} = \frac{3}{2}$$

The slope of the line through (2, 3) and (4, 6) is $\frac{3}{2}$.

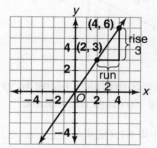

---

**Find the slope of each line.**

**1.**

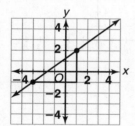

$$\text{slope} = \frac{\text{rise}}{\text{run}} = \text{\_\_\_\_\_}$$

**2.**

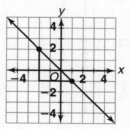

$$\text{slope} = \frac{\text{rise}}{\text{run}} = \text{\_\_\_\_\_}$$

**3.**

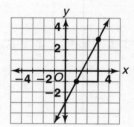

$$\text{slope} = \frac{\text{rise}}{\text{run}} = \text{\_\_\_\_\_}$$

**Draw a line with the given slope through the given point.**

**4.** $B(3, 5)$, slope = 3

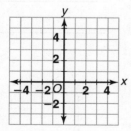

**5.** $Z(1, -1)$, slope = −1

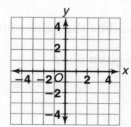

**6.** $S(1, -2)$, slope = 2

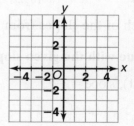

# Practice 10-3

**Finding the Slope of a Line**

**Find the slope of each line.**

1. _____

2. _____

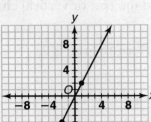

3. _____

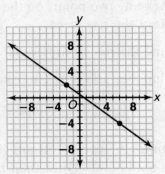

**Use the coordinate plane to graph the given points. Find the slope of the line through the points.**

4. $(-4, 6), (8, 4)$ _____     5. $(-1, 3), (4, 6)$ _____     6. $(-2, 3), (4, -6)$ _____

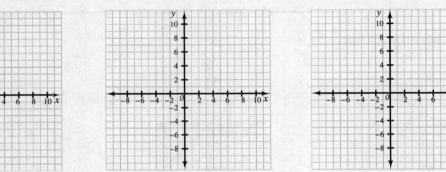

7. Which slope would it be easiest to push a heavy cart up, $\frac{1}{2}, \frac{1}{6}$, 3, or 5? _____

8. Which slope would probably give you the greatest speed down a hill when you are skiing, $\frac{1}{8}, \frac{1}{4}$, 1, or 2? _____

9. Which slope would be the most dangerous for a roofer trying to repair a roof, $\frac{1}{16}, \frac{1}{10}, \frac{1}{2}$, or $\frac{3}{2}$? _____

10. Which of the slopes from Exercise 9 would be the easiest for the roofer? _____

**Draw a line with the given slope through the given point.**

11. $P(5, 1)$, slope $= -\frac{1}{3}$

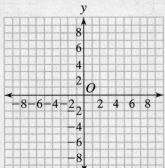

12. $K(-2, 4)$, slope $= 3$

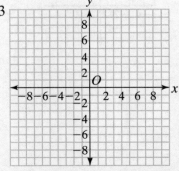

*Course 2* Chapter 10

# Reteaching 10-4

The graph of $y = x^2 - 1$ is a U-shaped curve called a **parabola.** To graph a parabola:

① Make a table of values.

| x | $x^2 - 1$ | y | (x, y) |
|---|---|---|---|
| −2 | $(-2)^2 - 1$ | 3 | (−2, 3) |
| −1 | $(-1)^2 - 1$ | 0 | (−1, 0) |
| 0 | $0^2 - 1$ | −1 | (0, −1) |
| 1 | $1^2 - 1$ | 0 | (1, 0) |
| 2 | $2^2 - 1$ | 3 | (2, 3) |

② Graph the points.

③ Draw the U shape.

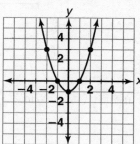

The graph of $y = 2|x|$ is called an **absolute value equation.** Its graph is V-shaped. To graph the equation:

① Make a table of values.

| x | $2|x|$ | y | (x, y) |
|---|---|---|---|
| −2 | 2 · 2 | 4 | (−2, 4) |
| −1 | 2 · 1 | 2 | (−1, 2) |
| 0 | 2 · 0 | 0 | (0, 0) |
| 1 | 2 · 1 | 2 | (1, 2) |
| 2 | 2 · 2 | 4 | (2, 4) |

② Graph the points.

③ Draw the V shape.

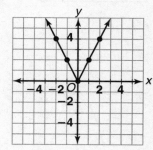

**Make a table of values for each equation. Then graph each equation.**

**1.** $y = x^2 - 2$

| x | y |
|---|---|
| −2 | |
| −1 | |
| 0 | |
| 1 | |
| 2 | |

**2.** $y = 2x^2 - 3$

| x | y |
|---|---|
| −2 | |
| −1 | |
| 0 | |
| 1 | |
| 2 | |

**3.** $y = \frac{1}{2}|x| + 1$

| x | y |
|---|---|
| −4 | |
| −2 | |
| 0 | |
| 2 | |
| 4 | |

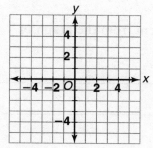

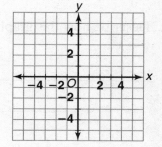

# Practice 10-4

**Exploring Nonlinear Relationships**

**Match each graph with an equation.**

**1.**

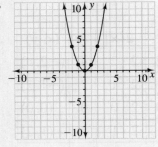

_____

**2.**

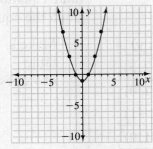

_____

**3.**

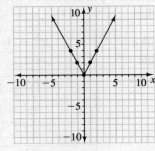

_____

**4.**

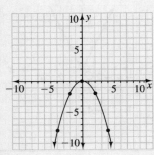

_____

**5.**

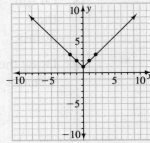

_____

**6.**

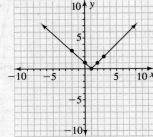

_____

**A.** $y = |x - 1|$

**B.** $y = x^2$

**C.** $y = -\frac{1}{2}x^2$

**D.** $y = |x| + 1$

**E.** $y = |2x|$

**F.** $y = x^2 - 1$

**7. a.** Complete the table below for the equation $y = x^2 + 2$.

| $x$ | −3 | −2 | −1 | 0 | 1 | 2 | 3 |
|-----|-----|-----|-----|---|---|---|---|
| $y$ |     |     |     |   |   |   |   |

**b.** Graph the ordered pairs and connect the points as smoothly as possible.

**c.** Describe how this graph is different from the graph of $y = x^2$.

_____

_____

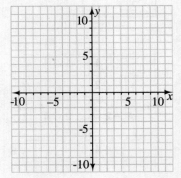

# Reteaching 10-5

**Problem Solving: Make a Table and Make a Graph**

You can solve problems by making a table and a graph. First, use the information in the problem to make a table. Then use the table to draw a graph. You can use the graph to answer questions or make predictions.

**Suppose there is a 60-in.-tall tree in your front yard. After a month the tree is 64 in. tall. After another month the tree is 66 in. tall. After the third month it is 68 in. tall. How tall is the tree after 6 months?**

**Read and Understand** Given the tree's height after each of the first three months, find the height of the tree after 6 months.

**Plan and Solve** Make a table to organize the information in the problem. Then make a graph to predict the height of the tree after 6 months.

| Month | Height (in.) |
|-------|--------------|
| 0 | 60 |
| 1 | 64 |
| 2 | 66 |
| 3 | 68 |

Use the table to create a graph. Use an interval of 1 on the *x*-axis and label it from 1 to 6 months. Use an interval of 2 on the *y*-axis and label it from 58 to 70 in.

It appears that the tree grows about 2 in. each month. So in 6 months the tree should be about 74 in. tall.

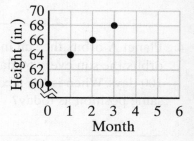

**Look Back and Check** Since the rate of increase is assumed to be constant, you can say that every month the tree grows 2 in.

---

**Solve the problem by making a table and a graph.**

1. The distance that an object falls when dropped from a height is given by the rule $d = \frac{1}{2}gt^2$ where $g = 32$ ft/sec/sec, and $t$ = time. What is the distance the object has fallen after 7 seconds?

    _____

2. Your older sister is working part-time at a novelty store. Some of the most often bought items are funny noses at $.29 each and buzzers at $.79 each. How much does a person owe if he/she buys 3 noses and 4 buzzers?

    _____

# Practice 10-5

**Problem Solving: Make a Table and Make a Graph**

**Choose a strategy or combination of strategies to solve each problem.**

1. A bookstore charges $7 per book but gives a $5 discount when five or more books are purchased. Jim always buys enough books to get the discount. If his purchase comes to $65, how many books did he buy?

   _____

2. A typical giant squid is about 240 in. long, which is 16 times the diameter of one of its eyes. What is the diameter of the eye?

   _____

3. Eileen prints art on T-shirts. She charges $18 to make the art pattern and $9 per shirt. How many shirts did she make if she was paid $54 for an order?

   _____

4. Planet A orbits the sun in a system once every 50 days. Planet B orbits the sun every 60 days and Planet C orbits the sun every 100 days. When is the next time all three planets will be in the same position as today?

   _____

5. Sean plans to drive his car to a park, 72 miles away. He needs to arrive at 10:00 a.m. to meet his friends. If he drives at an average speed of 48 mi/hr, when should he leave?

   _____

6. Terry wants to cover a box shaped like a rectangular prism. It is 8 cm wide, 10 cm long, and 12 cm high. Terry only has 600 cm2 of paper. Will there be enough paper to cover the box?

   _____

7. An orchard charges a fee of $2.00 to pick apples and $.75 for every pound of apples picked. How much would you pay to pick 20 pounds of apples at this orchard?

   _____

8. Gorillas and chimpanzees can learn sign language to communicate with humans. One gorilla knows 700 words. This is 50 fewer than 5 times the number that a chimpanzee knows. How many words does the chimpanzee know?

   _____

# Reteaching 10-6

Movements of figures on a plane are called
**transformations.** A translation, or slide, moves
all points the same distance and direction.

The translation $(x, y) \rightarrow (x + 4, y - 1)$ moves *each*
point to the right 4 units and down 1 unit.

$A(-3, 1)$ moves to $(-3 + 4, 1 - 1)$, where point
$A'(1, 0)$ is its **image.**

The square $ABCD$ moves to its image square $A'B'C'D'$.

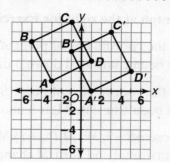

**Complete the following for the figure above.**

**1.** $B(-5, 5) \rightarrow B'(\underline{\quad}, \underline{\quad})$

**2.** $C(-1, 7) \rightarrow C'(\underline{\quad}, \underline{\quad})$

**3.** $D(\underline{\quad}, \underline{\quad}) \rightarrow D'(\underline{\quad}, \underline{\quad})$

**Graph each translation of figure *PRST.***

**4.** right 2 units

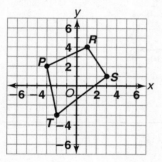

**5.** left 2 units, down 2 units

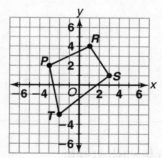

**6.** right 1 unit, up 3 units

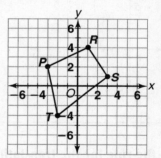

**Complete the rule for each translation.**

**7.** right 3 units, up 1 unit

$(x, y) \rightarrow$ _____

**8.** left 4 units, up 5 units

$(x, y) \rightarrow$ _____

**9.** left 1 unit, down 9 units

$(x, y) \rightarrow$ _____

**Write a rule for the translation.**

**10.** left 1 unit, down 3 units

_____

**11.** right 1 unit, up 2 units

_____

**12.** left 3 units, up 2 units

_____

# Practice 10-6

**Use the graph at the right for Exercises 1–4.**

1. Give the coordinates of point *A* after it has been translated down 3 units.

    _____

2. Give the coordinates of point *B* after it has been translated left 3 units.

    _____

3. Suppose $M(-7, 3) : M'(4, -1)$. What are the horizontal and vertical changes?

    _____

4. What are the coordinates of point *N* after it is translated right 8 units and up 5 units?

    _____

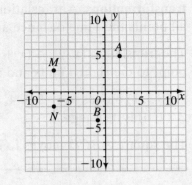

**Graph each translation of *ABCD*.**
**Give the coordinates of *A′*, *B′*, *C′*, and *D′*.**

5. *A* (2, 1), *B* (4, 5), *C* (7, 4), *D* (5, −1);
   right 2 units

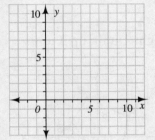

6. *A* (2, 1), *B* (4, 5), *C* (7, 4), *D* (5, −1);
   down 1 unit, left 2 units

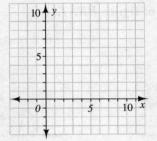

_____

**Write the rule for the translation shown in each graph.**

7.

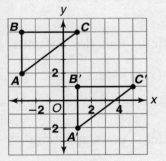

8.

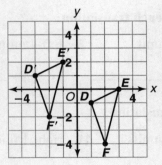

_____

Name _____ Class _____ Date _____

# Reteaching 10-7

**Symmetry and Reflections**

**Symmetry**

A figure is **symmetrical** if one side is a mirror image of the other. The line that divides a figure into two identical parts is called a **line of symmetry.**

The figure below has 2 lines of symmetry.

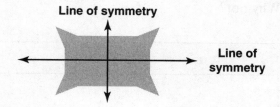

You can trace the figure and fold it along either line to see that the two halves match.

**Reflections**

A **reflection** is a transformation that creates a mirror image. $\triangle A'B'C'$ is the mirror image of $\triangle ABC$ across the x-axis. The x-axis is the **line of reflection.**

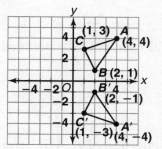

- When you reflect across the x-axis, the y-coordinates change sign.

- When you reflect across the y-axis, the x-coordinates change sign.

- When you reflect across a line of symmetry, the image is the figure itself.

---

**Draw the line(s) of symmetry. If there are no lines of symmetry, write *none*.**

1.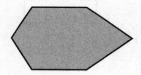
_____

2.
_____

3.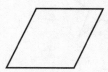
_____

**△ ABC is shown. Draw △ A'B'C' so it is a reflection of △ ABC over the specified axis. Then complete each statement.**

4. over the x-axis

$A(-4, 4) \rightarrow A'$
_____

$B(-2, 0) \rightarrow B'$
_____

$C(0, 2) \rightarrow C'$

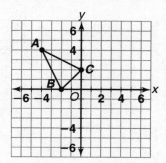

5. over the y-axis

$A(-4, 4) \rightarrow A'$
_____

$B(-2, 0) \rightarrow B'$
_____

$C(0, 2) \rightarrow C'$

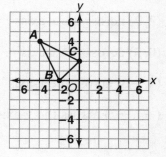

Name _____ Class _____ Date _____

# Practice 10-7

**Use the graph at the right for Exercises 1–3.**

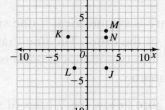

1. For which two points is the *x*-axis a line of reflection?

   _____

2. For which two points is the *y*-axis a line of reflection?

   _____

3. Points *L* and *J* are not reflections across the *y*-axis. Why not?

   _____

   _____

△ *A′B′C′* is a reflection of △ *ABC* over the *x*-axis. Draw
△ *A′B′C′* and complete each statement.

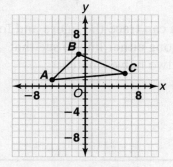

4. $A(-5, 1) \rightarrow A'(x, y)$ _____

5. $B(-1, 5) \rightarrow B'(x, y)$ _____

6. $C(6, 2) \rightarrow C'(x, y)$ _____

**Draw the lines of symmetry for each figure.**
**If there are no lines of symmetry, write *none*.**

7.

8.

9.

10.

**Graph each point and its reflection across the indicated axis. Write**
**the coordinates of the reflected point.**

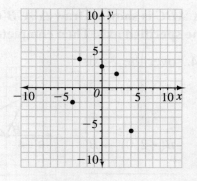

11. $(-3, 4)$ across the *y*-axis _____

12. $(-4, -2)$ across the *x*-axis _____

13. $(2, 2)$ across the *x*-axis _____

14. $(0, 3)$ across the *x*-axis _____

15. $(4, -6)$ across the *y*-axis _____

16. $(-4, -2)$ across the *y*-axis _____

# Reteaching 10-8

A **rotation** is a transformation that turns a figure about a fixed point. The fixed point is called the **center of rotation.**

A figure has **rotational symmetry** if it can be rotated less than 360° and fit exactly on top of the original figure.

The figure below has rotational symmetry.

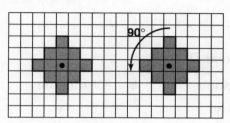

For a rotation of 90° or 180° about its center, the figure fits exactly on top of itself.

To draw a 180° rotation about point $A$, trace $\triangle ABC$. Place a pencil tip on point $A$ and rotate the tracing 180°. Mark points $A'$, $B'$, and $C'$. Then draw $\triangle A'B'C'$.

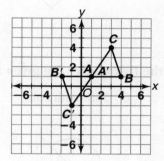

---

**Does each figure have rotational symmetry?**

**1.**

_____

**2.**

_____

**3.**

_____

**Draw the image of the figure after each rotation about point $O$.**

**4.** rotation of 90°

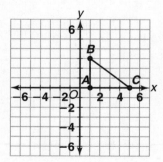

**5.** rotation of 180°

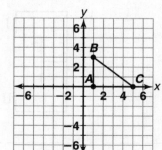

**6.** rotation of 270°

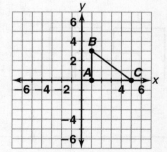

# Practice 10-8

**Does each figure have rotational symmetry? Explain.**

1.
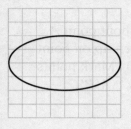
_____

2.
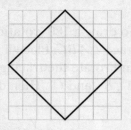
_____

3.

_____

4.
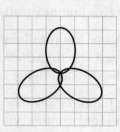
_____

**Draw the images of the figure after the given rotation about point *O*.**

5. 90° rotation
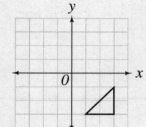

6. 180° rotation
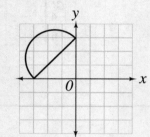

7. 270° rotation
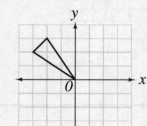

8. 180° rotation
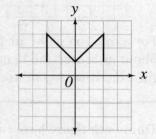

**Figure II is the image of Figure I. Identify the transformation as a translation, a reflection, or a rotation.**

9.
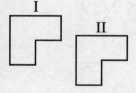
_____

10.
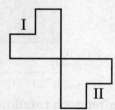
_____

11.
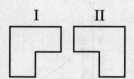
_____

12.
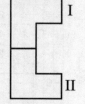
_____

# Reteaching 11-1

Aimee asked students in her grade how many CDs they own. She displayed her data in a **frequency table.** Each tally stands for 1 CD.

**Students' CD Collections**

| Number of CDs | 17 | 18 | 19 | 20 | 21 | 22 | 23 | 24 |
|---|---|---|---|---|---|---|---|---|
| Tally | ⦀⦀ I | I | ⦀⦀ | III | I | IIII | II | IIII |
| Frequency | 6 | 1 | 5 | 3 | 1 | 4 | 2 | 4 |

She displayed the same data in a **line plot.** Each ✗ stands for 1 CD.

Number of CDs Students Own

```
✗
✗      ✗
✗      ✗              ✗       ✗
✗      ✗   ✗          ✗       ✗
✗      ✗   ✗          ✗   ✗   ✗
✗   ✗  ✗   ✗   ✗      ✗   ✗   ✗
17  18 19  20  21  22  23  24
```

She also made a **histogram** to show the frequencies. The bars represent intervals of equal size. The height of each bar gives the frequency of the data.

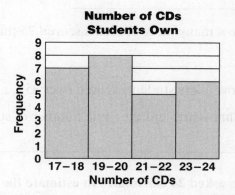

**Number of CDs Students Own**

**Use the frequency table for Exercises 1–3.**

1. Ms. Ortiz's class is planning a school garden. She asked her students how many rose bushes they want in the garden. She recorded the data in a frequency table. Complete the table.

| Number of Rose Bushes | 1 | 2 | 3 | 4 | 5 | 6 |
|---|---|---|---|---|---|---|
| Tally | I | IIII | III | ⦀⦀ I | I | I |
| Frequency | | | | | | |

2. Use the frequency table to make a line plot for the data.

3. Draw a histogram of the students' data.

# Practice 11-1

**Make a frequency table and a line plot for the data.**

1.  boxes of juice sold per day:

    26  21  26  24  27  23  24  22

    26  21  23  26  24  26  23

**Ms. Makita made a line plot to show the scores her students got on a test. At the right is Ms. Makita's line plot.**

2.  What does each data item or ✗ represent?

    _____

3.  How many more students scored 75 than scored 95?

    _____

4.  How many students scored over 85? _____

5.  What scores did the same number of students get?

    _____

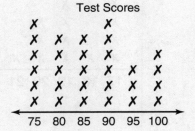

**Nathan asked 24 classmates to estimate the total number of hours (to the nearest quarter hour) they spend doing homework Monday through Thursday. The frequency table below shows their responses.**

6.  Can you tell from the table how many students do homework for two hours or less? Explain.

    _____

7.  How many more students do homework for at least 5 h than do homework for less than 4 h?

    _____

8.  Make a histogram for the data. Use the intervals in the table.

    **Hours Spent Doing Homework**

    | Number of Hours | Frequency |
    |:---:|:---:|
    | 1 – 1.75 | 1 |
    | 2 – 2.75 | 1 |
    | 3 – 3.75 | 2 |
    | 4 – 4.75 | 6 |
    | 5 – 5.75 | 8 |
    | 6 – 6.75 | 3 |
    | 7 – 7.75 | 2 |
    | 8 – 8.75 | 1 |

# Reteaching 11-2

A **spreadsheet** is one way to organize data.

Columns are labeled A, B, C, and so on. Rows are numbered 1, 2, 3, and so on. The box where column B and row 3 meet is called **cell** B3. The *value* in cell B3 is 10.

### Weekly Butter and Margarine Sales

|   | **A** | **B** | **C** |
|---|---|---|---|
| **1** | Day | Butter | Margarine |
| **2** | Monday | 9 | 7 |
| **3** | Tuesday | 10 | 9 |
| **4** | Wednesday | 7 | 6 |
| **5** | Thursday | 9 | 6 |
| **6** | Friday | 10 | 8 |
| **7** | Saturday | 11 | 9 |

• Spreadsheet column A gives the labels for the horizontal axis.

• Spreadsheet column B gives the heights for one set of bars and one set of points.

• Spreadsheet column C gives the heights for another set of bars and another set of points.

You can use the data from this spreadsheet to make a **double bar graph.** A double bar graph compares two sets of data. The **legend,** or key, tells what kinds of data the graph is comparing.

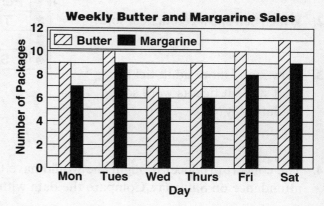

You can compare changes over time of two sets of data with a double line graph.

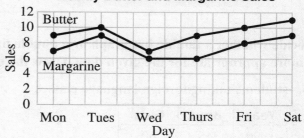

---

**Use the data in the spreadsheet for Exercises 1–4.**

1. What is the value in cell B4? cell C2?

   _____

2. In which cell is the year 2000? 1997?

   _____

3. Make a double bar graph from the spreadsheet. Include a legend.

### Percents of Families Who Prefer Frozen and Fresh Vegetables

|   | **A** | **B** | **C** |
|---|---|---|---|
| **1** | Year | Frozen | Fresh |
| **2** | 1997 | 61 | 39 |
| **3** | 1998 | 70 | 30 |
| **4** | 1999 | 78 | 22 |
| **5** | 2000 | 84 | 16 |

4. Make a double line graph from the spreadsheet. Include a legend.

# Practice 11-2

**Use the spreadsheet at the right for Exercises 1–4.**

1. What is the value in cell B3?

   _____

2. Which cell shows 65 tickets sold?

   _____

3. How many more adult tickets
   than student tickets were sold
   on Saturday?

   _____

4. The concert producer thought she would have the greatest
   attendance on Saturday. Compare the data with her expectation.

   _____

   _____

   _____

**Tickets Sold to Concert Performances**

|   | A | B | C |
|---|---|---|---|
| 1 | Performance | Adult Tickets | Student Tickets |
| 2 | Thursday | 47 | 65 |
| 3 | Friday | 125 | 133 |
| 4 | Saturday | 143 | 92 |

**Decide whether a double bar graph or a double line graph
is more appropriate for the given data. Draw the graph.**

5. students taking foreign language classes

| Year | Boys | Girls |
|------|------|-------|
| 1990 | 45 | 60 |
| 1991 | 50 | 55 |
| 1992 | 70 | 60 |
| 1993 | 55 | 75 |

6. extracurricular sport activities

| Sport | Boys | Girls |
|-------|------|-------|
| basketball | 40 | 30 |
| volleyball | 30 | 40 |
| soccer | 40 | 25 |

# Reteaching 11-3

**Other Displays**

Make a **stem-and-leaf plot** of the summer earnings data.

① Make a column of the tens digits of the data in order from least to greatest. These are the stems.

② Record the ones digits for each tens digit in order from least to greatest. These are the leaves.

③ Make a *key* to explain what the stems and leaves represent.

| Summer Earnings | | | | | |
|---|---|---|---|---|---|
| $35 | $35 | $38 | $15 | $52 | $40 |
| $20 | $23 | $56 | $12 | $14 | $58 |

① stems    ② leaves

```
  1 |          1 | 2 4 5
  2 |          2 | 0 3
  3 |          3 | 5 5 8
  4 |          4 | 0
  5 |          5 | 2 6 8
```

Make a **box-and-whisker plot** for the summer earnings data.

① List the data in order.

③ 1 | 2 means 12

least value → 12 14 15 20 23 35 35 38 40 52 56 58 ← greatest value

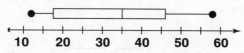

The lower quartile is 17.5.    The middle quartile is 35.    The upper quartile is 46.

② Use a number line to draw the box-and-whisker plot.

```
●———[——|———]——————●
 10  20  30  40  50  60
```

---

**1.** Complete the stem-and-leaf plot of this set of data.

| 24 | 36 | 64 | 42 | 59 |
|----|----|----|----|----|
| 61 | 16 | 63 | 54 | 39 |
| 36 | 45 | 15 | 27 | 51 |

```
1 | _ _
2 |   _
3 | _ _
4 | _ _
5 | _ _ _
6 | _ _ _

1 | 5 means ___
```

**2.** Brandy recorded these high temperatures for two weeks in July. Make a stem-and-leaf plot of her data.

| 92 | 86 | 91 | 90 | 85 |
|----|----|----|----|----|
| 82 | 84 | 78 | 79 | 83 |
| 84 | 89 | 86 | 87 |    |

**3.** Mr. Wang recorded these test scores. Make a box-and-whisker plot for the data.

| 66 | 83 | 58 | 65 | 66 |
|----|----|----|----|----|
| 66 | 82 | 55 | 57 | 71 |
| 40 | 43 | 41 | 56 | 71 |
| 74 | 81 | 85 | 63 | 62 |

# Practice 11-3

**The stem-and-leaf plot at the right shows the number of baskets
scored by one of ten intramural teams last season.
Use it for Exercises 1–4.**

1. How many data items are there?

   _____

2. What is the least measurement given?

   _____

3. What is the greatest measurement given?

   _____

4. In how many games did the team score less than 70 baskets?

   _____

| 5 | 2 | 6 | 9 |
|---|---|---|---|
| 6 | 0 | 4 | 6 |
| 7 | 1 | 5 |   |
| 8 | 4 | 8 |   |

8|4 means 84

**The box-and-whisker plot at the right shows the number of pages
read for book reports by a 7th grade literature class. Use it for
Exercises 5–7.**

5. What is the range of the data?

   _____

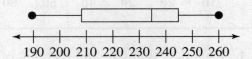

190 200 210 220 230 240 250 260

6. What is the lower quartile? The upper quartile?

   _____

7. Which quartile contains most of the data?

   _____

8. Make a stem-and-leaf plot and a box-and-whisker plot for the set
   of data.

   science test scores:  83    73    78    60    85

            92    95    85    99    68

# Reteaching 11-4    Problem Solving: Make a Table and Use Logical Reasoning

Travis, Seritta, Ariel, and Tess are going hiking, boating, biking, and surfing.

① Tess does not know how to surf.

② Ariel asked the hiker to show her a map.

③ Tess and Ariel talked with the biker and the boater.

④ Travis doesn't like water.

Tell who will do each activity.

**Read and Understand**   What do you need to find out? *The problem asks you to tell who will do each activity.*

**Plan and Solve**   Make a logic table. Use the clues from the problem. Write *yes* or *no* in each box.

Fact ① tells you Tess is not the surfer. Write *no* in the box where Tess and Surfer meet.

Fact ② says that Ariel is not the hiker. Write *no* for this.

Fact ③ says that Tess and Ariel are not the boater nor the biker. Write *no* in four boxes, leaving Ariel to be the surfer. Write *yes* in the box where Ariel and Surfer meet.

**Look Back and Check**   Complete the table. *Travis is the biker, Seritta is the boater, Ariel is the surfer, and Tess is the hiker.*

|         | Hiker | Boater | Biker | Surfer |
|---------|-------|--------|-------|--------|
| Travis  |       |        |       |        |
| Seritta |       |        |       |        |
| Ariel   |       |        |       |        |
| Tess    |       |        |       | no     |

|         | Hiker | Boater | Biker | Surfer |
|---------|-------|--------|-------|--------|
| Travis  |       |        |       |        |
| Seritta |       |        |       |        |
| Ariel   | no    | no     | no    | yes    |
| Tess    |       | no     | no    | no     |

|         | Hiker | Boater | Biker | Surfer |
|---------|-------|--------|-------|--------|
| Travis  | no    | no     | yes   | no     |
| Seritta | no    | yes    | no    | no     |
| Ariel   | no    | no     | no    | yes    |
| Tess    | yes   | no     | no    | no     |

---

**Complete the table to solve the problem.**

Iona, Sara, Pete, and Tim went to the Northwest Coast Indian Conference. They are from the Noottka, Salish, Haida, and Tlingit families. Pete and Sara had not seen a Haida for a year. The Tlingit gave Iona and Tim a wood carving. Iona is not the Noottka. Sara joined the Noottka at the evening ceremonies. The Tlingit is not a woman. Who is the Noottka? the Salish? the Haida? the Tlingit? _____

|         | Iona | Sara | Pete | Tim |
|---------|------|------|------|-----|
| Noottka |      |      |      |     |
| Salish  |      |      |      |     |
| Haida   |      |      |      |     |
| Tlingit |      |      |      |     |

# Practice 11-4

**Problem Solving: Make a Table and Use Logical Reasoning**

**Solve each problem by combining Use Logical Reasoning and Make a Table.**

1. Alicia, Barb, Cathy, Dahlia, and Ellen each arrive at school in a different way. One rides in a car pool, one rides her bike, one walks every day, one rides in her family car, and one rides the school bus. Cathy does not ride in a motor vehicle. Barb enjoys the bus ride along the country road. Ellen is last to be picked up on the car pool route. Alicia lives across the street from school. How does each of the girls arrive at school?

_____

_____

2. Four cousins are born in the same year. Stanley was born after Mark. David was born before Stanley, but David is not the oldest of the cousins. Greg was born last. What is the order of their births?

**Use any strategy or combination of strategies to solve each problem.**

3. Nick took some money from his piggy bank. He bought a book for $3.50 and he earned $3.00 for raking leaves. Now he has $4.50. How much did Nick take from his bank? _____

4. Find the median of all positive odd multiples of 3 that are less than 50. _____

5. How many different ways can you have $1 in change using nickels, dimes, quarters, and half-dollars?

6. Which number shown at the right is described below?

| | 85 | 41 |
|---|---|---|

   The difference of the digits is 3.
   It is a multiple of 3.
   It is greater than the average of 84 and 41.
   It is less than the product of 9 and 11.
   It is even.

52      74      69

30    96

**Theodore works for Mr. Jonas. Mr. Jonas agreed to start Theodore at $.01 the first day, $.02 the second day, $.04 the third day, $.08 the fourth day, and so on.**

7. How much does Theodore earn on the fifteenth day? _____

8. How much did Theodore earn in fifteen days?

# Reteaching 11-5

Carlos is curious about sports that students in his school like best. He cannot interview every student in the school. But he could interview a sample of the school **population.**

Carlos wants a **random sample.** A sample is random if everyone has an equal chance of being selected. How will Carlos get a random sample? He considers two possibilities:

- He can interview 30 students at a soccer game.

- He can interview 5 students in each of 6 class changes.

Carlos realizes that students at a soccer game probably like soccer better than other sports. That would not be a random sample. He decides on the interviews during class changes.

What question will he ask? He considers two possibilities:

- "Which sport do you prefer, football, soccer, baseball, or tennis?"

- "Which do you enjoy most, the slow sport of baseball or one of the more exciting sports like football, soccer, or tennis?"

The second question is **biased.** It makes one answer seem better than another. Carlos decides to ask the first question.

---

1. You want to find how many people in your community are vegetarian. Where would be the best place to take a survey?

   _____

**In each question biased or fair?**

2. Will you vote for the young inexperienced candidate, Mr. Soong, or the experienced candidate, Ms. Lopez? _____

3. Will you vote for Mr. Soong or Ms. Lopez? _____

**You plan to survey people to see what percent own their home and what percent rent. Tell whether the following will give a random sample. Explain.**

4. You interview people outside a pool supply store in the suburbs.

   _____

5. You interview people in the street near an apartment complex.

   _____

6. You mail a survey to every 20th person in the telephone book.

   _____

# Practice 11-5

**You want to survey students in your school about their exercise habits. Tell whether Exercises 1–2 are likely to give a random sample of the population. Explain.**

1. You select every tenth student on an alphabetical list of the students in your school. You survey the selected students in their first-period classes.

   _____

   _____

2. At lunchtime you stand by a vending machine. You survey every student who buys something from the vending machine.

   _____

   _____

**Is each question *biased* or *fair*? Rewrite biased questions as fair questions.**

3. Do you think bike helmets should be mandatory for all bike riders?

   _____

4. Do you prefer the natural beauty of hardwood floors in your home?

   _____

5. Do you exercise regularly?

   _____

6. Do you eat at least the recommended number of servings of fruits and vegetables to ensure a healthy and long life?

   _____

7. Do you prefer the look and feel of thick lush carpeting in your living room?

   _____

8. Do you take a daily multiple vitamin to supplement your diet?

   _____

9. Do you read the newspaper to be informed about world events?

   _____

10. Do you feel that the TV news is a sensational portrayal of life's problems?

    _____

# Reteaching 11-6

**Estimating Population Size**

Researchers tagged 100 fish in a pond and then released them back into the pond. Later they captured 60 fish and found that 3 were tagged. Estimate the number of fish in the pond.

① Write a proportion of tagged fish to total fish.

$$\frac{\text{tagged fish (pond)}}{\text{total fish (pond)}} = \frac{\text{tagged fish (sample)}}{\text{total fish (sample)}}$$

$$\frac{100}{n} = \frac{3}{60}$$

② Write cross products.

$$3n = 6{,}000$$

③ Solve.

$$n = 2{,}000$$

There are about 2,000 fish in the pond.

---

**Complete to estimate the number of deer in the woods.**

1. One year researchers tagged 80 deer. They later captured 15 deer and found 5 were tagged. Estimate the number of deer in the woods.

$$\frac{80}{n} = \frac{\boxed{\phantom{x}}}{\boxed{\phantom{x}}}$$

$$5n = 15 \cdot \text{_____}$$

$$n = \text{_____}$$

There are about _____ deer.

2. Two years later, researchers tagged 45 deer. They later captured 20 and found 3 were tagged. Estimate the number of deer in the woods then.

$$\frac{}{n} = \frac{}{20}$$

$$3n = \text{_____}$$

$$n = \text{_____}$$

There are about _____ deer.

**Use a proportion to estimate each animal population.**

3. In another project, researchers caught and tagged 85 sea lions in a bay. Later they caught and released 50 sea lions. Of those, 9 had tags. Estimate the sea lion population in the bay.

_____

4. Other researchers caught and tagged 5 spotted owls. Later they caught 7 owls. Of those, 4 were tagged. Estimate the number of spotted owls in that forest.

_____

5. An ecology class helped researchers determine the rabbit population in a nature preserve. One weekend, the students captured, tagged, and set free 32 rabbits. A month later, they captured 27 rabbits including 16 with tags. Estimate the number of rabbits in the nature preserve.

_____

6. Another ecology class helped researchers determine the pigeon population in a city park. In one day, the students captured, banded, and released 200 pigeons. Two weeks later, of the 24 pigeons they captured, 3 had bands. Estimate the pigeon population in the park.

_____

# Practice 11-6

Workers at a state park caught, tagged, and set free the species shown
at the right. Later that same year, the workers caught the number of
animals shown in the table below, and counted the tagged animals.
Use a proportion to estimate the park population of each species.

| Tagged Animals | |
|---|---|
| Bears | 12 |
| Squirrels | 50 |
| Raccoons | 23 |
| Rabbits | 42 |
| Trout | 46 |
| Owls | 24 |
| Foxes | 14 |
| Skunks | 21 |

| | Caught | Counted Tagged | Estimated Population |
|---|---|---|---|
| 1. Bears | 30 | 9 | |
| 2. Squirrels | 1,102 | 28 | |
| 3. Raccoons | 412 | 10 | |
| 4. Rabbits | 210 | 2 | |
| 5. Trout | 318 | 25 | |
| 6. Owls | 117 | 10 | |
| 7. Foxes | 54 | 9 | |
| 8. Skunks | 45 | 6 | |

A park ranger tags 100 animals. Use a proportion to estimate the
total population for each sample.

9. 23 out of 100 animals are tagged

_____

10. 12 out of 75 animals are tagged

_____

11. 8 out of 116 animals are tagged

_____

12. 5 out of 63 animals are tagged

_____

13. 4 out of 83 animals are tagged

_____

14. 3 out of 121 animals are tagged

_____

15. 83 out of 125 animals are tagged

_____

16. 7 out of 165 animals are tagged

_____

Use a proportion to estimate each animal population.

17. Total ducks counted: 1,100
Marked ducks counted: 257
Total marked ducks: 960

_____

18. Total alligators counted: 310
Marked alligators counted: 16
Total marked alligators: 90

_____

# Reteaching 11-7

**Using Data to Persuade**

There are 3 ways that graphs can be drawn to be misleading.

**1.** The interval on the vertical axis may not start at zero.

**2.** There may be a break in the graph.

**3.** The intervals on the horizontal or vertical axis may have unequal intervals.

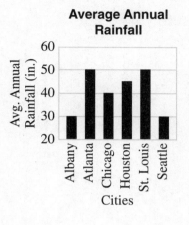

**Average Annual Rainfall**

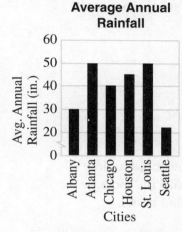

**Average Annual Rainfall**

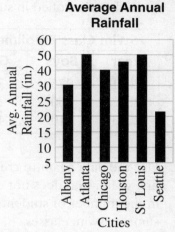

**Average Annual Rainfall**

Mean, median, and mode can also be used to mislead. Consider a set of data where most of the numbers are in a certain range. There are a few numbers that are either way above or way below the range. The mean is not a good measure of the data in this case.

---

**For each graph do the following:**
**(a) Tell what the graph shows. (b) What can you say about the graph?**

**1.**

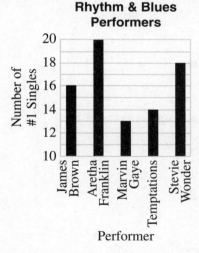

**Rhythm & Blues Performers**

**2.**

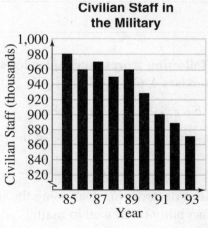

**Civilian Staff in the Military**

_____

_____

_____

_____

_____

_____

_____

_____

# Practice 11-7

**The table below shows the number of students
enrolled in swimming classes for 2001 to 2003.**

1. Use the data to create a double line graph
   that emphasizes the increase in the number
   of students enrolled in summer swim classes.

| Swim Class Enrollment | | |
|---|---|---|
| **Year** | **Boys** | **Girls** |
| 2001 | 375 | 360 |
| 2002 | 400 | 395 |
| 2003 | 410 | 420 |

2. Use the data again to create a second double
   line graph that does not emphasize the increase
   in the number of students enrolled in the
   summer swim classes.

3. Which graph could be used to request additional reserved
   times for swim classes at the pool?

   _____

   _____

**Vince has the following scores on chapter tests in his math class. Use
this data in Exercises 4–6.**

   95      89      83      90      83

4. Find the mean, median, and mode of his test scores.

   _____

5. Should Vince describe his tests using the mean, median, or mode
   to show his ability to do well in math?

   _____

   _____

6. Should his teacher use the mean, the median, or the mode to
   encourage Vince to check his work carefully on the next test?

   _____

   _____

# Reteaching 11-8

Gilbert is investigating the relationship between the number of credit cards a person has and the amount of credit card debt.

First, he made a table from his data.

### Credit Cards and Credit Card Debt

| Number of Cards | Amount of Debt |
|:---:|:---:|
| 1 | $0 |
| 1 | $1,000 |
| 1 | $5,000 |
| 2 | $3,000 |
| 2 | $5,000 |
| 3 | $10,000 |
| 3 | $5,000 |
| 3 | $8,000 |
| 4 | $10,000 |
| 5 | $19,000 |

Then he plotted the data in a scatter plot.

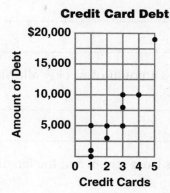

**Credit Card Debt**

Gilbert's scatter plot shows a **positive trend** in the data. That means as the number of credit cards goes up so does the amount of debt. As one value goes up, so does the other.

In a **negative trend,** one value goes up while the other goes down.

---

**Complete the scatter plot for the data.**

1. Dana surveyed her friends about how much TV they watch and their average test scores. Her results are shown below.

### Test Scores and TV

| TV Hours Per Day | Average Test Score | TV Hours Per Day | Average Test Score |
|:---:|:---:|:---:|:---:|
| 1 | 98 | 3 | 79 |
| 1 | 86 | 3 | 73 |
| 2 | 90 | 3 | 75 |
| 2 | 82 | 4 | 62 |
| 2 | 85 | 5 | 68 |

**Test Scores and TV**

2. Is the trend in the data negative or positive? Explain.

_____

3. Describe the relationship Dana likely found between test scores and TV time.

_____

# Practice 11-8

**Tell what trend you would expect to see in scatter plots comparing the
sets of data in Exercises 1–4. Explain your reasoning.**

1. a person's height and the person's shoe size

   _____

   _____

2. the age of a child and amount of weekly allowance that the child receives

   _____

   _____

3. the distance one lives from school and the length of the school day

   _____

   _____

4. the average number of hours a child sleeps and the age of the child

   _____

   _____

5. Make a scatter plot of the following data. Does the scatter plot
   show any trend? If so, what?                      _____

| Number of Hours of Practice | Number of Successful Free Throws out of 10 |
|:---:|:---:|
| 6 | 3 |
| 7 | 5 |
| 8 | 6 |
| 9 | 6 |
| 10 | 7 |
| 11 | 7 |
| 12 | 6 |
| 13 | 7 |

**Describe the trend in each scatter plot.**

6.                                    7.                                    8.

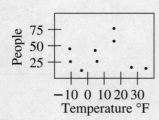          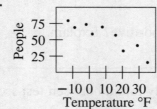          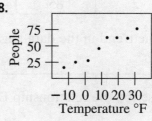

_____        _____        _____

# Reteaching 12-1

To find a **theoretical probability,** first list all possible **outcomes.** Then use the formula:

$$P(\text{event}) = \frac{\text{number of favorable outcomes}}{\text{total number of possible outcomes}}$$

A letter is selected at random from the letters of the word FLORIDA. What is the probability that the letter is an A?

- There are 7 letters (possible outcomes).

- There is one A, which represents a favorable outcome.

$$P(A) = \frac{\text{number of favorable outcomes}}{\text{total number of outcomes}} = \frac{1}{7}$$

The probability that the letter is an A is $\frac{1}{7}$.

Selecting a letter other than A is called *not* A and is the **complement** of the event A. The sum of the probabilities of an event and its complement equals 1, or 100%.

What is the probability of the event "*not* A"?

$$P(A) + P(\textit{not } A) = 1$$

$$\frac{1}{7} + P(\textit{not } A) = 1$$

$$P(\textit{not } A) = 1 - \frac{1}{7} = \frac{6}{7}$$

The probability of the event "*not* A,"

(selecting F, L, O, R, I, or D), is $\frac{6}{7}$.

---

**Spin the spinner shown once. Find each probability as a fraction, a decimal, and a percent.**

1. $P(5)$

$$\frac{\text{number of favorable outcomes}}{\text{total number of outcomes}}$$

$$= \frac{\boxed{\phantom{0}}}{5} \ \underline{\hspace{3cm}}$$

2. $P(\text{odd number})$

$$\frac{\text{number of favorable outcomes}}{\text{total number of outcomes}}$$

$$= \frac{2}{\boxed{\phantom{0}}} \ \underline{\hspace{3cm}}$$

**You select a card at random from a box that contains cards numbered from 1 to 10. Find each probability as a fraction, a decimal, and a percent.**

3. $P(\text{even number})$

_____

4. $P(\text{number less than 4})$

_____

5. $P(\text{not } 5)$

_____

**The letters H, A, P, P, I, N, E, S, and S are written on pieces of paper. Select one piece of paper. Find each probability.**

6. $P(P)$ _____

7. $P(\text{not vowel})$ _____

8. $P(\text{not } E)$ _____

**A number is selected at random from the numbers 1 to 50. Find the odds in favor of each outcome.**

9. selecting a multiple of 5

_____

10. selecting a factor of 50

_____

11. selecting a number that is not a factor of 50

_____

# Practice 12-1

**Probability**

**You spin a spinner numbered 1 through 10. Each outcome is equally likely. Find the probabilities below as a fraction, decimal, and percent.**

**1.** $P(9)$

**2.** $P(\text{even})$

**3.** $P(\text{number greater than 0})$

**4.** $P(\text{multiple of 4})$

_____    _____    _____    _____

**There are eight blue marbles, nine orange marbles, and six yellow marbles in a bag. You draw one marble. Find each probability.**

**5.** $P(\text{blue marble})$ _____

**6.** $P(\text{yellow marble})$ _____

**7.** What marble could you add or remove so that the probability of drawing a blue marble is $\frac{1}{3}$?

_____

**A box contains 12 slips of paper as shown. Each slip of paper is equally likely to be drawn. Find each probability.**

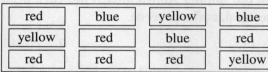

| red | blue | yellow | blue |
| yellow | red | blue | red |
| red | red | red | yellow |

**8.** $P(\text{red})$

**9.** $P(\text{blue})$

**10.** $P(\text{yellow})$

_____    _____    _____

**11.** $P(\text{red}) + P(\text{blue})$

**12.** $P(\text{red}) + P(\text{yellow})$

**13.** $P(\text{blue}) + P(\text{yellow})$

_____    _____    _____

**14.** $P(\text{red or blue})$

**15.** $P(\text{red or yellow})$

**16.** $P(\text{blue or yellow})$

_____    _____    _____

**17.** $P(\text{not red})$

**18.** $P(\text{not blue})$

**19.** $P(\text{not yellow})$

_____    _____    _____

**You select a letter randomly from a bag containing the letters S, P, I, N, N, E, and R. Find the odds in favor of each outcome.**

**20.** selecting an N

**21.** selecting an S

_____                        _____

# Reteaching 12-2

**Experimental Probability**

**Probability** measures how likely it is that an event will occur. For an **experimental probability,** you collect data through observations or experiments and use the data to state the probability.

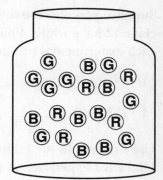

The jar contains red, green, and blue chips. You shake the jar, draw a chip, note its color, and then put it back. You do this 20 times with these results: 7 blue chips, 5 red chips, and 8 green chips. The experimental probability of drawing a green chip is

$$P(\text{green chip}) = \frac{\text{number of times "green chips" occur}}{\text{total number of trials}}$$

$$P(\text{green chip}) = \frac{8}{20} = \frac{2}{5} = 0.4 = 40\%$$

The probability of drawing a green chip is $\frac{2}{5}$, or 0.4, or 40%.

Sometimes a model, or simulation, is used to represent a situation. Then, the simulaton is used to find the experimental probability. For example, spinning this spinner can simulate the probability that 1 of 3 people is chosen for president of the student body.

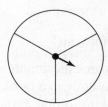

---

**Use the 20 draws above to complete each exercise.**

1.  What is the experimental probability of drawing a red chip? Write the probability as a fraction.

    $P(\text{red chip}) = \dfrac{\phantom{xx}}{20} = \underline{\hspace{2cm}}$

2.  What is the experimental probability of drawing a blue chip? Write the probability as a percent.

    $P(\text{blue chip}) = \underline{\hspace{1cm}} = \underline{\hspace{2cm}}$

**Suppose you have a bag with 30 chips: 12 red, 8 white, and 10 blue. You shake the jar, draw a chip, note its color, and then put it back. You do this 30 times with these results: 10 blue chips, 12 red chips, and 8 white chips. Write each probability as fraction in simplest form.**

3.  $P(\text{red})$ _____

4.  $P(\text{white})$ _____

5.  $P(\text{blue})$ _____

**Describe a probability simulation for each situation.**

6.  You guess the answers on a true/false test with 20 questions.

    _____

    _____

7.  One student out of 6 is randomly chosen to be the homeroom representative.

    _____

    _____

# Practice 12-2

**Suppose you observe the color of socks worn by students in your class: 12 have white, 4 have black, 3 have blue, and 1 has red. Find each experimental probability as a fraction in simplest form.**

1. P(white) _____

2. P(red) _____

3. P(blue) _____

4. P(black) _____

5. P(yellow) _____

6. P(black or red) _____

**Use the data in the table at the right for Exercises 7–12. Find each experimental probability as a percent.**

| Favorite Snack Survey Results | |
| --- | --- |
| Snack | Number of Students |
| Fruit | 8 |
| Granola | 2 |
| Pretzels | 3 |
| Chips | 7 |
| Carrots | 5 |

7. P(fruit) _____

8. P(granola) _____

9. P(pretzels) _____

10. P(carrots) _____

11. P(not fruit) _____

12. P(granola or chips) _____

13. Do an experiment to find the probability that a word chosen randomly in a book is the word *the*. How many words did you look at to find P(the)? What is P(the)?

_____

14. Suppose the following is the result of tossing a coin:

   heads, tails, heads, tails, heads.

   What is the experimental probability for heads?

_____

**Solve.**

15. The probability that a twelve-year-old has a brother or sister is 25%. Suppose you survey 300 twelve-year-old boys. About how many do you think will have a brother or sister? _____

16. a. A quality control inspector found flaws in 13 out of 150 sweaters. Find the probability that a sweater has a flaw. Round to the nearest tenth of a percent. _____

   b. Suppose the company produces 500 sweaters a day. How many will not have flaws? _____

   c. Suppose the company produces 600 sweaters a day. How many will have flaws? _____

17. Describe a simulated experiment that would test the following: Your newspaper arrives before 7:00 A.M. half of the time and after 7:00 A.M. half of the time. How many days would you expect to pass before your paper has arrived before 7:00 A.M. 5 days in a row? _____

Name _____ Class _____ Date _____

# Reteaching 12-3    Problem Solving: Make an Organized List and Simulate a Problem

When you use simulation to solve a problem, you must first develop a model. Then, conduct experiments to generate data.

You and a friend are equally skilled at playing checkers. Estimate how many games you will have to play until one of you wins 6 games.

**Read and Understand**    What do you want to find? *Find out how many games you can expect to play until one of you wins six games.*

**Plan and Solve**    Instead of playing the games, develop a simulation. Toss a coin to see who wins each game. Heads means you win. Tails means your friend wins. Keep track of the results.

Show the results of the simulation in a table. You tossed the coin 10 times before either 6 heads or 6 tails appeared. So you estimate that you would have to play 10 games before one of you would win 6 games.

| Tosses of a Coin | |
|---|---|
| **Result** | **Number** |
| Heads | $\cancel{||||}$ | |
| Tails | //// |

**Look Back and Check**    Would you get the same results if you repeated the simulation?

---

**Solve each problem by either making an organized list or by simulating the problem. Explain why you chose the method you did.**

1. There is one of four symbols on the inner wrapper of energy bars. The symbols are equally distributed among the wrappers. If you collect all four symbols, you get a free bar. Estimate how many bars you need to purchase to win a free bar.

   _____

   _____

   _____

2. A bank gives away one of six baseball cards each time you make a deposit. There is an equal chance of getting any one of the cards. Estimate how many deposits you will have to make to get all six cards.

   _____

   _____

   _____

3. A bakery puts a saying in each cookie. There are 36 different sayings, and there is an equally likely chance that any one of them will be inside any cookie. Estimate how many cookies Mary would have to buy to collect all 36 sayings.

   _____

   _____

   _____

4. Your 10 pairs of socks are in the dryer. Each pair of socks is a different color. Estimate how many socks you will have to pull out without looking to get two the same color.

   _____

   _____

   _____

# Practice 12-3

**Problem Solving: Make an Organized List and Simulate a Problem**

**Solve each problem by either making an organized list or by simulating the problem. Explain why you chose the method you did.**

1. A grocery store is running a contest. Every time you enter the store, you receive a card with the letter W, I, N, E, or R. You have an equally likely chance of receiving any one card. To win a prize, you must spell WINNER by collecting the cards. How many times will you have to enter the store to win a prize?

_____

_____

2. A chewing gum company wraps its product in a piece of paper with one of the digits 1 to 6 on the paper. When you collect wrappers that contain all 6 digits, you win a prize. Use a number cube to help you decide how many pieces of gum you will need to buy in order to get all 6 digits.

_____

_____

**Use any strategy to solve each problem. Show your work.**

3. In 1960, the submarine *Triton* traveled 36,014 miles journeying around the world. If the trip took 76 days, how many miles did the Triton average each day?

_____

4. After working for a company for a year, Melanie received a 10% raise in her salary. Later, the entire company took a 10% cut in pay because of budget difficulties. If Melanie started working at $2,000 a month, what would she now be receiving?

_____

5. At the mall on Saturday, Suki bought a pair of blue jeans for $15.55 and some books for $8.53. For lunch she spent $1.50 on juice and $3.25 on a sandwich. When she left the mall she had $5.27 left. How much money did Suki take to the mall?

_____

6. Mari plans to make a doll's quilt with 16 squares. Half of the squares will be solid red. The rest of the squares will be half calico print and half white. If each square is 9 inches on a side, how many square feet of each type of fabric will she need?

_____

# Reteaching 12-4

**Sample Spaces**

The set of all possible outcomes of an experiment is called the **sample space.**

You can use a *tree diagram* or a table to show the sample space for an experiment. The tree diagram below shows the sample space for spinning the spinner and tossing a coin.

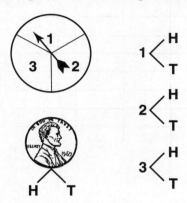

There are 6 possible outcomes: 1H, 1T, 2H, 2T, 3H, 3T. What is the probability of spinning a 3 and tossing heads? There is one favorable outcome (3H) out of 6 possible outcomes. The probabilty is $\frac{1}{6}$.

You can use the *counting principle* to find the number of possible outcomes: If there are *m* ways of making one choice and *n* ways of making a second choice, then there are *m* × *n* ways of making the first choice followed by the second.

Evelyn and Kara are planning to go skating or to a movie. Afterward they want to go out for pizza, tacos, or cheeseburgers. How many possible choices do they have?

- There are *two choices* for an activity and *three choices* for food.

- First choices × Second choices

$$2 \quad \times \quad 3 \quad = 6$$

There are 6 possible choices.

---

**Complete the tree diagram to show the sample space.**

1. Roll a number cube and toss a coin. What is the probability of getting (4, Heads)?

_ _ _ _ _ _ _ _ _ _ _ _

Number of outcomes _____

$P$(4, heads) = _____

**Use the counting principle.**

2. 4 kinds of yogurt and 8 toppings

   _____

3. 6 shirts and 9 pairs of slacks

   _____

4. 3 types of sandwiches and 3 flavors of juice

   _____

5. 4 types of bread and 6 different sandwich spreads

   _____

# Practice 12-4

**Make a table to show the sample space and find the number of outcomes. Then find the probability.**

1. A theater uses a letter to show which row a seat is in, and a number to show the column the seat is in. If there are eight rows and ten columns, what is the probability that you select a seat at random in column 1? _____

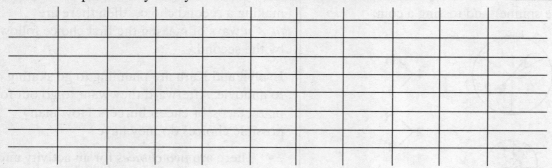

**Make a tree diagram. Then find the probability.**

2. A coin is tossed three times.
   a. Make a tree diagram that shows all the possible outcomes of how the coin will land.
   b. Find the probability that the coin will land heads up all three times or tails up all three times.

_____

**Use the counting principle.**

3. A pizza company makes pizza in three different sizes, small, medium, and large. There are four possible toppings, pepperoni, sausage, green pepper, and mushroom. How many different kinds of pizza with one topping are available? _____

4. You can choose from three types of sandwiches for lunch and three types of juice. How many possible lunch combinations of sandwich and juice can you have? _____

**Susan has red, blue, green, and yellow sweaters. Joanne has green, red, purple, and white sweaters. Diane's sweaters are red, blue, purple, and mauve. Each girl has only one sweater of each color, and will pick a sweater to wear at random. Find each probability.**

5. P(each girl chooses a different color)

_____

6. P(each girl chooses the same color)

_____

7. P(two girls choose the same color, and the third chooses a different color)

_____

8. P(each girl chooses a red sweater)

_____

# Reteaching 12-5

**Compound Events**

If you toss a coin and roll a number cube, the events are **independent.** The outcome of one event does not affect the outcome of the second event.

Find the probability of tossing a heads (H) and rolling an even number (E).

Find $P$(H and E). H and E are independent.

① Find $P$(H):

$$P(\text{H}) = \frac{1 \text{ heads}}{2 \text{ sides}} = \frac{1}{2}$$

② Find $P$(E):

$$P(\text{E}) = \frac{3 \text{ evens}}{6 \text{ faces}} = \frac{1}{2}$$

③ $P(\text{H and E}) = P(\text{H}) \times P(\text{E}) = \frac{1}{2} \times \frac{1}{2} = \frac{1}{4}$

If the outcome of the first event affects the outcome of the second event, the events are **dependent.**

A bag contains 3 blue and 3 red marbles. Draw a marble, then draw a second marble without replacing the first marble. Find the probability of drawing 2 blue marbles.

① Find $P$(blue).

$$P(\text{blue}) = \frac{3 \text{ blue}}{6 \text{ marbles}} = \frac{1}{2}$$

② Find $P$(blue after blue).

$$P(\text{blue after blue}) = \frac{2 \text{ blue}}{5 \text{ marbles}} = \frac{2}{5}$$

③ Find $P$(blue, then blue)

$P$(blue, then blue)
$= P(\text{blue}) \times P(\text{blue after blue})$
$= \frac{1}{2} \times \frac{2}{5} = \frac{1}{5}$

---

**In Exercises 1–6, you draw a marble at random from the bag of marbles shown. Then, you replace it and draw again. Find each probability.**

1. $P$(blue and red)    2. $P$(2 reds)    3. $P$(2 blues)

_____    _____    _____

**Next, you draw two marbles randomly *without* replacing the first marble. Find each probability.**

4. $P$(blue and red)    5. $P$(2 reds)    6. $P$(2 blues)

_____    _____    _____

**You draw two letters randomly from a box containing the letters M, I, S, S, O, U, R, and I.**

7. Suppose you do not replace the first letter before drawing the second. What is $P$(M and I)?

_____

8. Suppose you replace the first letter before drawing the second. What is $P$(M and I)?

_____

# Practice 12-5

**Each letter in the word MASSACHUSETTS is written on a card. The cards are placed in a basket. Find each probability.**

1. What is the probability of selecting two S's if the first card is replaced before selecting the second card?

   _____

2. What is the probability of selecting two S's if the first card is not replaced before selecting the second card?

   _____

**You roll a fair number cube. Find each probability.**

3. $P(3, \text{then } 5)$

   _____

4. $P(2, \text{then } 2)$

   _____

5. $P(5, \text{then } 4, \text{then } 6)$

   _____

6. $P(6, \text{then } 0)$

   _____

7. $P(9, \text{then } 4)$

   _____

8. $P(2, \text{then } 1, \text{then } 5)$

   _____

**Four girls and eight boys are running for president or vice president of the Student Council. Find each probability.**

9. Find the probability that two boys are elected.

   _____

10. Find the probability that two girls are elected.

    _____

11. Find the probability that the president is a boy and the vice president is a girl.

    _____

12. Find the probability that the president is a girl and the vice president is a boy.

    _____

**A box contains ten balls, numbered 1 through 10. Marisha draws a ball. She records its number and then returns it to the bag. Then Penney draws a ball. Find each probability.**

13. $P(9, \text{then } 3)$

    _____

14. $P(\text{even, then odd})$

    _____

15. $P(\text{odd, then } 2)$

    _____

16. $P(\text{the sum of the numbers is } 25)$

    _____

17. $P(\text{prime, then composite})$

    _____

18. $P(\text{a factor of } 8, \text{then a multiple of } 2)$

    _____

# Reteaching 12-6

**Permutations**

You can arrange the letters A, B, and C in different ways: ABC, ACB, and so on.
An arrangement in which order is important is a **permutation**.

How many ways can the three blocks be
arranged in a line?

① List the ways.

② Count the number of arrangements.

There are 6 possible arrangements.

ABC    ACB
BAC    BCA
CAB    CBA

You can use the counting principle as a shortcut.

| choices for<br>1st block | | choices for<br>2nd block | | choice for<br>3rd block | |
|---|---|---|---|---|---|
| 3 | × | 2 | × | 1 | = 6 |

A factorial can be used to show the product of all integers less than or equal to
a number.

3!    = 3    ×    2    ×    1    = 6

---

**Complete to find the number of permutations for each.**

**1.** In how many ways can you arrange 4
different books on a shelf?

4 × _____ × _____ × 1 = _____

**2.** In how many ways can the first, second, and
third prizes be awarded to 10 contestants?

_____ × _____ × _____ = _____

**Find the number of permutations for each.**

**3.** In how many different ways can the four
letters in BIRD be arranged?

_____

**4.** How many different ways can you frame
two of five pictures in different frames?

_____

**5.** How many different seating arrangements
are possible for a row of five chairs,
choosing from six people?

_____

**6.** A basket contains five different pieces of
fruit. If three people each choose one
piece, in how many different ways can they
make their choices?

_____

**Find the number of two-letter permutations of the letters.**

**7.** R, I, B

_____

**8.** H, E, L, P

_____

**9.** R, A, M, B, L, E

_____

**10.** C, A, N, D, L, E, S

_____

**Find the number of three-letter permutations of the letters.**

**11.** T, A, B

_____

**12.** R, A, D, I, O

_____

**13.** T, O, P, S

_____

**14.** W, A, L, R, U, S

_____

# Practice 12-6

**Start with the letters in the word STEP.**

1. Make an organized list of all the possible four-letter permutations of the letters.

2. How many of the permutations form real words? _____

**Find the number of permutations of each group of letters.**

3. C, H, A, I, R

   _____

4. L, I, G, H, T, S

   _____

5. C, O, M, P, U, T, E, R

   _____

**Find the number of three-letter permutations of the letters.**

6. A, P, Q, M

   _____

7. L, S, U, V, R,

   _____

8. M, B, T, O, D, K

   _____

**Solve.**

9. Suppose that first, second, and third place winners of a contest are to be selected from eight students who entered. In how many ways can the winners be chosen? _____

10. Antonio has nine different sweatshirts that he can wear for his job doing yard work. He has three pairs of jeans and two pairs of sweatpants. How many different outfits can Antonio wear for the yard work? _____

11. Ramona has a combination lock for her bicycle. She knows the numbers are 20, 41, and 6, but she can't remember the order. How many different arrangements are possible? _____

12. Travis is planting 5 rose bushes along a fence. Each rose bush has a different flower color: red, yellow, pink, peach, and white. If he wants to plant 3 rose bushes in between white and yellow rose bushes, in how many ways can he plant the 5 rose bushes? _____

# Reteaching 12-7

**Combinations**

An arrangement in which order does *not* matter is a **combination**.
For example, if you pair Raiz and Carla to play tennis, it is the same
as if you pair Carla and Raiz.

How many groups of 2 letters can you form from A, B, C, and D?

① Make an organized list.

② Eliminate any duplicates.

③ List the combinations.

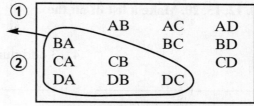

① 
② 

AB, AC, AD, BC, BD, CD

There are 6 possible combinations.

You can also get the number of combinations from the number of permutations.

$$\text{combinations} = \frac{\text{total number of permutations}}{\text{number of permutations of smaller group}} = \frac{4 \times 3}{2 \times 1} = 6 \text{ possible combinations}$$

---

**Use the letters C, O, M, P, U, T, E, R for Exercises 1–4.**

1. How many combinations of 2 vowels are there? Show an organized list with no duplicates.

   _____

   _____

   _____

2. How many combinations of 3 consonants are there? Show an organized list with no duplicates.

   _____

   _____

   _____

3. If you use C, O, M, P, U, T, E, R, S instead of C, O, M, P, U, T, E, R, how many combinations of 2 vowels are there?

   _____

4. If you use C, O, M, P, U, T, E, R, S instead of C, O, M, P, U, T, E, R, how many combinations of 3 consonants are there?

   _____

**Find the number of combinations.**

5. In how many ways can Robin pick 2 different kinds of muffins from a choice of wheat, raisin, blueberry, banana, garlic, and plain?

   _____

6. Sara has 24 tapes. In how many different ways can she take 2 tapes to school?

   _____

7. Augusto has purple, green, black, red, and blue T-shirts. In how many ways can he choose 3 for his vacation?

   _____

8. Abdul selects three light filters from a box of ten different filters. How many different sets could he choose?

   _____

# Practice 12-7

**Find the number of combinations.**

1. Choose 3 people from 4.

   _____

2. Choose 4 people from 6.

   _____

**Use the numbers 3, 5, 8, 10, 12, 15, 20. Make a list of all the combinations.**

3. 2 even numbers

   _____

4. 3 odd numbers

   _____

5. 1 even, 1 odd

   _____

   _____

6. any 2 numbers

   _____

   _____

7. You just bought five new books to read. You want to take two
   of them with you on vacation. In how many ways can you
   choose two books to take? _____

**Charmayne is organizing a track meet. There are 4 runners in her
class. Each runner must compete one-on-one against each of the
other runners in her class.**

8. How many races must Charmayne schedule? _____

9. Must Charmayne schedule permutations or combinations? _____

**A committee for the end-of-year party is composed of four eighth graders
and three seventh graders. A three-member subcommittee is formed.**

10. How many different combinations of
    eighth graders could there be if there are
    three eighth graders on the subcommittee?

    _____

11. How many different combinations of seventh
    graders could there be if the subcommittee
    consists of three seventh graders?

    _____

12. Find the probability that all 3 members
    on the subcommittee are eighth graders.

    _____

13. Find the probability that all 3 members
    on the subcommittee are seventh graders.

    _____